W9-BGJ-365

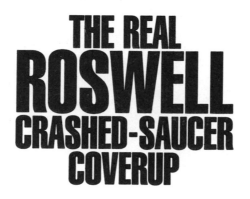

THE REAL
ROSWELL
CRASHED-SAUCER
COVERUP

THE REAL
ROSWELL
CRASHED-SAUCER
COVERUP

PHILIP J. KLASS

Prometheus Books
59 John Glenn Drive
Amherst, NewYork 14228-2197

Published 1997 by Prometheus Books

01 00 99 98 97   5 4 3 2 1

Library of Congress Cataloging-in-Publication Data

Klass, Philip J.
   The real Roswell crashed-saucer coverup / Philip J. Klass.
      p.   cm.
   Includes index.
   ISBN 1–57392–164–5 (cloth : alk. paper)
   1. Unidentified flying objects—Sightings and encounters—New Mexico—Roswell. 2. Government information—United States. I. Title.
TL789.5.N6K58   1997
001.942′09789′43—dc21   97–26355
                                                                          CIP

Printed in the United States of America on acid-free paper

Contents

Introduction

Beware the clever charlatan who can make an outright falsehood seem like a plausible truth.

—Anon.

If extraterrestrial spacecraft have been visiting Earth at least since
June 24, 1947, when the first Unidentified Flying Object (UFO)
report by pilot Kenneth Arnold made headlines around the nation,
sooner or later one could be expected to crash. While extraterrestrial (ET) technology would necessarily be much more advanced
than our own in order to visit Earth from their distant solar system,
it is unlikely that both ET operators and their technology could be
infallible. After all, we Earthlings have been producing aircraft for
many decades but sometimes they malfunction and even very
experienced airline and military pilots occasionally blunder.

Thus it is not surprising that barely three years after the first
UFO report in mid-1947, a book was published which claimed
that the U.S. government had recovered a crashed saucer and had
managed to keep that startling fact secret. The book *Behind the
Flying Saucers,* which quickly became a bestseller, was authored
by Frank Scully, a columnist for *Variety*—then known as the
"Bible of show business." Scully's book claimed that the recovered saucer had crashed in New Mexico in 1948. Scully's source

for this claim was a "Dr. Gee"—a pseudonym for a man who claimed to be a top scientist who had been brought in by the government to help analyze the crashed saucer's technology—and a Colorado businessman named Silas M. Newton.

Two years later, Tully's crashed-saucer tale was exposed as a hoax by investigative reporter J. P. Cahn. He revealed that "Dr. Gee" was a Mr. Leo GeBauer who was not a top scientist but the owner of a radio-parts store in Phoenix. Further, that Silas M. Newton had a reputation for questionable business practices. Shortly after Cahn's exposé was published in *True* magazine, Newton and GeBauer were arrested and charged with selling a device they called the "Doodlebug," which they claimed could discover oil deposits under ground. Within a year both men were convicted of operating a "confidence game" and having defrauded innocent victims (see Philip J. Klass, *UFOs: The Public Deceived,* p. 279).

It was not until more than two decades later that another claim of a secret crashed-saucer recovery attracted media attention. In early October 1974, UFOlogist Robert Carr, of Clearwater, Florida, held a press conference to publicize an upcoming UFO conference and announced that the U.S. Air Force (USAF) had recovered at least two crashed saucers, which he claimed had crashed near Aztec, New Mexico, in February 1948. Both craft, he claimed, along with twelve alien bodies, were being stored in Hangar 18 at the Wright-Patterson Air Force Base (WPAFB), near Dayton, Ohio.

Following Carr's press conference, the public affairs office at WPAFB was deluged with nearly one hundred news media inquiries about his crashed-saucer claims. The USAF response was: "There are no little green creatures or craft from space at Wright-Patterson Air Force Base now. There never have been. The report is without foundation." The public affairs office said there is no Hangar 18 at either of the two facilities that make up WPAFB, but there is a Building 18 at each site. Interested members of the media were invited to take a tour and inspect both buildings, one of which housed electrical power equipment and the other, the Aero Propulsion Laboratory.

In a subsequent interview in the October 16, 1974 edition of the *Tampa Tribune,* Carr was quoted as saying: "Five weeks ago I heard from the highest authority in Washington that before Christmas the whole UFO coverup will be ended." More than two decades have since passed without Carr's prediction coming true.

On July 29, 1978, at the annual conference of the Mutual UFO Network (MUFON)—the world's largest pro-UFO organization—the keynote speech was entitled: "Retrievals of the Third Kind: A Case Study of Alleged UFOs and Occupants in Military Custody." In the talk, long-time pro-UFOlogist Leonard H. Stringfield cited numerous crashed-saucer recovery reports he had heard. These came from persons who claimed to have been involved, nearly all of whom insisted on anonymity. One of Stringfield's anonymous sources reported recovery in 1948 of a crashed saucer 30 miles in Mexico, south of Laredo, Texas. Another claimed recovery in *1952* from near Edwards Air Force Base, California. Still another UFO reportedly crashed on *May 21, 1953,* near Kingman, Arizona. Still another source reported a UFO crash in *New Mexico in 1962. Importantly, there was no correlation in their tales.*

In the fall of 1980, three decades after Scully's crashed-saucer book became a bestseller, another was published: *The Roswell Incident* (Grosset & Dunlap) jointly authored by Charles Berlitz and William L. Moore. Berlitz had earlier written a bestseller on the Bermuda Triangle, which he claimed mysteriously swallowed up airplanes and ships. In the late 1970s, he and Moore had coauthored a book which claimed that the U.S. Navy had developed techniques during World War II that could make its ships invisible to the deadly German U-boats. But, according to their book, this remarkable technique was never used to protect sailors from untimely death because it gave them a headache or made them ill.

The Roswell Incident claimed that a flying saucer had crashed on a ranch near Corona, New Mexico, on July 2, 1947, and its debris had been recovered by two officers from the Roswell Army Air

Force Base approximately 75 miles southeast of the ranch. The book also cited a secondhand report that another UFO crashed at about the same time on the Plains of San Agustin, roughly 150 miles west of the Corona site. The Berlitz/Moore book did not immediately attract much media attention, because some of its claims were so patently nonsensical. For instance, the book claimed that Dwight D. Eisenhower was not told of the recovery of a crashed saucer for several years after he became President because "he did not possess the necessary clearances to be permitted access to such information." Moore subsequently acknowledged that the book contained many inaccuracies—which he attributed to Berlitz.

Even within the UFO movement, whose long-standing dogma has been that the U.S. government has long been involved in a "UFO coverup," relatively few pro-UFOlogists then accepted the Berlitz/Moore crashed-saucer claims as fact. But in the late 1980s, the prestigious Center for UFO Studies (CUFOS), in Chicago, became interested and funded an expedition to try to locate the "crash site" and possibly recover buried saucer debris. Key members of the expedition included Don Schmitt, director of special investigations for CUFOS, and Kevin Randle, who had earlier authored two pro-UFO books.

Randle and Schmitt's research, partially supported by CUFOS and the Fund for UFO Research (FUFOR), turned up many more persons whose *claimed* forty-year-old recollections seemed to confirm the crashed-saucer incident. Randle and Schmitt's book *UFO Crash at Roswell* (Avon Books), published in mid-1991, concluded that the U.S. government not only recovered a crashed saucer in 1947 but also the bodies of several extraterrestrials.

Still another book on the subject, *Crash at Corona* (Paragon House), was published in mid-1992, coauthored by long-time pro-UFOlogists Stanton T. Friedman and Don Berliner. Based on the testimony of a recently discovered "witness" named Gerald F. Anderson, Friedman and Berliner claim that the government recovered *two* crashed saucers in New Mexico in early July 1947, along with seven ET bodies *and one live ET.*

In March 1994, Randle and Schmitt published a second book, *The Truth About the UFO Crash at Roswell,* in which several of their witnesses sharply revised and expanded their earlier tales.

Recalling the old adage that "where there is smoke there must be fire," these four books and the many "witnesses" whom they quote have convinced many people that there has been a crashed-saucer coverup. Based on a number of USAF and Central Intelligence Agency (CIA) documents once classified "Secret" or "Top Secret"—some of which have been available to these Roswell researchers since the late 1960s—there is no doubt that there has been a coverup—*but not by the U.S. government.*

This coverup is being carried out by the authors of these books and by producers of television shows who exploit the "Roswell Incident" for their own financial gain. This charge will be documented in the pages that follow.

Before the collapse of the Soviet Union, it attempted to discredit the United States government, resorting to false charges and counterfeit documents—without notable success. Those who now falsely accuse the United States government of UFO and crashed-saucer coverup have achieved far greater success, judging from recent opinion polls. These polls typically indicate that at least half of American adults erroneously believe it is their government which is guilty of a UFO coverup. *This book is intended to identify those who are really the guilty parties.*

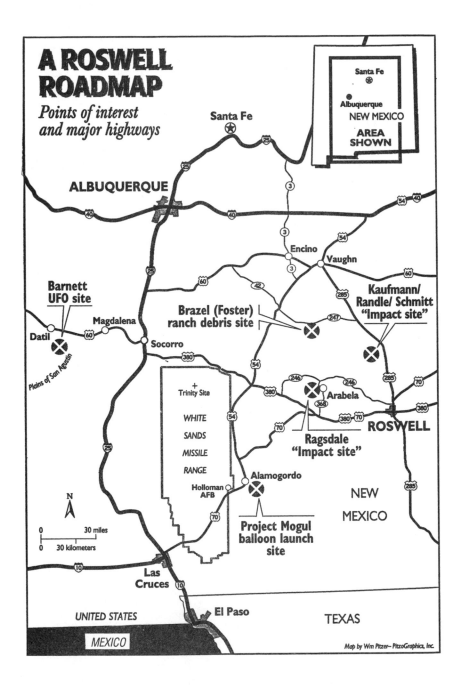

A ROSWELL ROADMAP

Points of interest and major highways

Santa Fe

ALBUQUERQUE

Santa Fe

Albuquerque
NEW MEXICO

AREA SHOWN

Encino

Vaughn

Barnett UFO site

Magdalena

Datil

Plains of San Agustin

Socorro

Brazel (Foster) ranch debris site

Kaufmann/ Randle/ Schmitt "Impact site"

+ Trinity Site

WHITE
SANDS
MISSILE
RANGE

Arabela

ROSWELL

Ragsdale "Impact site"

Alamogordo

Holloman AFB

Project Mogul balloon launch site

NEW MEXICO

N

0 — 30 miles
0 — 30 kilometers

Las Cruces

El Paso

UNITED STATES

TEXAS

MEXICO

Map by Wm Pitzer–PitzoGraphics, Inc.

1.

Contemporary Accounts

To better understand the mood of the nation immediately after the first UFO sighting on June 24, 1947 by private pilot Kenneth Arnold, it is useful to read an Associated Press (AP) story published on the front page of the July 6 edition of the *Roswell Dispatch*, the town's morning newspaper. The article carried the headline: "Nation's Perplexity over Flying Discs Deepens":

> The nation's perplexity over discs reported spinning through the skies deepened today in the wake of July 4 reports from virtually all parts of the country. There was no scientific explanation offered to fit the observations which spanned the nation from the Pacific to the Gulf of the Atlantic. A mass of evidence piled up swiftly as holiday throngs and fliers joined in telling of seeing bright, pancake-like objects skimming through the air at varying estimates of altitude and speed.
>
> Former skeptics joined the ranks of the believers as the flashing objects glittered before their eyes. Reliable observers such as Capt. E. J. Smith of United Air Lines, his co-pilot Ralph

Stevens and his stewardess, Marty Morrow, told of seeing the round flat objects for 12 minutes while flying west from Boise, Idaho, on Independence Day evening. Ex-airmen, picknickers, motorists, and housewives swelled the number of witnesses to the strange phenomena.

The first published report of "flying saucers" came from Kenneth Arnold, Boise, Ida., businessman pilot, who reported at Pendleton, Ore., on June 25 [Note: sighting date was June 24], that he had seen nine flying at 1200 miles an hour in formation, shifting position "like the tail of a kite," over Washington state's Cascade mountains. . . . Then the reports began to filter in, mostly from individuals. The discs were seen in Texas, in New Mexico, in Washington, Oregon, Idaho, Missouri, Colorado, California, Arizona, Nebraska.

Then the July 4 deluge hit. Two hundred persons in one group and 60 in another saw them in Idaho, hundreds saw them in Oregon, Washington and other states throughout the west. And for the first time, the eastern states had their reports. . . .

An Army Air Forces spokesman in Washington on July 3 said there was not enough fact to "warrant further investigation," but Air Materiel Command at Wright Field, Dayton, Ohio, said it was making a study. Saturday at Washington an Army researcher admitted "we're mystified" and the Navy said it "had no theories. . . ."

Two days after this article appeared, around noon on Tuesday, July 8, 1st. Lt. Walter G. Haut—a former B-29 bombardier-turned-public information officer at the Roswell Army Air Field (RAAF)—finished writing a short press release, got into his car, and drove a few miles north to deliver it to Roswell's two newspapers and two radio stations. Haut's release read:

The many rumors regarding the flying disk became reality yesterday when the intelligence office of the 509th Bomb Group of the Eighth Air Force, Roswell Army Air Field, was fortunate enough to gain possession of a disc through the co-operation [sic] of one of the local ranchers and the Sheriff's office of Chavez county.

The flying object landed on a ranch near Roswell sometime last week. Not having phone facilities, the rancher stored the disk until such time as he was able to contact the Sheriff's office, who in turn notified Major Jesse A. Marcel, of the 509th Bomb Group Intelligence office.

Action was immediately taken and the disc was picked up at the rancher's home. It was inspected at the Roswell Army Air Field and subsequently loaned by Major Marcel to higher headquarters.

When Haut arrived at the offices of the *Roswell Daily Record*, an evening newspaper, its deadline was fast approaching. Within several hours its July 8 edition was on the streets, bearing the five-column headline: "RAAF Captures Flying Saucer on Ranch in Roswell Region."

This article provided a few more details than Haut's release, which he supplied to the *Roswell Daily Record* reporter and which would prove significant in retrospect. These are italicized below:

The *intelligence office* of the 509th Bombardment group at Roswell Army Air Field announced at noon today that the field had come into possession of a flying saucer. According to information released by the department, *over authority of Maj. J. A. Marcel,* intelligence officer, the disk was recovered on a ranch in the Roswell vicinity after an unidentified rancher had notified Sheriff Geo. Wilcox here that he had found the *instrument* on his premises.

Maj. Marcel and a detail from his department went to the ranch and recovered the disk, it was stated. After the intelligence office here had inspected the instrument it was flown to "higher headquarters." *The intelligence office* stated that no details of the saucer's construction or its appearance had been revealed.

Mr. and Mrs. Dan Wilmot apparently were the only persons in Roswell who have seen what they thought was a flying disk. They were sitting on their porch at 105 South Penn. last Wednesday night [July 2] at about ten o'clock when a large glowing object zoomed out of the sky from the southeast, going in a northwesterly direction at a high rate of speed. . . . (Emphasis added)

(The remainder of the article offered more details on the Wilmot sighting.)

The newspaper sent its blockbuster story out over the Associated Press wire service, resulting in a deluge of inquiries. As reported in the July 9 *Roswell Dispatch*, the town's morning newspaper:

Sheriff Wilcox was the object of a storm of inquiries from papers in San Francisco, Boston, Los Angeles, New York, New Orleans, Baltimore, St. Louis, Denver, Albuquerque, Milwaukee, Santa Fe, Chicago, Washington and Mexico City. The longest call came from London, England, where the London Daily Mail and other newspapers desired information. The major radio networks, including N.B.C., C.B.S., Trans Radio plus the Associated and United Press and International News Service also contacted Wilcox. Others in the cavalcade were Paramount News and International News Photo.

Those who called Wilcox in the hope of obtaining more details on the recovered disk were disappointed. The newspaper account noted that *"No member of the local sheriff's office saw the article at any time"* (emphasis added). Maj. Marcel was unavailable because he and the material recovered from the ranch were flying to Eighth Air Force Headquarters, Fort Worth, Texas.

On Tuesday evening, July 8, at 6:17 P.M. central daylight time, the Federal Bureau of Investigation (FBI) office in Dallas sent a teletype to FBI Director J. Edgar Hoover in Washington and to the FBI office in Cincinnati—the closest FBI office to Wright Field/Dayton—that read:

XXXXXXXX [name of individual which was deleted when the FBI released its UFO-related documents in mid-1970s under

Freedom of Information Act request] HEADQUARTERS EIGHTH AIR FORCE, TELEPHONICALLY ADVISED THIS OFFICE THAT AN OBJECT PURPORTING TO BE A FLYING DISC WAS RECOVERED NEAR ROSWELL, NEW MEXICO, THIS DATE. THE DISC IS HEXAGONAL IN SHAPE AND WAS SUSPENDED FROM A BALLOON BY CABLE, WHICH BALLON [sic] WAS APPROXIMATELY TWENTY FEET IN DIAMETER. [Deleted name] FURTHER ADVISED THAT THE OBJECT FOUND RESEMBLES A HIGH ALTITUDE WEATHER BALLOON WITH A RADAR REFLECTOR, BUT THAT TELEPHONIC CONVERSATION BETWEEN THEIR OFFICE AND WRIGHT FIELD HAD NOT BORNE OUT THIS BELIEF. DISC AND BALLOON BEING TRANSPORTED TO WRIGHT FIELD BY SPECIAL PLANE FOR EXAMINATION. INFORMATION PROVIDED THIS OFFICE BECAUSE OF NATIONAL INTEREST IN CASE AND FACT THAT NATIONAL BROADCASTING COMPANY, ASSOCIATED PRESS, AND OTHERS ATTEMPTING TO BREAK STORY OF LOCATION OF DISC TODAY. [Deleted name] ADVISED WOULD REQUEST WRIGHT FIELD TO ADVISE CINCINNATI OFFICE RESULTS OF EXAMINATION. NO FURTHER INVESTIGATION BEING CONDUCTED.

At roughly the same time, the *Fort Worth Morning Star-Telegram* received a call from Eighth Air Force Headquarters inviting the newspaper to send out a reporter for a briefing on the recently recovered "flying disk." The newspaper sent a young reporter, J. Bond Johnson. His story, published in the next morning's edition under the headline " 'Disk-overy' Near Roswell Identified as Weather Balloon by FWAAF Officer," read:

An object found near Roswell, N.M., was stripped of its glamor as a "flying disk" by a Fort Worth Army Air Field weather officer who late Tuesday identified it as a weather balloon.

Warrant Officer Irving Newton, of Medford, Wis., a forecaster at the base weather station, said the object was a ray wind [Rawin] target used to determine the direction and velocity of winds at high altitudes.

Newton said there were some 80 weather stations in the United States using this type of balloon and that it could have come from any of them. "We use them because they can go so much higher than the eye can see," Newton explained. A radar set is employed to follow the balloon and through a process of triangulation the winds aloft are chartered [*sic*], he said. When rigged up, Newton stated, the object looks like a six-pointed star, is silvery in appearance and rises in the air like a kite, mounted to a 100-gram balloon. . . .

The weather device was flown to Fort Worth Army Air Field by B-29 from Roswell Army Air Field at 10 a.m. Tuesday at the command of Brig. Gen. Roger Ramey, 8th Air Force commanding officer here. *It had been found three weeks previously* by a New Mexico rancher, W. W. Brazell [*sic*], on his property about 85 miles northwest of Roswell. Brazell, whose ranch is 30 miles from the nearest telephone and has no radio, knew nothing about flying disks when he found the broken remains of the weather device scattered over a square mile of his land.

He bundled the *tinfoil and broken wooden beams of the kite and the torn synthetic rubber remains of the balloon* together and rolled it under some brush, *according to Maj. Jesse A. Marcel,* Houma, La., 509th Bomb Group intelligence officer at Roswell who brought the device to FWAAF. On a trip to town at Corona, N.M., Saturday night [July 5], Brazell heard the first reference to the "silver flying risks [*sic*]," Major Marcel related.

Brazell hurried home, dug up the remnants of the kites and balloon on Sunday and Monday [July 7] headed for Roswell to report his find to the sheriff's office. This resulted in a call to the Roswell Army Air Field and to Major Marcel's being assigned to the case. Marcel and Brazell journeyed back to the ranch, where Marcel took the object into the custody of the Army. After Col. William H. Blanchard, 509th commanding officer, reported the incident to General Ramey, he was ordered to dispatch the object to Fort Worth Army Air Field immediately.

About that time, word broke from Roswell that a flying disk finally had been found. After his first look, Ramey declared all it was was a weather balloon. The weather officer verified his view. (Emphasis added)

Reporter Johnson had brought along his camera and took photos showing Marcel holding some of the debris in Ramey's office, as well as photos of meteorologist Newton, Ramey, and his chief of staff, Col. Thomas J. DuBose. Johnson hurried back to his office to develop the photos and to write his story in time for the next morning's edition. Johnson's story also was sent out on the Associated Press wire service Tuesday evening.

Johnson was under great deadline pressure to get his story written in time for the next morning's edition. But with the benefit of hindsight, it is regrettable that his opening sentence and the story's headline referred to the recovered debris as a "weather balloon." The unfamiliar parchment paper coated with tinfoil and wooden beams were from a radar corner-reflector cluster carried by a weather balloon to enable its location and movements to be tracked by a ground radar.

Prior to the invention of radar during World War II, meteorologists used balloon-borne "radiosondes"—a small box designed to measure barometric pressure, temperature, and humidity, and transmit back this data via a small radio transmitter. The barometric pressure provided a rough indication of the balloon's altitude enabling meteorologists to determine air temperature and humidity at different altitudes. But there was no way to determine the balloon's geographic location when the data was measured.

If the balloon could be tracked by radar, its location could be determined precisely at all times. However, the rubberlike material used for balloons does not reflect radar energy. For this reason, the balloon was outfitted to carry a "corner-reflector" which served to focus radar energy and reflect it back to the radar. To enable the balloon to rise to very high altitude, the corner-reflector was constructed of the lightest possible materials, much like a kite. The "faces" of the corner-reflector need to be perpendicular to one another and have a metal surface to reflect radar energy. The solution was to make a corner reflector structure using balsawood sticks attached to a stiff parchmentlike paper to which a thin aluminum foil was attached (see figure 5).

Shortly after Johnson's story went out on the AP wire from Fort Worth on the evening of July 8, Brazel was interviewed in the offices of the *Roswell Daily Record* for a feature story that would be published the following afternoon. Also present was Jason Kellahin, from the Associated Press bureau in Albuquerque, along with his associate Robin Adair, who had driven nearly 200 miles to report on the exciting incident. But by the time they had arrived at the Roswell newspaper office, its AP wire had reported that the object was only a "weather balloon."

Brazel's firsthand account of the debris he had found, headlined "Harassed Rancher Who Located 'Saucer' Sorry He Told About It," appeared in the July 9 (evening) edition of the *Roswell Daily Record*:

> W. W. Brazel, 48, Lincoln county rancher living 30 miles south east of Corona, today told his story of finding what the army at first described as a flying disk, but the publicity which attended his find caused him to add that if he ever found anything else short of a bomb he sure wasn't going to say anything about it.
>
> Brazel *was brought here late yesterday by W. E. Whitmore,* of radio station KGFL, had his picture taken and gave an interview to the Record and Jason Kellahin, sent here from the Albuquerque bureau of the Associated Press to cover the story. The picture he posed for was sent out over AP telephoto wire sending machine specially set up in the Record office by R. D. Adair, AP wire chief sent here from Albuquerque for the sole purpose of getting out his picture and that of [S]heriff George Wilcox, to whom Brazel originally gave the information of his find.
>
> Brazel related that on *June 14* he and an 8-year-old son, Vernon, were about 7 or 8 miles from the ranch house of the J. B. Foster ranch, which he operates, when they came upon a large area of bright wreckage made up on [*sic*] *rubber strips, tinfoil, a rather tough paper and sticks.* At the time Brazel was in a hurry to get his round made and he did not pay much attention to it. But he did remark about what he had seen and on July 4 [Friday] he, his wife, Vernon and a daughter [Bessie], age 14, went back to the spot and gathered up quite a bit of the debris.
>
> The next day he first heard about the flying disks, and he wondered if what he had found might be some remnants of one

of these. Monday [July 7] he came to town [Roswell] to sell some wool and while here he went to see [S]heriff George Wilcox and "whispered kinda confidential like" that he might have found a flying disk.

Wilcox got in touch with the Roswell Army Air Field, and Maj. Jesse A. Marcel and a man in plain clothes accompanied him home, where they picked up the rest of the pieces of the "disk" and went to his [Brazel's] home to try to reconstruct it. According to Brazel they simply could not reconstruct it at all. They tried to make a kite out of it, but could not do that and could not find any way to put it back together so that it would fit.

Then Major Marcel brought it to Roswell and that was the last he heard of it until the story broke that he had found a flying disk. Brazel said that he did not see it fall from the sky and did not see it before it was torn up, so he did not know the size or shape it might have been, but he thought it might have been about as large as a table top. *The balloon that held it up*, if that was how it worked, must have been about 12 feet long, he felt, measuring the distance by the size of the room in which he sat. *The rubber* was smoky gray in color and scattered over *an area about 200 yards in diameter.*

When the debris was gathered up *the tinfoil, paper, tape and sticks made a bundle about three feet long and 7 or 8 inches thick, while the rubber made a bundle about 18 or 20 inches thick. In all, he estimated, the entire lot would have weighed maybe five pounds.* There was no sign of any metal in the area which might have been used for an engine and no sign of any propellers of any kind, although at least one *paper fin had been glued onto some of the tinfoil.*

There were no words to be found anywhere on the instrument, although there were *some letters* on some of the parts. *Considerable scotch tape and some tape with flowers printed upon it had been used in the construction.* No strings or wire were to be found but there were some *eyelets in the paper* to indicate that some sort of attachment may have been used.

Brazel said he had previously found two weather observation balloons on the ranch, but that what he found this time did not in any way resemble either of these. "I am sure what I found was not any weather observation balloon," he said. "But if I find anything else besides a bomb they are going to have a hard time getting me to say anything about it."(Emphasis added)

It is hardly surprising that rancher Brazel, a somewhat retiring person who had not himself made any claims about the debris he had found, was embarrassed by the news media furor that resulted from Haut's press release.

The Wednesday morning *Roswell Dispatch,* which had been scooped by its evening rival on the original crashed-saucer story, carried a two-tier banner headline for its story identifying the object as a balloon-borne radar target: "Army Debunks Roswell Flying Disk As World Simmers With Excitement." That evening the *Roswell Daily Record* carried a banner headline for its story: "Gen. Ramey Empties Roswell Saucer." The following day, both Roswell newspapers carried a picture of Maj. Marcel in Gen. Ramey's office, holding debris from a balloon-borne radar target, which had been taken by reporter J. Bond Johnson.

The photo shows Marcel smiling, but it is doubtful that the smile reflected his true feelings under the circumstances. As reported in the July 9, 1947 *Washington Post,* ". . . officers at the Roswell, N.M. air base received a blistering rebuke from the Army A.F. Headquarters in Washington, the United Press reported, for announcing that a 'flying disc' had been found on a New Mexico ranch."

Two decades later, in 1967, long-time pro-UFOlogist Ted Bloecher published *Report on the UFO Wave of 1947,* whose chronological listing showed a total of 853 UFO reports that had been carried by the news media during the last week of June and the month of July. Bloecher did not consider the Roswell "crashed saucer" incident worthy of being included in his lengthy list. He offered the following explanation: "Through a series of clumsy blunders in public relations . . . the story got blown up out of all proportion."

Two decades later, in early October 1966, the USAF—in

response to criticism by pro-UFO groups of its investigations of UFO reports—awarded a contract to the University of Colorado to conduct an independent study. Dr. Edward U. Condon, who headed the study, and his deputy, Robert Low, invited the two leading pro-UFO groups to recommend the most impressive UFO cases which they believed the Colorado group should investigate. Both NICAP (National Investigations Committee on Aerial Phenomena), then the nation's largest pro-UFO group, and APRO (Aerial Phenomena Research Organization) agreed to do so. But neither NICAP nor APRO included the Roswell Incident on their list of important UFO cases.

2.

Major Marcel's
Thirty-Year-Old Recollections

But for a couple of chance encounters in the late 1970s, the "Roswell Incident" would today not even be an obscure footnote in the history of UFOs. Rancher Brazel died in 1963. Marcel, who resigned from the USAF in 1950 during the Korean War to return to his hometown of Houma, Louisiana, to operate a radio-TV repair shop, was now retired and in his early seventies.

The first UFOlogist to hear Marcel's thirty-plus-year-old recollections of the Roswell Incident was Stanton T. Friedman. Friedman, trained as a nuclear physicist, worked in that field for fourteen years for five different companies. Since being laid off in 1971, he has earned much of his income as a pro-UFO lecturer and writer. Friedman was in Baton Rouge, Louisiana, on February 21, 1978, for a lecture and was participating in a TV talk show on UFOs. One of Marcel's friends, who worked at the station, told Friedman of hearing Marcel tell of his involvement in recovering a crashed saucer. This prompted Friedman to call Marcel the next day for details.

Marcel was unable to recall even the year when the incident

had occurred and he had not kept any newspaper clippings about the seemingly remarkable event. As Friedman himself would later admit, at the time he "found it hard to get very excited" about Marcel's tale.

Several months later, on April 7, 1978, based on Friedman's suggestion, Marcel participated (from his home) in a talk show on UFOs on a Chicago radio station. Another participant was long-time pro-UFOlogist Leonard H. Stringfield, who had recently emerged as the UFO Movement's crashed-saucer specialist. Stringfield had briefly discussed such reports in his then recently published book *Situation Red* (Doubleday, 1977). And, as earlier noted (see the Introduction), Stringfield had focused on crashed-saucer recovery reports in his talk at the 1978 MUFON conference in Dayton, Ohio. Stringfield was not sufficiently impressed with Marcel's story to obtain a tape of the radio interview from the Chicago station.

However, Stringfield did take written notes during the talk show, which were used for a very brief report on Marcel's crashed-saucer story that Stringfield included in the paper he delivered at the MUFON conference. (Stringfield later published this "updated" version.) According to Stringfield's notes, Marcel recalled finding many metal fragments and what appeared to be *"parchment"* strewn over a one-mile square area at the Brazel ranch. Marcel said the "metal fragments varied in size up to *six inches in length*, but were the *thickness of tinfoil.* . . . They were of great strength. They could not be bent or broken, no matter what pressure we applied" (emphasis added). Marcel said the area where the debris was found was thoroughly checked "but *no fresh impact depressions were found in the sand.* The area was not radioactive" (emphasis added).

By the late 1970s, Friedman was collaborating with William L. Moore for his upcoming book with Berlitz which would be published in late 1980. In early 1979, Friedman was hired by Group I International, of Hollywood, to assist in producing a UFO movie subsequently titled *UFOs Are Real.* In May 1979, the film crew and Friedman spent a day in Houma, interviewing Marcel. In one of Marcel's appearances in the movie, he tried to recall what happened in General Ramey's office thirty-two years earlier: "The newsmen saw very little of the [recovered] material, very small portion of it. And none of the important things, like these [wood] members that had these hieroglyphics or markings on them. They (newsmen) wanted me to tell them about it and *I couldn't say anything. And when the General came in, he told me not to say anything—that he would handle it*" (emphasis added). (During one part of the Marcel interview, not included in the final film, he said: *"As far as newspeople, I never talked to any of them"* [emphasis added].)

Friedman appeared in the movie shortly after Marcel and said: *"We have verified every statement made by Jesse Marcel"* (emphasis added). This claim is flatly contradicted by the article published in the July 9, 1947 *Fort Worth Morning Star-Telegram* (see pp. 17–18). The article, written by reporter J. Bond Johnson, specifically attributes several of the statements to Marcel, i.e., "... according to Maj. Jesse A. Marcel, Houma, La. . . ." and "... Major Marcel related." Furthermore, the article contains details about Brazel's discovery and recovery of the debris which would not be known to anyone else in Ramey's office but Marcel. No one else in Ramey's office would have known that Marcel's hometown was Houma, Louisiana.

This discrepancy and others that follow are *not* intended to suggest that Marcel was intentionally lying in 1979. Rather it demonstrates that any person's attempt to recall events that occurred nearly a third of a century earlier can be seriously flawed. This is especially true for persons in their later years.

An even more significant flaw in Marcel's recollections was his statement, quoted in the Berlitz/Moore book (p. 68), that

> General Ramey allowed some members of the press in to take a picture of the stuff. They took *one* picture of me on the floor holding up some of the less-interesting metallic debris. The

press was allowed to photograph this, but were not allowed far enough into the room to touch it. *The stuff in that one photo was pieces of the actual stuff we found.* It was not a staged photo. Later, they cleared out our wreckage and *substituted some of their own. Then they allowed more photos.* Those photos were taken while the actual wreckage was already on its way to Wright Field. *I was not in these.* I believe these were taken with the general and one of his aids. (Emphasis added)

A decade later, negatives for the photos that were taken in Gen. Ramey's office on July 8, 1947 were located by Kevin Randle and Don Schmitt in the archives of the *Fort Worth Star-Telegram* at the University of Texas at Arlington Library. *Two* of the photos showed Marcel holding what he had described as "the actual stuff we found." Another photo showed Gen. Ramey examining what Marcel claimed was "substituted" material and two others showed Ramey and his executive officer, Col. Thomas J. DuBose, examining the *same* material. Another photo, located in the United Press International (UPI) files, shows meteorologist Newton examining the *same* debris.

Even cursory examination shows that the debris in all the photos is identical. And the material in the photos closely matches the description given by rancher Brazel at roughly the same time in the offices of the Roswell Daily Record *some 400 miles to the west. More importantly, the material resembles the debris from a balloon-borne radar-reflecting device, as Gen. Ramey had announced at the time.*

Recall that during Brazel's interview at the *Roswell Daily Record*, he said the recovered debris included rubber, tinfoil, paper, tape, sticks, and "Scotch tape." That after he and Marcel had recovered the debris, they "tried to make a kite out of it, but . . . could not find any way to put it back together so that it would fit." If the debris that Brazel described and the debris visible in the photos taken in Ramey's office was from an extraterrestrial spaceship, what an extraordinary coincidence that ETs would construct their spacecraft from materials—including "Scotch tape"—which so closely resemble those used in a balloon-borne radar corner-reflector!

In a paper presented at the 1981 MUFON Conference in Cambridge, Massachusetts, Friedman admitted that, "Both Bill Moore and I, when first looking at the prints of the pictures made . . . in General Ramey's office, *worried about the material in the pictures really being from a balloon*" (emphasis added). The Berlitz/Moore book includes two of these photos but they are so very heavily "cropped" that *almost none* of the crinkled foil-like debris is visible.

In late August 1947, after many hundreds of UFO sightings had been reported, the White House and top Pentagon officials were under pressure to explain what UFOs might be. Brig. Gen. George Schulgen, deputy chief of staff for intelligence requirements, requested the views of Lt. Gen. Nathan Twining, commander of the Air Materiel Command at Wright Field in Dayton, Ohio, where the Army Air Forces' (AAF) technical experts and laboratories were located. If strange debris had been recovered from the Brazel ranch, it would have been sent to Wright Field (now Wright-Patterson Air Force Base), *as Marcel reported in his interviews in the late 1970s.*

On September 23, 1947, Twining replied to Schulgen in a memo originally classified "Secret," which provided what he said was the "considered opinion of this Command." The Berlitz/Moore book quotes *most* of the Twining letter, including the following which appeared in italics:

> (a) *The phenomenon reported is something real and not visionary or fictitious.*
> (b) *There are objects probably approximately the shape of a disc, of such appreciable size as to appear to be as large as man-made aircraft.*

Berlitz and Moore also quoted, using italics, Twining's statement that, "*The reported operating characteristics . . . lend belief to the possibility that some of the objects are controlled either manually, automatically or remotely.*"

But Berlitz and Moore *omitted* the following caveat in the Twining letter: "Due consideration must be given the following. . . . *The lack of physical evidence in the shape of crash recovered exhibits which would undeniably prove the existence of these objects*" (emphasis added). Having omitted this significant caveat, the Berlitz/Moore book says: "It is understandable that the Twining memo makes no reference to the Roswell disc. . ." (p. 138). *Understandable?* That debris from an ET craft, which might possibly be the precursor of an ET invasion or attack, had been sent to Wright Field—but nobody thought to inform its commander so he could immediately alert the Pentagon and the White House? Or that Lt. Gen. Twining, who would later rise to become Chairman of the Joint Chiefs of Staff, would intentionally lie to a high-ranking Pentagon official?

This omission of vitally important "hard data" is understandable only if Berlitz and Moore were intentionally trying to cover up information that could demolish the credibility of their crashed-saucer book.

When the Randle/Schmitt book was published in 1991, it, too, would quote the same portions of the Twining letter, but would omit the revealing statement about the "lack of physical evidence in the shape of crash recovered exhibits which would undeniably prove the existence of these objects." As with Berlitz and Moore, Randle and Schmitt would have the gall to accuse the U.S. government of "coverup."

3.

Major Marcel's Puzzling Actions

It is not surprising that Maj. Marcel did not recognize the Brazel ranch debris. When he entered the Army Air Corps in 1942, his initial training was in analysis of aerial reconnaissance photos to locate potential targets for bombing and to assess the damage effects of bombing. In 1945, he underwent four weeks of training in the use of radar for aircraft navigation and the use of airborne radar imagery to locate targets and assess bomb damage. Because Marcel was never trained as a meteorologist, he would not be familiar with techniques developed to enable weather balloons to be tracked by radar by means of corner-reflectors.

On the basis of statements made by Marcel in the late 1970s, which are often quoted in crashed-saucer books and seen in TV programs, it would appear that he instantly recognized the extraordinary nature of the debris recovered from the Brazel ranch. But in fact, when Marcel was interviewed in May 1979 for the movie *UFOs Are Real,* he said that when he returned to the Roswell Army Air Field he turned the debris over to "one of the boys" in his office. Marcel said: "I didn't pay too much attention to that [debris] at first, until one of the boys came to me and said, 'You know the metal that was in there, I tried to bend that stuff and it won't bend.' " Marcel added: *"I didn't go back to look at it myself because we were busy in the office and I had quite a bit of work to do"* (emphasis added). But this revealing statement by Marcel ended up on the "cutting room floor" and was not used in the movie, nor was it included in the Berlitz/Moore book.

Marcel did know that tests of captured German V-2 ballistic missiles were under way at the Army's White Sands Missile Range—less than 150 miles south of the Brazel ranch. Less than a month before the debris was found, Roswell newspapers reported that a V-2 rocket malfunction caused the missile to head south and impact in Mexico. Two weeks earlier, another errant V-2 had headed east and impacted near Alamogordo, New Mexico. If Marcel quickly recognized that the debris used some very advanced technology, as he would claim thirty-plus years later, he should have suspected that it might be something involved with Army V-2 missile tests. And he should promptly have called the White Sands Missile Range. Yet he did not, so far as is known.

Another possibility that should have occurred to Marcel as an intelligence officer, was that the debris might be a secret Soviet reconnaissance device, intended to spy on America's nuclear weapons laboratories in Los Alamos and Albuquerque, and on the White Sands missile test facility. Still another potential target for Soviet reconnaissance was the Roswell airfield which was home base for B-29s capable of carrying nuclear weapons. If the debris that Brazel discovered was related to V-2 or other new secret weapon tests at White Sands, obviously there should be no public disclosure without first checking with White Sands and obtaining Pentagon approval. If the debris came from a Soviet reconnaissance device which was covertly spying on sensitive U.S. facilities, any decision to make this fact public should be made by President Harry Truman or at least by a top Pentagon official.

Yet within several hours after Marcel returned with the Brazel ranch debris, Lt. Haut was distributing a press release announcing that a "flying disk" had been recovered. Haut now claims that he received a telephone call from Roswell base commander Col. William H. Blanchard telling him to issue the release. But this claim is challenged by the wording of the article published in the July 8 *Roswell Daily Record.* The reporter to whom Haut gave his release recognized the extraordinary nature of its claim. Being a good reporter he knew that the claim needed to be attributed to someone in authority at the base. And so after asking, he rewrote Haut's release as follows: "The *intelligence office* of the 509th Bombardment group at Roswell Army Air Field announced at noon today . . . According to information released by the department, *over the authority of Maj. J. A. Marcel,* intelligence officer . . ." (emphasis added). Col. Blanchard's name did not appear anywhere in the article.

Another challenge to Haut's current recollections can be found in the Berlitz/Moore book based on a 1979 interview with Marcel. When he was asked how the press learned about the debris recovered from the Brazel ranch, Marcel responded: "It was the public information officer, Haut I believe his name was, who called the AP and later wrote the press release. I heard he wasn't authorized to do this, and I believe he was severely reprimanded for it, I think all the way from Washington" (p. 68).

Additional clues as to who was held responsible for issuing the press release may be gained from the fact that shortly after the incident, Haut was transferred to another job. And a few months later, Haut resigned from the USAF "for personal reasons." At about the same time Marcel was transferred to a desk-job in Washington and he resigned from the USAF roughly two years later. Col. Blanchard, however, rose to the rank of a four-star general and was vice chief of staff of the USAF when he suffered a fatal heart attack.

Berlitz and Moore report that shortly after Marcel was transferred to Washington he was assigned to a program which used high-flying aircraft to collect air samples to determine when the USSR had exploded its first nuclear weapon. The book quotes

Marcel as saying: "When we finally detected that there had been an atomic explosion, it was my job to write the report on it. In fact, when President Truman went on the air to declare that the Russians had exploded a nuclear device, *it was my report that he was reading from*" (emphasis added). The record shows that White House disclosure of the Soviet nuclear test was made via a press release and that Truman did *not* go on the radio to announce the event.

Possibly the most puzzling aspect of Marcel's actions—*if* his 30-plus-year recollections were correct—is the way the Brazel ranch material was handled after he returned to his office. If the object that crashed was an advanced Soviet reconnaissance device constructed from new types of materials, the precious material should have been handled very carefully until it could be analyzed by AAF scientists. Yet when Marcel was interviewed in 1979 for the movie *UFOs Are Real*, he said: "These little members could not be broken, could not be burned—*I even tried to burn them. . . . We even tried making a dent in it with a 16 lb. sledge-hammer and there was still no dent in it*" (emphasis added).

This claim is contradicted by the photos taken in Ramey's office, including the two with Marcel which clearly show that portions of the foil-covered paper are bent and crumpled. This was noted by pro-UFOlogist Joe Kirk Thomas, in an article published in the January 1991 *MUFON UFO Journal*, based on high-quality reproductions of the Ramey office photos published in its September 1990 issue.

Thomas referred to another article by William L. Moore, and his new collaborator Jaime Shandera, which claimed the Ramey office photos showed "genuine remnants of a crashed UFO." Thomas characterized their claim as "Absurd. In fact, a casual examination of the *Journal* photographs gives ample evidence that all the statements made by the Air Force as to the nature of the debris are true. . . ." Kirk noted that portions of the foil-covered parchment were clearly bent.

4.

Correct Chronology of Key Events

During one of several interviews with Marcel in 1979, as recounted in the Berlitz/Moore book (p. 63), he was asked how he first learned of the debris discovered on the Brazel ranch. Marcel replied:

> We heard about it on July 7 [Monday] when we got a call from the county sheriff's office at Roswell. I was eating lunch at the officers' club when the call came through saying that I should go out and talk to Brazel. The sheriff said that Brazel had told him there was a lot of debris scattered around.
>
> I finished my lunch and went into town to talk to this fellow. When I had heard what he had to say, I decided that this was a matter that had better be brought to the attention of the colonel [Base Commander Blanchard] right away and let him decide what ought to be done. I wanted Brazel to accompany me back to the base with his truck, but he said he had some things to do first and could he meet me somewhere in an hour or so. I arranged for him to meet me at the sheriff's office, and went back to see the colonel.

In my discussion with the colonel, we determined that a downed aircraft of some unusual sort might be involved, so the colonel said I had better get out there, and to take whatever I needed and go. I and a CIC [Counter-Intelligence Corps] agent from West Texas by the name of Cavitt [Marcel couldn't recall his first name] followed this man [Brazel] out to his ranch, with me driving my staff car [a '42 Buick] and Cavitt in a Jeep Carry-all. There were almost no roads, and at spots we literally had to go right across country. It was as close to the middle of nowhere as you could get. Anyhow, we got there very late in the afternoon and had to spend the night with this fellow. All we had to eat was some cold pork and beans and some crackers.

Two pages after Berlitz and Moore quote Marcel as saying he got a call on *Monday, July 7* from Sheriff Wilcox while having lunch at the officers' club, the authors erroneously state that Brazel came to Roswell "on Sunday July 6." And they quote Marcel as saying that after collecting "all the debris we could handle . . . That afternoon, July 7, we headed back to Roswell and arrived there *in the early evening* [emphasis added]. When we arrived there, we discovered that the story that we had found a flying disc had leaked out ahead of us. We had an eager-beaver PIO [public information officer] on the base who had taken it upon himself to call the AP on this thing. We had several calls that night, and one reporter even came over to the house. . . . The next morning [i.e., Tuesday, July 8] that written press release went out, and after that things really hit the fan."

Marcel's 1979 recollections are flawed and inconsistent with the known facts. On Tuesday evening, July 8, when rancher Brazel was interviewed in the offices of the *Roswell Daily Record* he was quoted as saying that he had come to Roswell on *Monday, July 7.* And the *Fort Worth Morning Star-Telegram* article of July 9, citing the chronology of events related by Marcel in Ramey's office, said that on "Monday [Brazel] headed for Roswell to report his find to the sheriff's office." Further, during Brazel's briefing in the Roswell newspaper offices, he said he had driven to Roswell to "sell some wool." The offices of sheep-shearing contractors would not be open on Sunday—especially that particular Sunday because July 4 fell on a Friday, providing a then rare three-day holiday.

Despite the foregoing, the Randle/Schmitt book also claims that Brazel came to Roswell on *Sunday, July 6* and that Marcel returned to base on the early evening of Monday, July 7. If true, the debris should have been promptly flown to Fort Worth Monday night instead of delaying until the following afternoon.

The correct scenario is that Marcel and the CIC man reached the Brazel ranch shortly before dusk on July 7. Early the next morning (July 8), Marcel, Brazel, and the CIC man (Cavitt) went out to the debris field to recover debris that Brazel had not earlier collected and then Marcel and Cavitt departed for Roswell. If they departed for Roswell by 8 A.M.—allowing roughly three hours driving time—they would have arrived at the base around 11 A.M. Marcel would have notified Col. Blanchard, who would have informed Gen. Ramey who instructed Blanchard to have Marcel fly the debris to his headquarters near Fort Worth.

Judging from the wording of the press release which Haut began distributing shortly after noon, Marcel and the debris were then en route to Fort Worth. Allowing two hours flying time, Marcel and the debris probably arrived around 4 P.M. in Fort Worth—which was on central daylight time—an hour ahead of Roswell Mountain daylight savings time.

At 6:17 P.M. central time, on July 8, the FBI office in Fort Worth sent the teletype message to FBI Headquarters in Washington that it had been informed by an Eighth Air Force spokesman that the recovered disk was a balloon-borne radar reflector, as reported in chapter 1 (p. 12). The *Fort Worth Morning Star-Telegram* story by Johnson probably went out on the AP wire around 7 to 8 P.M. Tuesday night. And its contents would thus be known to reporters who were meeting with Brazel in the offices of the *Roswell Daily Record.*

The books by Randle and Schmitt and Friedman and Berliner claim that the balloon-borne radar reflector explanation was concocted by Gen. Ramey and that none of the debris photographed in Ramey's office was authentic. Further, they claim that the account given by rancher Brazel in the offices of the *Roswell Daily Record* was riddled with falsehoods. Friedman and Berliner suggest that Brazel was bribed while Randle and Schmitt imply he was intimidated by threats by unnamed AAF officers. (Friedman/Berliner, *Crash at Corona*, p. 82; Randle/Schmitt, *The Truth About the UFO Crash at Roswell*, pp. 31, 127)

If the balloon-borne radar reflector was a spurious "cover story" concocted by Ramey, there was no way in which the details could have been communicated to Brazel before he met with reporters in the Roswell newspaper offices. Unbeknown to Ramey, Marcel, or other AAF officials, Mac Brazel had decided to drive to Roswell Tuesday and was visiting Walt Whitmore, owner of radio station KGFL. Jud Roberts, KGFL manager, had chanced to stumble on the "crashed disc" story on Monday when he called Sheriff Wilcox to inquire if he had any newsworthy items to report. At the time, Brazel was there waiting for Marcel to arrive and he talked briefly with Roberts.

It would be logical for Roberts to ask Brazel to come to the station for an interview, only to learn that Brazel had to escort Marcel back to his ranch. Roberts would then have suggested that Brazel come to the station the next day—Tuesday. It is known with certainty that Brazel was visiting Whitmore who brought him to the offices of the *Roswell Daily Record* for an interview, as reported in the newspaper's July 9 edition. Because Brazel's whereabouts Tuesday afternoon were unknown to anyone in the Air Force, it would have been impossible for Ramey to inform Brazel what he should say at the newspaper offices to match what Marcel would say in Ramey's office.

Yet Brazel's account, as published in the July 9 *Roswell Daily Record*, very closely matches the one quoting Marcel, which was published in the July 9 *Fort Worth Star-Telegram*. For example, Brazel said he first discovered the debris "on *June 14*" (emphasis added). Marcel said it had been found "three weeks previously."

Berlitz/Moore, Randle/Schmitt, and Friedman/Berliner erroneously claim the debris was not found by Brazel until *July 2* or *July 4*.

The Fort Worth newspaper article quoted Marcel as saying that the debris consisted of *"tinfoil and broken wooden beams of the kite and the torn synthetic remains of the balloon . . ."* (emphasis added). Brazel's description was "rubber strips, tinfoil, a rather tough paper and sticks . . . the rubber was smoky gray in color. . . . Considerable Scotch tape and some tape with flowers printed upon it had been used in the construction. . . ."

If Brazel had been instructed or bribed to lie, there was no need for him to lie about the *date* when he first discovered the debris. All he needed to remember to say was: "Gen. Ramey is correct, it was some kind of weather balloon." *But in fact, the Roswell article concludes by quoting Brazel as contradicting Ramey: "I am sure what I found was not any weather observation balloon."*

If the balloon-borne radar corner-reflector were a concocted story, Ramey would be seriously constrained in devising a cover story because of other witnesses. For example, according to the 1979 recollections of Mac Brazel's daughter, who had helped him retrieve the debris, it included "pieces of heavily waxed paper and a sort of aluminum-like foil. . . . Some of the metal foil pieces had a sort of tape stuck to them. . . ." Mac Brazel's older son Bill, who reported finding pieces of the debris in subsequent months, told William L. Moore: ". . . it weighed almost nothing. There was some wooden-like particles . . . like balsa wood in weight. . . . It was pliable but wouldn't break. Of course, all I had was a few splinters."

When KGFL's Roberts filed a story with United Press on Tuesday afternoon, based on his brief telephone interview with Brazel in the sheriff's office, he wrote: "Sheriff Wilcox quoted Brizell [*sic*] as saying that 'it more or less seemed like tinfoil.'" Roberts's story cited a "report from Carrizozo, N.M. [which] said that a disc was found 35 miles southeast of Corona. The report—which was not substantiated—merely said that it was 'a rubber substance and tinfoil encased.'"

At Marcel's suggestion, his son, Dr. Jesse A. Marcel Jr., a

physician then living in Helena, Montana, was interviewed in 1979. Dr. Marcel—who was only eleven at the time of the incident—recalled that his father had brought some of the debris home and that the "material was foil-like stuff, very thin, metallic-like but not metal, and very tough," according to the Berlitz/ Moore book.

Dr. Marcel said that his father, who had been away for "a couple of days," arrived home after midnight and had awakened his family to show them the debris. If Maj. Marcel had stopped at his house to show his family the debris *before* bringing it to the base, it would have been shortly *before noon* on Tuesday, not after midnight, and he would have been away from home for little more than *one* day, not a "couple days." The more likely explanation is that Marcel returned from Fort Worth late Tuesday night and brought back some samples of the debris to show his family what had kept him away from home for nearly two days.

On August 10, 1990, I sent Dr. Marcel a photocopy of pictures taken in Gen. Ramey's office showing his father and others holding the debris. Dr. Marcel replied on October 10 saying that he found "a certain superficial resemblance to the debris that was brought into our house that night, in that there were a lot of metallic fragments, very similar to the parts that were spread out on the floor of, I believe, General Ramey's office." However, based on Dr. Marcel's thirty-plus-year-old recollections * he added that the pictures taken in Ramey's office "did not include the type debris that was brought into our house that evening, admittedly some of the more interesting artifacts. I cannot dispute that perhaps the picture does depict at least a portion of that debris, though. . . ."

---

*Dr. Marcel's recollections differ from his father's in one significant detail. In 1980, New Orleans TV station WWL's Johnny Mann produced a five-part series on UFOs and Maj. Marcel was featured in two segments. In one segment, he said: *"It took me a while to realize that there was something strange about it"* (emphasis added). But Dr. Marcel, who appears in the same program, said: "The *very first time* [emphasis added] I saw that [material] and picked up the I-beam, I knew there was something very unusual." If Dr. Marcel's recollections are correct it means that as a boy of eleven, he was much smarter than his father in his ability to spot material with unusual characteristics.

If the object that crashed on the Brazel ranch was an honest-to-goodness extraterrestrial craft, how fortuitous for Gen. Ramey that it was constructed from materials, including "Scotch tape," whose appearance so closely resembled those then being used to construct a balloon-borne radar corner-reflector.

5.

A Second Saucer Crash?

Approximately eight months after Stanton Friedman first talked with Jesse Marcel, he had heard another tale of a crashed UFO in New Mexico which was said to include recovery of several ET bodies. Following Friedman's UFO lecture in Bemidji, Minnesota, on October 24, 1978, he was approached by Mr. and Mrs. Vernon Malthais who gave their recollections of a story told them in early 1950 by a friend, Grady L. ("Barney") Barnett. Barnett, now deceased, was a civil engineer employed by the U.S. Soil Conservation Service and in 1947 was living in Socorro, New Mexico—roughly 80 miles west of the Brazel ranch.

As later recounted by Friedman, Mr. and Mrs. Malthais said Barnett told them he had been working west of Socorro, when he chanced upon a crashed saucer, about 25 feet in diameter, and the bodies of several small strange-looking creatures. Barnett claimed he was joined by a group of archeologists from the University of Pennsylvania. Shortly, a military party arrived at the scene and ordered Barnett and the University of Pennsylvania group to depart, after swearing them to secrecy. Mrs. Malthais

41

recalled that Barnett "repeated several times that their [ET] eyes were *small* and oddly spaced," according to the Berlitz/Moore book. (*This was prior to the emergence of the "UFO-abduction cult" and the "standard ET" which reportedly has very large eyes.*)

Author Moore later located and interviewed the man who had been Barnett's supervisor at the time, J. F. Danley. According to Moore, Danley recalled that "Barney came into the office one afternoon all kind of excited and said to me: 'You know those flying-saucer things they've been talking about? Well, they're real.' Then he said something about he's just had a look at one of them. I was real busy at the time and wasn't in any mood to buy a story like that, so I just turned around to him and said: 'Bull——!' He didn't explain anything else about it." Danley told Moore that "I got to thinking about it later that maybe I shouldn't have been so rough with him because he wasn't the sort to go around making up stories like that, but when I asked him about it a day or two later all he said was out on the flats, that it looked like a saucer, and that he didn't care to talk about it any more."

If Barnett's crashed-saucer story was true, as a long-time employee of the U.S. government, he would know that he risked loss of his job and retirement pension, or worse, if he violated his (alleged) oath to keep the crashed saucer secret. Yet clearly, if the tale were true, he had violated his oath by revealing the incident to Danley as well as to Mr. and Mrs. Malthais.

At the 1982 MUFON conference, held July 2–4 in Toronto, Canada, Moore presented a paper summarizing the results of his and Friedman's continuing research since the Berlitz/Moore book was published two years earlier. Moore said that he and Friedman had "expended considerable time and effort trying to uncover some lead [*sic*] as to who the members of the 'archaeological expedition' may have been that were mentioned by Barnett as having been additional witnesses to the San Agustin crash. From a variety of sources, we succeeded in compiling a list of individuals who had been on the Plains [of San Agustin] in one capacity or another in 1947. . . ." Moore said, "A few people on the list were located, but seemed to know nothing of value."

Three years later, at the 1985 MUFON conference held June 28–30 in St. Louis, Missouri, Moore provided another update on his and Friedman's efforts. Moore *claimed*, without offering any evidence, that "the presence of University of Pennsylvania students at archaeological digs in the area in 1947 (as well as 1948 and 1949) has been confirmed." But he added that "exhaustive efforts to identify the students in question have been essentially fruitless."

Mr. and Mrs. Malthais originally could not recall when or where Barnett claimed he had seen the crashed saucer and Barnett's supervisor, Danley, also had similar difficulty. Moore reported in 1985 that "efforts to corroborate Danley's recollections of the date and location of the event have also been without success in spite of several lengthy research trips into the Socorro-Magdalena-Datil area. In short, while the Barnett claim may in fact be true, efforts to substantiate it have been repeatedly frustrated by a *marked lack of additional corroborating accounts. Indeed, the whole scenario, based as it is on only Danley's recollection of time and place, may well be substantially in error . . ."* (emphasis added).

Moore admitted "that earlier attempts to tie it [Barnett's crashed-saucer story] to the Roswell Incident [Brazel ranch debris] were somewhat overzealous and definitely premature." Moore concluded that "the Barnett investigation seems to have reached an insurmountable impasse from which nothing in the way of new evidence seems likely to emerge in the foreseeable future."

Barely four years later, in the fall of 1989, the Barnett crashed-saucer tale would be featured on a national TV network show, "Unsolved Mysteries." After seeing a repeat broadcast in early 1990, a Springfield, Missouri, man named Gerald F. Anderson would call in to claim that he and four members of his family—all now deceased—also had encountered the same crashed saucer.

Anderson claimed that the TV version was in error because *one of the four ETs was still alive.* (Anderson's account and its major discrepancies will be discussed in chapter 9.)

By this time, Randle and Schmitt would be claiming that Barnett had been on the Brazel ranch when he found the crashed saucer with four ET bodies—*not 150 miles to the west on the Plains of San Agustin as Berlitz and Moore first reported and Anderson claimed.* Moore and his new collaborator, Jaime Shandera, would challenge both Anderson's claim and the Randle/Schmitt hypothesis. And Stanton Friedman would have broken with Moore, his longtime friend and collaborator, and would endorse Anderson's story and sharply challenge key elements of the Randle/Schmitt scenario. Friedman would claim that *two* saucers suffered a midair collision and that one of them crash-landed on the Brazel ranch while the other managed to fly 150 miles to the west to crash-land on the Plains of San Agustin. Randle and Schmitt would challenge Anderson's story as well as Friedman's claim that *two* saucers had been recovered.

Thus, by mid-1991, there were three "crashed-saucer camps" whose leaders agreed only that one or more crashed saucers had been recovered by the Army Air Forces in New Mexico in July 1947. But they disagreed sharply as to which "witness" claims and recollections were true and which were false. Moore and Shandera insisted that the debris shown in *all* of the photos taken in Gen. Ramey's office were genuine artifacts from a crashed ET craft. Randle and Schmitt challenged this and claimed that the debris shown in *all* of the photos was from a balloon-borne radar corner-reflector which had been substituted for the crashed-saucer debris. Friedman and Berliner opted to *ignore* this key issue and they did not include even one of the Ramey office photos in their book.

All of these crashed-saucer book authors chose to withhold hard evidence in the form of once "Secret" documents from the files of the Central Intelligence Agency which had been released in 1978 and revealed the CIA's assessment of UFOs. And these crashed-saucer book authors also opted to withhold the conclu-

sions of the once "Top Secret" USAF/Navy intelligence report on what the Pentagon believed UFOs were and where they came from, which had been declassified in the spring of 1985. The contents of these documents would have demolished the crashed-saucer claims.

6.

The CIA's Once-Secret UFO Papers

On December 17, 1978—more than a year before publication of the Berlitz/Moore book on Roswell—the CIA released roughly nine hundred pages of UFO-related material from its files, including internal documents once classified "Secret." The agency's action was the result of the Freedom of Information Act (FOIA) which had been enacted by the U.S. Congress nearly four years earlier. FOIA enabled U.S. citizens to obtain information from any government agency, including the CIA, unless that agency could demonstrate that release of the information would significantly hurt national security.

The first UFO group to take advantage of FOIA was Ground Saucer Watch (GSW), in Phoenix, Arizona, headed by William Spaulding. On June 7, 1975, Spaulding filed an FOIA request to obtain a copy of a report by a panel of high-level scientists, headed by Dr. H. P. Robertson, which the CIA had convened in early 1953 to assess the UFO mystery. Before the month was over, Spaulding received a copy of the Robertson Panel report, originally classified "Secret."

On September 12, 1977, a more comprehensive FOIA request was filed with the CIA in GSW's behalf by Peter A. Gersten, a New York City attorney with a long-standing interest in UFOs and deep suspicions of government coverup. In the FOIA action, Gersten asked the CIA to release any information it had on a number of specific UFO incidents. To Gersten's great surprise, the CIA responded on August 17, 1978, asking that GSW change its FOIA request to ask the agency to conduct "a reasonable search" of its files and to release *all* UFO material—except for any that could damage national security. Gersten revised the FOIA request and a few months later the CIA released some nine hundred pages of material.

One of the earliest documents in the collection was an internal memorandum dated March 15, 1949, written by a Dr. Stone in the CIA's Office of Scientific Intelligence (OSI) to a Dr. Machle, also of OSI. Stone's memo—written nearly two years *after* the claimed recovery of a crashed saucer in New Mexico—concluded:

> Studies on the various possibilities [explanations for UFOs] have been made by Dr. Langmuir of GE [a world-renowned scientist and Nobel Prize winner], Dr. Valley of MIT [Massachusetts Institute of Technology expert on air defense], Dr. Lipp of Project Rand [an Air Force "Think Tank"], Dr. Hynek of Ohio State [University],* and [USAF] Aero Medical Lab. That the objects are from outer space or are an advanced aircraft of a foreign power is a possibility, but the above group have concluded that it is highly improbable. In discussions of this subject with Mr. Deyarmond at Wright Patterson Air Force Base, he seemed to think, and I agree, that "flying disks" will turn out to be another "sea serpent." *However, since there is even a remote possibility that they may be interplanetary or foreign aircraft, it is necessary to investigate each sighting.* (Emphasis added)

---

*Dr. J. Allen Hynek, a professor of astronomy at Ohio State University in the late 1940s, was hired by the USAF to serve as a consultant in its UFO investigations after the USAF discovered that many UFO reports were generated by bright celestial objects. In the early 1970s, after the USAF shut down its Project Blue Book UFO investigation office, Hynek created his Center for UFO Studies (CUFOS).

If the U.S. government already had physical evidence that some UFOs were ET craft, then it was deliberately wasting the time and talent of some of the nation's top scientists, and CIA technical analysts.

The CIA's UFO papers show that the agency first became actively involved in the UFO issue in mid-1952—a year in which the USAF received 1,501 UFO reports—nearly twice the combined total reported during the five years since the first report by pilot Kenneth Arnold. In early April, the very widely read and influential *LIFE* magazine carried a feature story on UFOs which was headlined: "Have We Visitors from Space?" Two months later, in June, the USAF received 149 UFO reports—*ten times the monthly average of the previous year. The following month, the USAF received more than three times as many UFO reports as in June.*

The final straw came on July 20 when the news media learned that several mysterious, unidentified "blips" had been spotted on the recently installed radar at Washington's National Airport shortly after midnight. If UFOs were ET craft, as the *LIFE* article suggested, perhaps they were reconnoitering the air defenses of the nation's capital preparatory to an attack. If so, ETs found the nation's capital undefended. Word of the mysterious radar blips belatedly reached the USAF's Air Defense Command and it dispatched a single F-94C interceptor from the closest base in Delaware. But by the time the interceptor arrived it was daylight and the mysterious blips had disappeared from the radar scopes. In response to news media inquiries, the Pentagon responded that the incident was under investigation.

One week later, during the night of July 26–27, another group of mysterious blips appeared on the same Washington National Airport radar, prompting banner newspaper headlines around the nation. The July 29 edition of Washington's *Times Herald* reported "A.F. Officials Seek to Quell Public Alarm," and said that Air Force UFO experts had been "summoned to Washington for a conference on the second appearance of mysterious objects here within a week." One of these was Capt. Edward J. Ruppelt, who in the spring of 1951 had been named to head the USAF's UFO investigations office—now called Project Blue Book—at Wright-Patterson AFB near Dayton, Ohio.

At 10 A.M., Ruppelt received a call from the White House, from Brig. Gen. Landry who said he was calling at the request of President Harry S. Truman "to find out what was happening in the skies over Washington," according to the book *The UFO Controversy in America* (Indiana University Press, 1975), authored by David Jacobs. "Later, Ruppelt learned that Truman had been listening in on the conversation," the book reported. *If one or more crashed saucers and several ET bodies had been recovered five years earlier in New Mexico, apparently nobody thought to inform the nation's commander in chief of what might be the precursor of an ET attack. Or else Truman had a short memory for what should have been an unforgettable event.*

The Pentagon held a press conference at which Maj. Gen. John Samford, director of USAF Intelligence, presided. He said that USAF radar experts suspected the mysterious radar blips were caused by a sharp temperature inversion which causes some radar energy to be refracted downward and reflected back by surface objects, such as automobiles and buildings.

Subsequent investigation by the Civil Aeronautics Administration (CAA) (now the Federal Aviation Administration [FAA]) would confirm that the mysterious radar blips were the result of a temperature inversion and inadequate training of the Washington controllers in the shortcomings of early vintage radars. The CAA investigators found that such mysterious blips had appeared many times on radars in Chicago, Cleveland, and Boston—particularly during temperature inversions—but controllers there recognized them as spurious targets. CAA scientists had themselves observed such spurious targets on the night of August 13, 1952, at a long-range radar covering the Washington area. The blips moved in the direction of the prevailing winds aloft at twice wind velocity—exactly as theory indicates they should. But the results of this CAA investigation would not be published until May 1953.

If the news media—being unfamiliar with the limitations of radar—questioned the validity of the temperature-inversion explanation, the White House also began to wonder whether the USAF's assurances that there were no unidentified vehicles in our skies were valid. It was this that prompted the CIA to initiate its own investigation shortly after the second "UFOs over Washington" incident. Details of the CIA's involvement, classified "Secret" at the time, first became public in late 1978, thanks to the FOIA.

For example, a few days after the Washington incident, a memo from Edward Tauss, then acting chief of the CIA's Weapons and Equipment Division, responded to an inquiry from his superior about UFOs. In the August 1 memo, Tauss noted that only about 10 percent of the UFO sightings reported to the USAF remained unexplained. And he added that "it is probable that if complete information were available for presently 'unexplainable' reports, they too" could be explained. However, Tauss added that "so long as a series of reports remains 'unexplainable' *(interplanetary aspects and alien origin not being thoroughly excluded from consideration)* caution requires that Intelligence continue coverage of the subject" (emphasis added).

Tauss recommended that the agency continue to monitor the UFO situation. He added: "It is strongly urged, however, that no indication of CIA interest or concern reach the press or the public, in view of their probable alarmist tendencies to accept such interest as 'confirmatory' of the soundness of [claims that there are] 'unpublished facts' in the hands of the U.S. Government." (Charges of government UFO coverup had earlier been made by Donald Keyhoe, a retired Marine Corps pilot-turned-freelance-writer, who authored many articles and several books on the subject. Keyhoe later helped create NICAP and headed the organization.) Tauss concluded his memo by noting that arrangements had been made for CIA analysts to receive a "thorough and comprehensive briefing related to this subject" on August 8 by the USAF's Air Technical Intelligence Center (ATIC) at Wright-Patterson AFB. If one or more crashed saucers had been recovered in

New Mexico, or elsewhere, they would have been sent to the laboratories at WPAFB for analysis and the results would have been reported to ATIC.

Top CIA officials were briefed on the results of the Office of Scientific Intelligence's initial UFO investigation in mid-August 1952, based on the dates of several briefing papers released under FOIA—all of them originally classified "Secret." One of these briefing papers, dated August 14, said the objective of the CIA's UFO survey was to:

> . . . make an evaluation of the Air Force study, its methodology and coverage, the relation of its conclusions to various theories which have been propounded and to try to reach some conclusions as to the intelligence implications of the problem—if any. *In view of the wide interest within the Agency,* this briefing has been arranged so that we could report on the survey. It must be mentioned that outside knowledge of Agency interest in Flying Saucers carries the risk of making the problem even more serious in the public mind than it already is, which we and the Air Force agree must be avoided.
>
> In order to supply both the breadth and depth to the survey we have reviewed our own intelligence, going back to the Swedish sightings of 1946; reviewed a large number of individual official [UFO] reports, recent press and magazine coverage and the main popular books. Indexes of the Soviet press were scanned [for mention of any Russian UFO sightings]. We interviewed a representative of the Air Force Special Study Group. Following this, we spent a day at Wright Field in a thorough discussion with the officers conducting the ATIC study, and finally we took the problem to a selected group of our own consultants, all leaders in their scientific fields. (Emphasis added)

This initial briefing paper, dated 14 August 1952, described the history of the UFO mystery and then presented "four major theories" which had been advanced to explain UFO sighting reports:

First, that it is a U.S. secret weapon development. This has been denied officially at the highest level of government and to make doubly certain we queried Dr. Whitman, Chairman of the Research and Development Board. *On a Top Secret basis,* he too denies it. . . .

The second theory is that these are a Russian development. Though we know that the Russians have done work on elliptical and delta wing principles, we have absolutely no intelligence of such a technological advance as would be indicated here in either design or energy source. Further, there seems to be no logical reason for the security risk that would be involved [in flying Soviet craft over the United States] and there has been no indication of a reconnaissance pattern. However, there is a totally unsupported thesis that this may be a Russian high altitude development of the World War II Jap[anese] balloon effort using preset flares and the resulting US press reports to check flight tracks.

The third theory is the man from Mars—space ships—interplanetary travelers. Even though we might admit that intelligent life may exist elsewhere and that space travel is possible, *there is no shred of evidence to support this theory at present.*

The fourth major theory is that now held by the Air Force, that the sightings, given adequate data, can be explained either on the basis of misinterpretation of known objects, or of as yet little understood natural phenomena. (Emphasis added)

The second CIA briefing paper, dated August 15 and also classified "Secret," began:

In the next few minutes, I intend to touch briefly upon the official [USAF] explanations of the great majority of sightings of unidentified flying objects (or UFOs) and mention possible phenomena which may account for some of the open [unexplained] cases. Before we elaborate upon the current explanations I would like you to keep in mind certain facts which are common to all reports. First is the earnestness of those making reports. These people are certain that they have seen *something*. Secondly, objects sighted almost always are reported to be against the sky thereby providing no point of reference. Thirdly, without a reference point, a valid estimation of size, speed, distance of relative motion [*sic*] is virtually impossible. *Finally, no debris or material evidence has ever been recovered following an unexplained sighting.* (Emphasis added)

On September 24, 1952, H. Marshall Chadwell, the director of the CIA's Office of Scientific Intelligence wrote a memo for the Director of Central Intelligence which summarized the findings of the UFO survey conducted by his group and their implications for national security. The CIA official noted that the USAF's then current policy of investigating UFO reports on a case-by-case basis

does not solve the more fundamental aspects of the problem . . . to determine definitely the nature of the various phenomena which are causing these sightings, and to discover means by which these causes, and their visual or electronic effects, may be identified immediately. The CIA consultants stated that these solutions would probably be found on the margins or just beyond the frontiers of our present knowledge in the fields of atmospheric, ionospheric and extraterrestrial [i.e., cosmic rays] phenomena, with the added possibility that the present dispersal of nuclear waste products might also be a factor. . . .

The flying saucer situation contains two elements of danger which, in a situation of international tension, have national security implications. These are: Psychological—With worldwide sightings reported, it was found that, up to the time of the investigation, there had been in the Soviet press no report or comment, even satirical, on flying saucers. . . . With a State-controlled press, this could only result from an official policy decision. The question, therefore, arises as to whether or not these sightings: (1) could be controlled, (2) could be predicted, and (3) could be used from a psychological warfare point of view, either offensively or defensively. *The public concern with the phenomena . . . indicates that a fair proportion of our population is mentally conditioned to the acceptance of the incredible. In this fact lies the potential for the touching-off of mass hysteria and panic.* (Emphasis added)

The second element of danger which Chadwell cited in his memo was:

> [*Air Vulnerability:*] The United States Air Warning System will undoubtedly always depend upon a combination of radar screening and visual observation. The U.S.S.R. is credited with the present capability of delivering an air attack against the United States, yet at any given moment now, there may be current a dozen *official* unidentified sightings plus many unofficial ones. At any moment of attack, we are now in a position where we cannot, on an instant basis, distinguish hardware [Soviet bombers] from phantoms [UFO reports], and as tension mounts we will run the increasing risk of false alerts and the even greater danger of falsely identifying the real as phantom. . . . (Emphasis added)

Chadwell recommended research into atmospheric and other natural phenomena that might be triggering UFO reports as well as techniques to more accurately distinguish enemy bombers from nonthreatening UFO reports. His memo also recommended actions that would logically be carried out by the CIA, such as determining the "present level of Soviet knowledge regarding these phenomena (and) possible Soviet intentions and capabilities to utilize these phenomena to the detriment of the United States security interests."

Chadwell's memo concluded: "I consider this problem to be of such importance that it should be brought to the attention of the National Security Council in order that a community-wide coordinated effort towards its solution may be initiated." On October 2, Chadwell wrote a follow-up memo which contained a draft memorandum for the Director of Central Intelligence to sign and submit to the National Security Council proposing that the CIA join the USAF in an expanded-scope UFO effort.

The CIA's Deputy Director for Intelligence, James Q. Reber, in a memo dated October 13, 1952, acknowledged that "determination of the scientific capabilities of the USSR to create and control

Flying Saucers as a weapon against the United States is a primary concern of the CIA/OSI." But he added that "its review of existing information does not lead to the conclusion that the saucers are USSR created or controlled." Reber's memo reveals that he was opposed to the CIA becoming actively involved in investigating UFOs. He argued that "the institution of fundamental scientific research is the primary responsibility of the Defense Department." He added: "It is far too early in view of the present state of our knowledge regarding Flying Saucers for psychological warfare planners to start planning how the United States might use U.S. Flying Saucers against the enemy. When intelligence has submitted the National Estimate on Flying Saucers there will be time and basis for a public policy to reduce or restrain mass hysteria."

To help resolve this internal CIA controversy, Chadwell proposed that a panel of top scientists be convened to examine the most impressive cases and evidence in the USAF's possession. Once-"Secret" CIA documents released in late 1978 show that the UFO issue was discussed at the December 4, 1952 meeting of the Intelligence Advisory Committee, consisting of top intelligence officials from the Defense Department, USAF, Army, and Navy; CIA, FBI, Atomic Energy Commission, and State Department. The group endorsed the idea that the CIA should "enlist the services of selected scientists to review and appraise the available [UFO] evidence in the light of pertinent scientific theories."

The panel of five scientists, which convened in Washington on January 14, 1953, was chaired by Dr. H. P. Robertson, a physicist from the California Institute of Technology who earlier had been director of research for the Pentagon's Weapon System Evaluation Group. Another panel member was Dr. Luis Alvarez, a Nobel Prize winner and recognized expert on radar and electronics. During the three days the panel met, it considered seventy-five of the USAF's "best documented" cases, including two where observers had taken home movies of UFOs. The Robertson Panel's conclusions, summarized in a report then classified "Secret," included: "We firmly believe that there is no residuum of cases which indicates phenomena which are attributable to foreign artifacts capable of hostile acts, and that there is no evidence that the phenomena indicate a need for the revision of current scientific concepts."

This Robertson Panel report echoed CIA concerns that public preoccupation with UFOs might interfere with an effective air defense against a Soviet bomber attack. It also expressed concern that the Soviets might exploit public interest in UFOs to *"induce hysterical behavior and harmful distrust of duly constituted authority"* (emphasis added).

The Robertson Panel conclusions resolved the issue of whether the CIA should become actively involved in investigating UFOs, as Chadwell had proposed. But it raised a new bureaucratic issue: who would be saddled with maintaining files of UFO reports and newspaper clippings sent in by embassies and overseas agents? In a memo dated January 27, 1953, Lt. Col. Frederick C. E. Ober (USAF), a member of the Physics and Electronics (P&E) Division of the Office of Scientific Intelligence, argued *against* a recommendation that his office be responsible for maintaining UFO files—but to no avail.

Several months later, Todos M. Odarenko—who headed the P&E Division—wrote a memo dated July 3, 1953, to complain that a careful analysis of incoming UFO clippings and material required the full-time services of two analysts and one file clerk. Odarenko's memo indicated that he had decided to downgrade the effort to "inactive" so it could be handled on a part-time basis by one analyst and one file clerk. Two years later, on August 8, 1955, Odarenko wrote a memo to his boss in which he said: *"In view of the fact that no positive intelligence of significance has been produced under the subject [UFO] project, it is recommended that the project be terminated and the files thereof be placed in dead storage"* (emphasis added).

The CIA's UFO papers released in late 1978 included a memo, dated March 26, 1956, from the agency's Deputy Director for Intelligence, Robert Amory Jr. In the memo to Herbert Scoville Jr., then Assistant Director for Scientific Intelligence, Amory said he had recently read an article in a French magazine about a UFO incident in France. Amory asked: "Are we keeping in touch with the Air Force [UFO] center on these things?" Amory's memo concluded: "Outlandish as it may seem, I do feel that OSI has the responsibility to keep its finger on this general subject if for no other purpose than to arm the front office with the refutation of the more spectacular reports." Scoville responded saying that the French magazine article "gives the impression that the sighting has been considerably exaggerated to produce a more sensational story." He added that if the incident were rigorously investigated "most likely an identification could be made." In response to his superior's suggestion, Scoville said his office "will follow the general subject closely, and keep you informed on the more spectacular published reports." However, there is no evidence in the CIA papers that Scoville's commitment was carried out because of more pressing duties resulting from the USSR's impressive advances in ballistic missile and space technology then under way.

It is important to emphasize that these internal CIA memoranda—many of them originally classified "Secret"—were written roughly twenty years before Congress passed the Freedom of Information Act which would result in their being made public. They provide incontrovertible evidence that if one or more crashed saucers and ET bodies were recovered from New Mexico in 1947, word of this historic event had not been reported to top CIA officials or President Truman as of mid-1952—some five years later.

7.

The "Cosmic Watergate"

"The Roswell Incident: Beginning of the Cosmic Watergate" was the title of the paper presented by Stanton Friedman at the 1981 MUFON conference, held July 25–26 in Cambridge, Massachusetts. In the published proceedings, Friedman's paper opened with a quotation attributed to Albert Einstein: *"The right to search for truth implies also a duty: one must not conceal any part of what one has recognized to be the truth"* (emphasis added).

The CIA's UFO papers had been made public more than two years before. In Friedman's twenty-two-page (single-spaced) published paper, he referred only briefly to the CIA papers, saying "it is quite clear that the 900 pages released by the CIA were merely the top [sic] of the iceberg, since they internally contain references to at least 200 other documents." *But Friedman withheld from his audience all of the information in the CIA documents cited in the previous chapter which would have demolished his claims of recovered crashed saucers and government coverup!*

Friedman acknowledged criticism of the Berlitz/Moore book "because of the Berlitz reputation for sensational, but inaccurate reporting of the so-called Bermuda Triangle mystery." Friedman explained that Berlitz had been invited to write the book because he had excellent contacts in the publishing world. "Thanks to Charles [Berlitz], 'The Roswell Incident' is now in print in more than 10 countries. For example, the English publishers met with Charles, who submitted a four-page outline, before the research was completed or any manuscript was prepared. They agreed to a 50,000 [British] pound (over $100,000) payment for the privilege of publishing the book, knowing as did the other foreign publishers that the Berlitz name would make it a success."

Friedman said Berlitz "insisted on adding a number of sensational, irrelevant stories" but added, "I think any intelligent reader of the book can separate the directly relevant research from the window dressing." Friedman admitted that "there were some bad moments" during his and Moore's research. "Both Bill Moore and I, when first looking at the prints of the pictures made by the Fort Worth Star Telegram in General Ramey's office, *worried about the material in the pictures really being from a balloon"* (emphasis added).

The next year at the 1982 MUFON conference held in Toronto, Canada, July 3–4, Moore presented a paper titled "The Roswell Investigation: New Evidence in the Search for a Crashed UFO." Moore's paper, as published in the conference proceedings, began:

> Rumors and stories about crashed UFOs and dead alien bodies have abounded for more than 30 years. Although various books, magazine articles and monographs have been published on the topic since as far back as 1950, the evidence needed to substantiate even one of these stories remained obscure until relatively recently. Now, as a result of an exhaustive investigation conducted over the last three and one-half years by myself, physicist Stanton T. Friedman and, to a lesser extent, author and linguist Charles Berlitz, *solid evidence for such an event has begun to emerge.* (Emphasis added)

Moore said the evidence he would present, along with other evidence, would be included in a new book he planned to write, tentatively titled *The Roswell Evidence*. (The book was never published.) Although Moore's 1982 MUFON paper ran 20 single-spaced typewritten pages in the conference proceedings, *there was not even a brief mention of the CIA papers that had been made public more than three years earlier.*

Moore spoke again three years later at the 1985 MUFON conference held in St. Louis, Missouri, June 28–30. His paper, titled "Crashed Saucers: Evidence in Search of Proof," totaled fifty single-spaced typewritten pages in the conference proceedings. Slightly less than half was devoted to debunking the Frank Scully crashed-saucer tale of the early 1950s while the remainder covered the Roswell Incident. Moore said that during the more than seven years since he and Friedman began their Roswell investigation, they had interviewed "no less than 91 different individuals who were able to provide varying degrees of information about the incident. Of those, 30 would have to be regarded as first-hand, or key, witnesses in that they were in some way personally involved either with the discovery, recovery or subsequent coverup." Moore said he had traveled more than 200,000 miles in his research into the Roswell Incident.

But in the twenty-six pages that Moore devoted to the Roswell Incident there was not a single mention of the contents of the CIA papers made public more than six years earlier.

At the same MUFON conference, Moore's partner Stanton Friedman spoke on "Flying Saucers, Noisy Negativists and Truth." In his published paper, Friedman criticized my then new book *UFOs: The Public Deceived* (Prometheus Books, 1983). Its first five chapters focused on CIA involvement with UFOs and included much of the material quoted in the preceding chapter. But Friedman did not even mention *any* of the contents of the CIA papers because this would demolish his Roswell crashed-saucer claims. Knowing that the public is unfamiliar with military security practices, Friedman devised a clever scheme to explain why there was no mention of *any* crashed saucer in the CIA papers. He would use the same ploy later when other once highly classified USAF letters and memoranda surfaced.

Friedman would claim that the Roswell crashed-saucer recovery was classified "Top Secret," and this explained why it was never mentioned in CIA (and USAF) documents which were only classified "Secret." In fact, all of the high-level CIA personnel involved in the agency's 1952 UFO investigation had "Top Secret" clearances. They could have classified their mid-August 1952 report to the Director of Central Intelligence "Top Secret" if its contents warranted. *More importantly, they would not intentionally lie to the DCI by reporting that "no [UFO] debris or material evidence has ever been recovered . . . ,"* knowing that he would report the agency's findings to President Truman.

This ridiculous Friedman claim was demolished in early March 1985 when a once "Top Secret" intelligence document was declassified and released by the National Archives. The document, titled "Analysis of Flying Object Incidents in the U.S.," had been prepared by the USAF's Directorate of Intelligence and the Office of Naval Intelligence. The document, identified as Air Intelligence Report No. 100-203-79, was dated *10 December 1948—some sixteen months after an ET craft allegedly was recovered in New Mexico.*

This report was an effort by top USAF and Navy intelligence experts to assess for the White House and for top Pentagon officials what was responsible for generating the rash of UFO reports since the first one by Kenneth Arnold some eighteen months earlier. As stated on the report's opening page: "PROBLEM: TO EXAMINE pattern of tactics of 'Flying Saucers' (hereinafter referred to as flying objects) and to develop conclusions *as to the possibility of [their] existence"* (emphasis added). The report noted that UFO reports had been received from seemingly reliable observers such as military and civilian pilots, and that some of the reports might have been triggered by "weather balloons, rockets, experimental flying wing aircraft or celestial phenomena." But the document focused on the possibility that some UFO reports might be secret Soviet reconnaissance vehicles, developed by talented German scientists who had been captured and brought back to the USSR at the end of World War II. *At no place does the report even speculate that any UFOs might be ET craft.*

If the U.S. government had recovered a crashed ET craft in New Mexico in July 1947, this once Top Secret report reveals that nobody informed top officials of the USAF and Navy who were responsible for defending against attack by enemy craft. (Other once highly classified documents which reveal there was no crashed ET craft will be reported in subsequent chapters.)

Ironically, the first UFOlogist to see Air Intelligence Report No. 100-203-79 was *Stanton Friedman*, who was in Washington in early March 1985 to attend a conference. During a visit to the National Archives, Friedman learned that this document, along with many others from USAF intelligence files dating back to 1947, had just been declassified. This was in response to a Freedom of Information Act request by UFO-researcher Robert G. Todd, of Ardmore, Pennsylvania. Because this document, prepared by top USAF and Navy intelligence officials, was formerly classified "Top Secret," it demolished the Moore and Friedman excuse that the reason there was no mention of a crashed saucer in any of the CIA papers was that they were *only* classified "Secret."

Friedman promptly informed Moore of this document and sent him a copy. The August 31, 1985 issue of *Focus* newsletter, which Moore published, began: "In March, 1985, the National Archives in Washington D.C., released more than 1,000 pages of previously classified files originating with the Air Force Directorate of Intelligence between 1947 and 1954. *The most significant of these items* was the previously Top Secret 'Air Intelligence Study No. 203: Analysis of Flying Object Incidents in the United States,' dated 10 December, 1948 . . ." (emphasis added). Moore noted that this report had been published in its entirety in the July 1985 issue of the *MUFON UFO Journal.*

But Moore did not inform readers of the document's implica-

tions for his Roswell crashed-saucer claims. When Moore spoke at the 1985 MUFON conference, he cited recently discovered circumstantial evidence that appeared to support his crashed-saucer story but there was *no mention* of the Air Intelligence Report. In Friedman's 1985 MUFON talk, he devoted much time to lambasting me and others for questioning crashed-saucer claims. But he made no mention of the once Top Secret Air Intelligence Report of 1948 that demolished his crashed-saucer claims.

Although Moore and Friedman have spoken at several subsequent MUFON conferences, neither has ever discussed the contents or implications of the once-Secret CIA papers or once-Top Secret Air Intelligence Report. Instead, they repeatedly accuse the U.S. government of coverup. Their actions recall the quotation from Albert Einstein with which Friedman began his 1981 MUFON paper: "The right to search for the truth implies also a duty: one must not conceal any part of what one has recognized to be the truth."

Either Friedman has intentionally ignored this duty or he is unable to recognize "the truth" when he sees it.

8.

Mortician's ET Autopsy Tale

Not long after 1st Lt. Walter G. Haut wrote the flying disk press release which had created so much unwanted publicity for the Army Air Force—soon to become the U.S. Air Force—he was transferred to another job: commander of the base security guard. The following spring Haut decided to resign from the USAF and left in August 1948. Initially he opened a collection agency in Roswell but soon shifted to selling insurance. By the late 1970s, when Haut was interviewed by Moore and Friedman, he had left the insurance business and was now operating a small art gallery and picture-framing shop in Roswell.

During my first meeting with Haut in Roswell in early December 1991, I found him to be an extremely affable person and quite cooperative although he knew I was skeptical of the Roswell crashed-saucer tale. Haut told me that for more than thirty years he had believed Gen. Ramey's crashed-weather-balloon/radar-target explanation until 1980 when Jesse Marcel returned to Roswell to film a TV series on UFOs for a New Orleans station. Although Haut and Marcel had both remained at RAAF for about a year after the flying disk incident, Haut told me that Marcel had never once hinted to him that the weather-balloon/radar-target explanation was not true.

On August 17, 1948, Marcel had been transferred to a desk-job at the Strategic Air Command (SAC) headquarters, then at Andrews AF Base near Washington, D.C. Barely two years later, during the Korean War, Marcel decided to resign and gave "undue hardship" as his reason. Marcel had suffered some ridicule as a result of the flying disk incident, according to Gen. Gene Tighe who had worked under Marcel as a young officer. "Marcel's reputation suffered dramatically at SAC," according to Tighe, because of the Roswell Incident.

After Marcel resigned he returned to his hometown of Houma, Louisiana, about 40 miles southwest of New Orleans. There he set up a radio-TV repair shop that he operated until he retired in the mid-1970s—several years before he was "discovered" by Friedman. In early 1979, Friedman was hired as a consultant by a Hollywood producer to make a "documentary" on UFOs called *UFOs Are Real.* In May 1979, the Hollywood film crew interviewed Marcel, giving him his first taste of "celebrity-hood."

Some of Marcel's filmed recollections—quoted in the book by Berlitz/Moore (p. 66)—were quite accurate. For example, Marcel said that a lot of the debris "looked like parchment." (Radar targets of that era were constructed from a parchmentlike material to which was attached a thin metal foil. The metal foil reflected radar energy and the parchment provided structural rigidity.) Marcel recalled that the debris included "pieces of metal . . . so thin, just like the tin-foil in a pack of cigarettes." He recalled trying to bend the material but "it would not bend. We even tried making a dent in it with a 16-lb. sledge-hammer, and there still was no dent in it." The foregoing portion of Marcel's recollections is widely quoted—but *not* his clarification of what he meant. "Now by bend, I mean *crease.* It was possible to flex this stuff back and forth, even to wrinkle it, but you could not put a crease in it that would stay. . . . I would almost describe it as a metal with plastic properties." (This is the type of structural rigidity that parchment paper covered with thin aluminum is intended to provide.)

Marcel recalled that the debris included "small beams about three-eighths or a half inch square." (Marcel's son, who was eleven at the time, would later claim that they were "I-beam"-shaped rather than square.) Maj. Marcel said the beams "looked something like balsa wood and were about the same weight, except they were not wood at all. They were very hard, although flexible, but would not burn." Marcel's aging recollections that he attempted to burn these lightweight beams and that an associate tried to dent the metal-foil material are suspect. If the material seemed that extraordinary, it should have been carefully preserved and sent to Air Force laboratories at Wright Field for analysis. It seems surprising that Marcel would attempt his own tests using a sledgehammer and cigarette lighter. Marcel also recalled that these small sticks had "some sort of hieroglyphics [i.e., symbols] on them that nobody could decipher." He said that "those symbols were pink and purple."

Yet there are other examples of Marcel's recollections that are clearly flawed. For example, the Berlitz/Moore book quotes Marcel as recalling that he and Cavitt had arrived back at Roswell

> in the early evening. When we arrived there, we discovered that the story we had found a flying disk had leaked out ahead of us. We had an eager-beaver PIO [public information officer/Lt. Haut] on the base who had taken it on himself to call the AP [Associated Press] on this thing. We had several calls that night, and one reporter even came to the house, but of course I couldn't confirm anything to them. . . . The next morning that written press release went out and after that . . . the phone rang right off the hook. I heard that the brass [AAF officials] "fried him" later for putting out that press release, but then I can't say for sure. . . . (p. 67)

It is known with certainty that Marcel and Cavitt arrived at the Brazel ranch around dusk on Monday, July 7; departed early the

MORTICIAN'S ET AUTOPSY TALE

next morning for RAAF; and by midday Marcel was flying the debris to Gen. Ramey in Fort Worth. Further, that Haut did not distribute his "flying disk" press release until around noon on July 8—*after Marcel had returned to Roswell and was en route to Fort Worth.*

By late 1979, Marcel was becoming a famous "UFO-celebrity." On December 8 he was interviewed by Bob Pratt, a reporter for the *National Enquirer* tabloid newspaper. Pratt's story appeared in the February 28, 1980 edition under the headline: "Former Intelligence Officer Reveals . . . I PICKED UP WRECKAGE OF UFO THAT EXPLODED OVER U.S." Pratt's article quoted Marcel as saying: "It was nothing that came from this earth."

Not long afterward, Johnny Mann of New Orleans TV station WWL decided to produce a series on UFOs and to feature Marcel who lived in nearby Houma. Mann offered to fly Marcel back to Roswell—his first return in forty-two years—to film his interview. Mann also wanted to film an interview with Walter Haut, which led to the first reunion of Haut and Marcel in forty-two years. It was during this visit, Haut told me, that he first heard Marcel reject Gen. Ramey's explanation. When the Mann TV show was broadcast in the fall of 1980, it showed Haut saying: "It must have been something of, out of the ordinary." Mann interrupted to ask: "Not of this world?" Haut responded: "Out of this world." *But neither Marcel nor Haut—nor Marcel's son (Dr. Jesse Marcel Jr.) who was also interviewed on Mann's show—made any mention of ET bodies.*

During my 1991 interview with Haut, I asked when he had first heard anyone claim that ET bodies had been recovered. He said he thought it was "in the early 1980s." This was shortly after publication of the Berlitz/Moore book which reported Barnett's claim of seeing ET bodies on the Plains of San Agustin—150 miles west of the Brazel ranch. I asked Haut: *"Before* the Berlitz/Moore book was published, did any of the local people come up to you and say, 'I hear there were [ET] bodies'?" Haut replied: *"Not a soul."*

When I asked Haut when he had first heard about former mortician Glenn Dennis's story of a nurse who had been involved in an ET autopsy at the Roswell base, Haut replied: "Two or three years ago," i.e., in the late 1980s. Max Littell, another longtime Roswell resident who was present during my interview, commented: "About the same time that he told me about it." Haut added: "I happen, personally, to believe Glenn. *He's a friend of many, many years.*"

I asked Haut how he had learned of the nurse/ET autopsy story. He replied: "I was out at the [local] air show and a party came up to me and said, 'You know, there's a guy here in town that knows an awful lot about this UFO situation and I've never heard anybody quote him.' " Haut continued: "I kind of looked skeptical because I figured it would be some 'weirdo off the wall,' and I said 'Who?' And this party said 'Glenn Dennis.' And I said what the heck would he know? And this party told me that he [Dennis] was a mortician for Ballard's [Funeral Home] at that time and he had some involvement. And the party told me: 'I don't know but what I've heard he had some involvement in relation to the bodies.' "

I asked Haut if he had then called his longtime friend to try to verify this startling news and he said he had not. However, Haut said that during a later conversation with Stanton Friedman he had suggested that Friedman talk to Dennis. Friedman did so and during his visit to Roswell in early August 1989, he became the first UFOlogist to hear Dennis's nurse/ET autopsy story. Haut declined to identify the person who tipped him off to Dennis's story, but there is good reason to believe it was Robert J. Shirkey, a close friend of Dennis. Shirkey was interviewed by TV producer George Knapp in August 1989 for a series on UFOs for Las Vegas TV station KLAS which was broadcast in November of that year.

At one point in the show, the narrator said: "Numerous witnesses say they saw the crashed disk, the bodies of dead aliens inside. But the military seized the evidence and swore them to secrecy. Walter Haut says flat out that the story of the weather balloon was a coverup. *So does Bob Shirkey.* Shirkey was the officer who ordered up the B-29 that transported the strange debris [to Fort Worth]. He saw the wreckage. . . . Shirkey also had knowledge of the alien bodies. *The information is from a close friend who ran the town funeral parlor in the 40s. It has never been made public until now"* (emphasis added).

Shirkey then appeared and said he had been asked by a friend: "Did you see the sketches in the paper of the humanoids or bodies? [The *Roswell Daily Record* published an artist's concept of an ET face in its June 8, 1987 edition as part of a series on UFOs.] He said, 'Well, I can tell you that's what they looked like.' He said, 'our funeral parlor had the contract. *And they came in and took all of the baby-size or youth-size caskets we had*' " (emphasis added). Shirkey accompanied Friedman when he drove to Lincoln, New Mexico, to interview Dennis who was then manager of a small hotel.

During the interview, which Friedman tape-recorded, Dennis said the Ballard Funeral Home provided ambulance service as well as embalming for the Roswell Army Air Field (RAAF). One afternoon, according to Dennis, he received a call from the RAAF mortuary officer who asked how many small sealed caskets Ballard had in stock. Later, according to Dennis, the mortuary officer called to ask how to move bodies which had been exposed to sunlight for several days. Still later, another call came asking how embalming fluid might affect body tissues.

Later that afternoon, Dennis said, he drove a slightly injured airman out to the base hospital. He decided to park in back and go inside in the hope of seeing an attractive young nurse who had recently been assigned to RAAF. While walking into the rear of the hospital, Dennis said he saw several old-style square military ambulances being guarded by two military police (MPs). The doors were open and inside Dennis said he saw strange-looking wreckage. When Dennis entered the hospital, he said he saw more MPs and unfamiliar military officers who challenged his presence.

Suddenly, Dennis told Friedman, the pretty young nurse dashed into the hall, spotted him and said: "How in the hell did you get in here?" She added: "My God, you are going to get killed." (Dennis told me that the nurse had been raised in a very religious Catholic family and intended to become a nun when she finished her military service.) At that point, according to Dennis, two MPs "grabbed me by the arms and carried me clear outside. ... They told me to get my ass out of there" and followed him all the way back to the mortuary. Dennis told Friedman that several hours later he received a call threatening to jail him "if you open your mouth."

The next day, according to Dennis, the young nurse called him and suggested they have lunch at the RAAF officers' club. At lunch, she said that the previous afternoon when she had gone into a room to obtain supplies, she had encountered two doctors performing autopsies on two small, strange-looking creatures and the remains of a third. She said the doctors insisted she stay and assist them. In the officers' club, Dennis said, the young nurse took out a pad of paper and drew five sketches showing the faces with bald heads and large black eyes, and their arms and hands. The sketches showed four fingers with tiny suction cups at the tips, no thumbs or fingernails.

When I interviewed Dennis in Roswell on December 9, 1991, he told me that the young nurse offered to give him her sketches of the creatures on the condition that he take a "sacred oath" never to disclose what she had revealed to him or her identity.

Dennis said that shortly after this meeting, the young nurse was transferred to England. He said he wrote her there, and received a cryptic response that she would explain everything later. When he sent her a second letter, Dennis said it was returned unopened and marked "Deceased."

Inasmuch as Dennis claimed he took a "sacred oath" to protect the nurse's secret, one might expect that he would have hidden her ET sketches in his apartment, or perhaps even rented a small safety deposit box in a local bank. Instead, Dennis says he put the ET sketches in his files at the Ballard Funeral Home. And when he left his job at Ballard, *he left the ET sketches behind.* When Dennis told Friedman his tale of the (alleged) nurse and her sketches,

Friedman suggested they go to the Ballard Funeral Home to see if they were still in the files. At this point, one might have expected Dennis to remember his "sacred oath" and have refused Friedman's suggestion, but Dennis agreed. When they visited Ballard, Dennis told me, they discovered that *all* of the old files were still there—*except for 1947, with the ET sketches.*

At this point, one might have expected Dennis to be thankful that the ET sketches were missing, so that he would not have violated his "sacred oath." *Instead, Dennis—who is an amateur sculptor—decided that he would himself try to redraw the ET sketches, based on his forty-plus-year-old recollections.* Dennis then did so and gave the sketches to an artist friend to "get them correct."

When Dennis related the foregoing to me in late 1991, including his "sacred oath," I noted that his recreation of the nurse's ET sketches had been published in the new Randle/Schmitt book *UFO Crash at Roswell,* and asked how the authors had obtained the sketches. Dennis replied: "That's what I would like to know, because I gave it to only one person," and he went on to say that that person—whom he refused to identify—claimed he was not responsible. When I asked: "Does he swear under solemn oath that he did not [give the sketches to Randle/Schmitt], Dennis replied: "I did not ask him for a solemn oath, *because I don't believe in solemn oaths.*" Then Dennis laughed.

(Several years later, during an interview with UFO/Roswell researcher Karl Pflock, Dennis admitted that he himself *had* given the ET sketches to Randle and Schmitt; to Mark Wolf, a TV-video producer; and also to Stanton Friedman.)

If Dennis's tale of the young nurse were true, and if she were still alive, she would be an invaluable witness to support claims of a crashed saucer and ET bodies. Dennis claims that after his second letter was returned marked "Deceased," he learned from RAAF personnel that the young nurse had been killed in a military aircraft accident. But investigation by Randle and others failed to find any military airplane accident during late 1947 or early 1948 in which one, or more, nurses was involved.

On January 31, 1991, Dennis was interviewed in Roswell by a UFO researcher named Anne MacFie who published a partial transcript of the interview in the April 1992 issue of the *MUFON UFO Journal*. When MacFie asked Dennis if he had tried to contact the nurse "to see if she would talk now that others have," Dennis replied: "I don't know where she is. She did join an order after she got out of the Army." When MacFie asked if the nurse was still alive, Dennis responded: "I heard she died three years ago, but that's only hearsay."

Randle/Schmitt's first book, *UFO Crash at Roswell*, published in mid-1991, was the first public report on Glenn Dennis and his alleged nurse friend. Randle and Schmitt welcomed Dennis's story because it seemed to add credence to their claim that the debris recovered from the Brazel ranch could only be from an extraterrestrial spaceship. Their own investigation into the Barney Barnett/Plains of San Agustin story had failed to locate any responsible person who had heard of a saucer crash on the Plains of San Agustin. But Randle and Schmitt were not yet ready to dismiss Barney Barnett's story as simply a "tall tale."

To resolve this dilemma, Randle and Schmitt arbitrarily decided that when Barnett (allegedly) saw a crashed saucer with several ET bodies, he had *not* been near the Plains of San Agustin, but had actually been some 150 miles east on the Brazel ranch. Further, Randle and Schmitt concluded that the debris discovered by Brazel had resulted from an explosion, but the damaged craft had managed to fly several miles before crashing on the Brazel ranch at what they called the "impact site." If ET bodies had been recovered from the Plains of San Agustin, they would have been taken to an Air Force base in Albuquerque, rather than transported to the more distant Roswell Army Air Field.

But Stanton Friedman continued to endorse the Plains of San Agustin "impact site." He theorized that two UFOs had collided over the Brazel ranch, one of which had landed nearby and the other had managed to fly 150 miles west to the Plains of San Agustin, and that *ET bodies had been recovered from both sites.*

Or, that a single UFO had exploded over the Brazel ranch but managed to fly 150 miles before crash-landing on the Plains of San Agustin. In early 1990, Friedman found a new "witness" to support his belief that an ET craft had crashed on the Plains of San Agustin.

9.

A New "Firsthand Witness"

The "Unsolved Mysteries" program on the Roswell Incident, originally broadcast September 20, 1989, was rebroadcast on January 24, 1990, and reportedly seen by more than thirty million viewers. Viewers were invited to call a toll-free number if they had any information on the incident. One caller, Gerald F. Anderson, of Springfield, Missouri, insisted that the TV show made a serious error in failing to report that *one ET had survived the crash.* Anderson said he was certain because in July 1947, when he was only five years old, he and four members of his family had stumbled across the crashed saucer on the Plains of San Agustin. (All other family members involved in the incident had since died.)

Anderson was supplied with the addresses of Stanton Friedman and Kevin Randle, wrote to them, and soon afterward was interviewed via telephone by both men. Friedman was delighted to have Anderson's affirmation of Barnett's Plains of San Agustin story—especially because Anderson confirmed Barnett's report that a party of archeologists from the University of Pennsylvania also had stumbled across the crashed saucer.

Anderson claimed that even though he was only five at the time and more than forty years had elapsed, *he remembered the name of the archeological group's leader: Dr. Buskirk.* Although Anderson said he had not seen Dr. Buskirk for more than forty years, he later was able to recall his appearance sufficiently well to construct a sketch of Buskirk's face using "Identikit" techniques used by law enforcement agencies. While Friedman accepted Anderson's story, Randle was suspicious of Anderson's tale, based on a nearly hour-long telephone interview on February 4, 1990, which Randle tape-recorded.

Later that year, Friedman received "physical evidence" which seemed to substantiate Anderson's story, sent by a person claiming to be Anderson's cousin Vallejean Anderson, allegedly a Catholic nun. The evidence consisted of several pages of a *handwritten* diary, dated early July 1947, in which Anderson's Uncle Ted Anderson (Vallejean's father) briefly described the crashed-saucer incident. The accompanying note read: "With this mailing I want no more involvement in this sorry scenario, nor does my mother. Both Maria [her sister] and I have been transferred to another convent and our Mother has been moved."

Robert Bigelow (a wealthy Las Vegas businessman) agreed to fund a laboratory analysis of the diary pages to determine the age of the ink, based on its chemical composition. Friedman submitted them to the Brunelle Forensic Laboratories in Fairfax, Virginia, for analysis. On October 18, 1990, Richard L. Brunelle wrote Friedman to report the results. "This particular ink formulation matches a Sheaffer Skrip black fountain pen ink formulation *that was first manufactured in 1974. The combination of dyes present in this ink was not used until approximately 1970*" (emphasis added). This was more than twenty years after the diary allegedly had been written.

When Friedman disclosed these test results to Anderson, he had a ready explanation: His Uncle Ted had decided to make a number of copies of the original 1947 diary for members of the family. Instead of using a Xerox machine, his uncle had decided to make each copy by hand. Friedman credulously accepted this explanation, ignoring the fact that Anderson's uncle had been killed in 1965 in an auto accident—*some years before the ink used for the diary pages was introduced.*

I first learned of Anderson's claims in an article published in the March 1991 issue of the *MUFON UFO Journal,* which reprinted a feature article on Anderson's story which had appeared in the December 9, 1990 edition of the *Springfield News-Leader.* The article said that Anderson had been employed as a deputy in the sheriff's office of Taney County, Missouri, prompting me to call Sheriff Charles Keithly on May 14, 1991. He told me that Anderson had been "fired" after two years because of "unsatisfactory" performance. When I asked the sheriff if Anderson had ever mentioned his childhood experience with a crashed saucer, Keithly replied: "The first time I ever heard that tale was when I read the story in our Springfield newspaper."

Later, when I talked to Anderson's former wife and asked if he had ever mentioned the crashed-saucer incident to her during their many years of married life, she replied: "Never." She added that he "likes to tell tall tales and he can actually make people believe them." One possible explanation for Anderson's failure to ever mention the crashed UFO incident to his wife or his associates was offered by him in a feature article published in the April 7, 1991 edition of the *Northwest Arkansas Times:* "Anderson said *he never gave the incident much thought until recently . . .*" (emphasis added).

According to Mr. and Mrs. Malthais, who first reported the Barnett/Plains of San Agustin story to Friedman in late 1978, Barnett had said that the archeological team which had also stumbled onto the crashed saucer was from the University of Pennsylvania. Because UFOlogist Tom Carey lives in the vicinity of the University of Pennsylvania, he had conducted a rigorous search of university archives, hoping to find some reference to such an archeological team which had been working in New Mexico in 1947. But Carey's search had been in vain.

When Carey learned of Anderson's claim that the group was headed by a "Dr. Buskirk," Carey renewed his search. In the process, he discovered a book that had been published five years earlier, in 1986, by a Dr. Winfred Buskirk. At that time, Buskirk lived in Albuquerque and had been trained as an archeologist. When Carey obtained a copy of Anderson's Identikit sketch of Buskirk and a copy of the book jacket with Dr. Buskirk's picture taken in 1947, there was a strong resemblance. Because Buskirk had moved from Albuquerque since his book had been published, Carey had considerable difficulty in locating him, but finally did so in June 1991. Buskirk categorically denied the Plains of San Agustin crashed-saucer story. He explained that during the three summer months of 1947 he and his wife were in Arizona at the Fort Apache Reservation conducting research for his Ph.D., as later reported in his book.

For Carey, who had spent much time and effort trying to substantiate the Barnett/Plains of Agustin crashed-saucer story, Buskirk's credible denial must have been a disappointment. But Carey's success in locating Dr. Buskirk would prove to be the key to exposing Anderson's tall tale. *Carey discovered that Buskirk had been a teacher at the Albuquerque High School at the same time as Gerald Anderson was a student there in the late 1950s.* By that time, Buskirk was a bit heavier than he had been in 1947, which explains why Anderson's Identikit sketch showed a somewhat rounder-faced Buskirk. Yet Anderson insisted that he had not seen Buskirk since 1947 on the Plains of San Agustin.

Buskirk, now eighty-three years old, could not recall with certainty whether Anderson had been a student in the anthropology course which he taught. When Anderson later learned that Carey had located Buskirk, Anderson denied having taken a course in anthropology. But when Kevin Randle tried to obtain a copy of Anderson's school records, he promptly notified Albuquerque school authorities not to release them.

One of Anderson's staunchest supporters at this time was John S. Carpenter, a UFOlogist and hypnotherapist who also lived in

Springfield, Missouri. Carpenter had used regressive hypnosis to help Anderson recall details of his crashed-saucer experience. Anderson's recall *seemingly* was good enough to enable him to prepare a map which pinpointed the crash site so that Friedman and others could visit it and search for ET artifacts. In mid-1992, using funds supplied by Robert Bigelow, a team consisting of Anderson, Friedman, Carpenter, Bigelow, and longtime UFOlogist Don Berliner visited the Plains of San Agustin. They were impressed with the accuracy of Anderson's (allegedly) forty-four-year-old recollections of the area, but found no ET artifacts.

The September 1991 issue of the *MUFON UFO Journal* carried a lengthy article by Carpenter which revealed that Anderson had successfully passed a several-hour polygraph test on July 24, 1991, dealing with his crashed-saucer story. The test was given by an examiner who had been recommended by the American Polygraph Association who reported finding "no evidence whatsoever of deception," according to Carpenter. He noted that "this may be the only firsthand crash/retrieval witness to undertake and pass a polygraph test." Near the end of the article, Carpenter commented briefly on Carey's recent contact with Dr. Buskirk, saying that "there is no absolute proof that any Buskirk from Albuquerque is the same Buskirk from the crash site." Carpenter reminded readers that federal law prohibits the release of a person's school records without that person's written consent.

Carpenter's article prompted me to write him on September 30, 1991, to pose several questions, including the following:

- "Have you asked Anderson if while he was a student in the Albuquerque High School he ever took a course in Anthropology? If so, what was his answer? If you have never asked, will you do so now?"

- "Is Anderson willing to authorize officials of the Albuquerque High School to make public a transcript of the courses he took while he was a student there—withholding his grades if Anderson so desires?"

Carpenter replied promptly, on October 3, saying that he *had* earlier posed my first question and that Anderson responded "that he believed he had only taken a Sociology course." Carpenter added that Anderson had sent him a photocopy of a transcript "clearly duplicated from microfilm records. . . . It shows that he indeed took a Sociology course as he had suspected." But Carpenter admitted that the "transcript" he received from Anderson was a bit ambiguous: "It would be fairly easy at a quick glance to think that Gerald took Anthropology if someone had asked that leading question because of the tiny lines and close proximity."

I promptly replied to Carpenter on October 7, pointing out that a great deal was riding on Anderson's veracity "and the critical issue was whether or not he took a course in Anthropology under Dr. Buskirk or a course in Sociology (under a different teacher) as indicated by the photocopy of the high school transcript he supplied to you." My letter said that this critical issue could "be resolved if Anderson were willing to authorize the current Principal of the Albuquerque High School to carefully examine the original transcript and issue a public statement as to whether Anderson did, or did not, take a course in Anthropology in 1957." My letter concluded: "Do you think that Anderson would be willing to authorize such an independent analysis?"

Three months would pass before Carpenter replied despite my reminder letters of November 27 and January 5, 1992, asking if he had passed along my October 7 suggestion to Anderson and, if so, what had been Anderson's response. Carpenter finally replied to my January 5 letter with handwritten comments on a copy of my letter. He revealed that I was not the first to suggest that Anderson authorize Albuquerque officials to study his school records and issue a statement as to whether he had, or had not, taken a course in Anthropology. *Carpenter indicated that the same suggestion had also been made by Friedman, by Mark Rodeghier—scientific director of CUFOS (Center for UFO Studies)—and by Fred Whiting, a Fund for UFO Research (FUFOR) official.*

Carpenter said that Anderson was considering the suggested

action but had not yet made a decision. He added: "Gerald doesn't care what anybody thinks at the present time." I responded on January 13, 1992, posing two questions for Carpenter, knowing of his strong endorsement of Anderson's veracity.

- "If Anderson sought your advice, would you suggest that he ought to agree to the proposal to prove his veracity?" Carpenter responded promptly, if cryptically: "He did, and I did."

- "Has Anderson's refusal (so far) to approve this proposal raised any doubts in your mind as to the veracity of his claim that he did not take a course under Dr. Buskirk?" Carpenter responded: "Not necessarily." He explained that Anderson has "been under other pressures recently (unrelated) and tends to back off to regroup and minimize overall stress."

After learning from Carpenter that Friedman also believed Anderson should authorize Albuquerque school officials to resolve the Anthropology course issue, I wrote Friedman to try to get him to pressure Anderson to take such action. From my previous dealings with Friedman I had learned that money is for him a strong motivator. So on August 8, 1992, I offered to pay Friedman $1,000 if he could get Anderson to provide me within thirty days a "notarized statement which requests the Principal [of the Albuquerque High School] or the Superintendent [of the school system] to examine Anderson's transcript and issue a public statement as to whether Anderson did, or did not, take a course in Anthropology." But if Anderson failed to take such action within thirty days, Friedman would have to pay me $100. *Friedman never responded to my offer.*

The same month that I made this offer, Friedman's new book *Crash at Corona,* coauthored by Don Berliner, went on sale with Gerald Anderson as a featured "witness." In the book, Friedman reported that Anderson had passed a polygraph test which was given July 24, 1991. *But Friedman omitted any mention of the fact that several weeks before the polygraph test, Dr. Buskirk had been located and that he had categorically denied Anderson's crashed-saucer tale. Friedman also omitted any mention of Anderson's determined efforts to withhold school records which could show whether he had taken a course in Anthropology under Buskirk.*

Nine months after the Friedman/Berliner book was published, John Carpenter demonstrated his forthright candor in a lengthy article published in the March 1993 issue of the *MUFON UFO Journal.* Carpenter admitted that "recent events have now cast grave doubts on Gerald's story and his own truthfulness with us." Carpenter admitted that Anderson had fabricated a counterfeit telephone bill, to challenge Kevin Randle's claim that he had interviewed Anderson by telephone for nearly an hour on February 4, 1990. Anderson claimed they had talked for only *twenty-six minutes* and offered as evidence what he claimed to be a photocopy of his telephone bill. (Randle had a fifty-six-minute tape recording of the interview.) Friedman finally decided to check with Anderson's telephone company to obtain a copy of his February 1990 phone bill and asked Anderson to accompany him. Anderson declined. When Friedman obtained an authentic copy of the bill, it showed that Randle was correct and that Anderson had fabricated a counterfeit version.

Carpenter also revealed that the typeface on Anderson's counterfeit phone bill matched that of the brief note that had accompanied the bogus "diary pages" which purportedly had been sent to Friedman by Anderson's cousin Vallejean. Carpenter added that "the style and phrasing of the [note's] content sounds very much like the manner in which Gerald communicates." Carpenter also acknowledged the possibility that the ambiguous high school transcript which he had received from Anderson "may have been doctored as well."

Despite these and other clever tricks perpetrated by Anderson, Carpenter was reluctant to dismiss *all* of Anderson's claims as bogus. For example, Carpenter asked: "How could Gerald draw specific features of New Mexico desert terrain accurately while sitting in Springfield, Missouri?" Carpenter seemingly forgot that earlier in his article he noted that Anderson liked to vacation in Colorado, just north of New Mexico. Carpenter acknowledged that Anderson "may have made a motorcycle vacation jaunt just before our [1991] research expedition to Datil, New Mexico," to look for the "crash-site."

Rather than consider that Anderson might have acquired crashed-saucer details from books, TV shows, and from Friedman, Carpenter speculated: "Could it be that Gerald was given genuine data about a crash on the Plains of San Agustin in order to leak it deliberately? In this manner he could feel that he was being honest about much of the information and could even pass the polygraph test. . . . Or did his father really experience something that Gerald wanted to share after he saw the 'Unsolved Mysteries' episode? Or is it just an elaborate hoax with no obvious goal, gain or point?" (Carpenter forgot that the 1990 *Springfield News-Leader* article said that Anderson hoped to write a book about his crashed-saucer experience.) Carpenter concluded: "One thing I know for certain, I can no longer trust anything my old friend Gerald Anderson wishes to tell me."

Carpenter's candor stands in sharp contrast to Friedman's "deafening silence" on his book's star witness, Gerald Anderson. Friedman's behavior in connection with Anderson recalls the sage observation of French philosopher Charles Peguy: "He who does not bellow the truth when he knows the truth makes himself the accomplice of liars and forgers."

10.

Debris Photographer Located

The 1980 Berlitz and Moore book, *The Roswell Incident*, contained two photos taken in the office of Brig. Gen. Roger Ramey in Fort Worth, Texas, on July 8, 1947, reportedly showing the debris that Maj. Jesse Marcel had recovered from the Brazel ranch. One photo showed General Ramey looking at a piece of debris being held by his chief of staff, Col. Thomas J. DuBose, while the other—heavily cropped—showed Marcel holding a piece of the debris. (See figures 2 and 3.)

Early in the Randle/Schmitt investigation, they located the negatives for these and four more pictures which had been taken in Ramey's office by a young reporter for the *Fort Worth Star-Telegram*, J. Bond Johnson. (The negatives and other *Star-Telegram* archival material had been turned over to the University of Texas's Arlington Library.) Randle later was able to locate Johnson, who now lived in Southern California, and first interviewed him by telephone on February 27, 1989. Randle tape-recorded the interview with Johnson's permission.

Shortly after this first interview, Randle and Schmitt authored an article in the March/April 1989 issue of the *International UFO Reporter* (*IUR*), published by the Center for UFO Studies (CUFOS). The article, headlined: "Fort Worth, July 8, 1947: The Coverup Begins," was based on Johnson's *initial* recollections, that he had taken only *two* pictures in Ramey's office, one showing Ramey crouched near the material and the second showing Ramey with Colonel DuBose. The *IUR* article said: "It was obvious from the pictures that the material was nothing extraordinary."

The Randle/Schmitt article said that Marcel had earlier recalled that after bringing the Brazel ranch debris to Ramey's office, "Ramey wanted to know exactly where it had been found, so they left the office and went to the map room. When they returned, *the real debris was gone, replaced by a torn weather balloon*" (emphasis added). Because Johnson did not then recall that he had taken any pictures of Marcel, the article said that two photos of Marcel were probably taken by the base's public information officer, Maj. Charles A. Cashon, *before Johnson arrived on the base.* "The weather balloon was spread out on the floor, two pictures with Marcel were taken, and then *Ramey told Marcel to leave the room and avoid any reporters* [emphasis added]," according to Randle and Schmitt.

The claim that Marcel was photographed with bogus debris contradicted his own recollections when he was interviewed by Moore and Friedman in 1979, as reported in the Berlitz/Moore book (p. 68). Marcel recalled:

> Gen. Ramey allowed some members of the press in to take a picture of this stuff. They took *one* picture of me on the floor holding up *some of the less-interesting metallic debris. . . . The stuff in that one photo was pieces of the actual stuff we had found.* It was not a staged photo. Later, they cleared out our wreckage and substituted some of their own. Then they allowed more photos. Those were taken while the actual wreckage was already on its way to Wright Field. I was not in these. I believe these were taken with the general and one of his aids. (Emphasis added)

Examination of the photos proved that Marcel's 1979 recollection was in error because *all* of the pictures taken in Ramey's office showed the same debris. Another of Marcel's 1979 recollections—that he was not allowed to talk to the press—and the Randle/Schmitt article's claim that Marcel departed Ramey's office before reporter Johnson arrived are *flatly contradicted by Johnson's article in the July 9, 1947 edition of the Fort Worth Morning Star-Telegram.* The Johnson article, which referred to Marcel's presence and even quoted him, follows:

An object found near Roswell, N.M. was stripped of its glamor as a "flying disk" by a Fort Worth Army Air Field weather officer who late Tuesday identified it as a weather balloon.

Warrant Officer Irving Newton of Medford, Wis., a forecaster at the base weather station, said the object was a ray wind [Rawin] target used to determine the direction and velocity of winds at high altitudes.

Newton said there were some 80 weather stations in the United States using this type of balloon and that it could have come from any of them. "We use them because they can go so much higher than the eye can see," Newton explained. A radar set is employed to follow the balloon and through a process of triangulation the winds aloft are chartered [*sic*], he added. When rigged up, Newton stated, the object looks like a six-pointed star, is silvery in appearance and rises in the air like a kite, mounted to a 100-gram balloon. Newton said he had sent up balloons identical to this one during the invasion of Okinawa to determine ballistics information for heavy guns.

The weather device was flown to Fort Worth Army Air Field by B-29 from Roswell Army Air Field at 10 a.m. Tuesday at the command of Brig. Gen. Roger Ramey, 8th Air Force commanding officer here. *It had been found three weeks previously* by a New Mexico rancher, W. W. Brazell [*sic*], on his property about 85 miles northwest of Roswell. Brazell, whose ranch is 30 miles from the nearest telephone and has no radio, knew nothing about flying disks when he found the broken remains of the weather device scattered over a square mile of his land.

He bundled *the tinfoil and broken wooden beams of the kite and the torn synthetic rubber remains of the balloon* together and rolled it under some brush, *according to Maj. Jesse A. Marcel, Houma, La.*, 509th Bomb Group intelligence officer at Roswell who brought the device to FWAAF. On a trip to town at Corona, N.M., Saturday night [July 5], Brazell heard the first reference to the "silver flying risks" [*sic*], *Major Marcel related.*

Brazell hurried home, dug up the remnants of the kites and balloon on Sunday and Monday [July 7] headed for Roswell to report his find to the sheriff's office. This resulted in a call to the Roswell Army Air Field and to Major Marcel's being assigned to the case. Marcel and Brazell journeyed back to the ranch, where Marcel took the object into the custody of the Army. After Col. William H. Blanchard, 509th commanding officer, reported the incident to General Ramey, he was ordered to dispatch the object to Fort Worth Army Air Field immediately.

About that time, word broke from Roswell that a flying disk finally had been found. After his first look, Ramey declared all it was was a weather balloon. The weather officer verified his view. (Emphasis added)

The November/December 1990 issue of IUR revealed that Johnson had revised his earlier opinion, expressed to Randle during his first telephone interview, that the material he had photographed in Ramey's office was a bogus substitute. Johnson now believed it was the authentic Brazel ranch debris. This was an embarrassing development for Randle and Schmitt and so the same issue of *IUR* devoted twelve pages—roughly half its total—to quoting what Johnson had originally told Randle, to show that Randle and Schmitt had not misquoted him.

This *IUR* article revealed that shortly after Randle's early 1989 interview, Johnson had begun to have doubts that Ramey had substituted bogus debris:

He [Johnson] asked us in August 1989 whether we thought it could have been the real stuff. This was our first indication that Johnson was beginning to change his story. . . . Now he wanted to know if it couldn't have been the real thing. *We replied, as we have all along, that it wasn't. The real debris had* not *been photographed in Ramey's office.* (Emphasis added)

Portions of Randle's early tape-recorded interviews reveal how Johnson's initial opinion could have been influenced by Randle's own strong views. During the first interview, Johnson said he had recently seen a TV show about the Roswell Incident (a show which promoted the idea of a coverup). Shortly after Johnson said he was uncertain whether Ramey's explanation was true, Randle commented: "They realized that it [the debris] was something extremely unusual. That it really was an alien spacecraft. Then Ramey comes up with this weath_r-balloon nonsense." Johnson responded: "Right. That was a hoax, I think . . . I think I was duped." Randle responded: "Yes. You and all the rest of the reporters were duped."

It is clear from listening to the tape recording of Randle's several interviews with Johnson—which Randle later supplied to me—that Johnson's *initial* recollections of what had occurred forty-plus years earlier were confused and, in some cases, flawed. For example, whereas Johnson recalled taking only two photos in Ramey's office, the hard evidence indicates that he took six. In the initial interview with Randle, Johnson said he did not recall having met Major Marcel—yet he had quoted Marcel in the story he wrote about his visit to Ramey's office.

Randle and Schmitt's *IUR* article implied that Johnson changed his views because he had been manipulated by two Randle and Schmitt rivals working in the Roswell crashed-saucer field: William L. Moore and his then research associate, Jaime Shandera. Moore and Shandera insisted that *all* of the photos taken in Ramey's office on July 8, 1947, show the *authentic* debris recovered from the Brazel ranch—*and that this was the wreckage from a crashed UFO*. Randle and Schmitt insisted that all of the pictures clearly show the remains of a weather balloon and radar target, which they claim was substituted for the authentic Brazel ranch debris. Obviously, both teams could not be correct.

One person still alive in 1989 might resolve this crucial issue: Thomas J. DuBose, Ramey's chief of staff. But when DuBose was interviewed in mid-1990 by Schmitt and shortly afterward by Shandera, they came up with sharply contradictory answers. Both claimed that DuBose had confirmed their previous views.

11.

Aging Witness, Confused Memory

In mid-August 1990, Donald Schmitt and Stanton Friedman flew to Florida to interview Thomas J. DuBose, who had been Gen. Ramey's chief of staff in July 1947. Because DuBose was nearly ninety years of age, they used regressive hypnosis, administered by a professional hypnotherapist, in the hope of enhancing DuBose's aging recollections. (Clinical specialists in hypnosis, such as Dr. Martin T. Orne, past president of the International Society of Hypnosis, stress that hypnosis is *not* a "magic road to the truth." Under hypnosis, a subject is prone to confabulation— "recalling" events as they now believe they should have occurred, with the benefit of hindsight and newly acquired information, rather than as the events actually did occur.)

DuBose's ambivalent, often contradictory, recollections, as later reported by Schmitt and Friedman, make it clear that age, plus the passage of more than forty years, had taken their toll. DuBose's recollections flatly contradicted well-established facts such as the day when rancher Brazel first came to Roswell to report finding the unusual debris to Sheriff George Wilcox. *Rather*

than challenge DuBose's obviously flawed recollections, Schmitt
and Friedman were quite willing to change the date of Brazel's
visit from Monday, July 7, to Sunday, July 6.

According to DuBose's recollection, he had received a phone
call from Maj. Gen. Clements McMullen *several days before* the
Ramey "press conference" where the debris photos were taken.
McMullen was then vice commander of the Strategic Air Command—which included the Eighth Air Force—and SAC's headquarters were located just outside of Washington, D.C. DuBose
said Gen. McMullen told him that some unusual debris had been
recovered by the Roswell Army Air Field (RAAF). Further, that
DuBose should call RAAF base commander Col. Blanchard and
instruct him to promptly fly the curious debris to McMullen in
Washington. If McMullen was eager to examine the debris, *it*
could be flown nonstop from Roswell to Washington in one of
RAAF's B-29s.

DuBose said that McMullen warned him that "no one was to
discuss [this matter] with their wives, me with Ramey, with anyone," according to an article written by Schmitt, published in the
April 1991 issue of the *MUFON UFO Journal.* But instead of the
debris being flown directly to Washington on a B-29, DuBose said
it was flown to Fort Worth on a short-range medium bomber, a B-
25 or B-26. DuBose said he met the flight from RAAF, was given
a small sealed container and turned it over to FWAAF base commander Col. Alan Clark, who promptly took off in a B-25 to fly it
to Gen. McMullen in Washington. (The short-range B-25 would
need to make a refueling stop en route.)

When DuBose was asked "when were the photographs [in
Ramey's office] taken?" he replied: "Must have been three or four
days after that." Schmitt and Friedman were understandably surprised and so DuBose was asked: "It wasn't the same day?" He
replied: "No, it was two or three days later." This should have
been a red warning flag that DuBose's recollections were seriously flawed. Instead, to try to accommodate DuBose's recollections, Schmitt wrote: "The earliest that any debris could have been

available was [Sunday] July 6, 1947, when Mac Brazel took some samples to Roswell. That must be the debris to which DuBose is referring. . . ."

There can be no doubt that Brazel came to Roswell and reported the unusual debris on *Monday, July 7, 1947*. According to a feature article on the front page of the July 9, 1947 edition of the *Roswell Dispatch* (a morning newspaper), "The furor started *Monday*, when W. W. Brazel, a rancher living on the old Foster place, 25 miles southeast of Corona, came into the office and reported finding an object which fitted the descriptions of the flying discs. . . . *No member of the local sheriff's office saw the article [debris] at any time*" (emphasis added).

That evening's edition of the *Roswell Daily Record* carried a feature story, based on an interview with Brazel the previous night, which said: "*Monday* he came to town to sell some wool and while here he went to see Sheriff George Wilcox . . ." (emphasis added) (see chapter 1, p. 20). And the article by reporter Johnson in the July 9 *Fort Worth Morning Star-Telegram*, based on Maj. Marcel's account in Ramey's office, said: "Brazell [*sic*] hurried home, dug up the remnants of the kites and balloon on Sunday and *Monday* headed for Roswell to report his find to the sheriff's office" (emphasis added).

Rather than admit that DuBose's recollections were flawed, Randle, Schmitt, and Friedman in *all of their articles and subsequent books claim that Brazel came to Roswell on Sunday, July 6, and that he brought some of the debris with him which was then flown to Fort Worth on Sunday, July 6, and on to Washington— which is flatly contradicted by the sheriff's office and by Marcel's recollections in the late 1970s.* In addition to this serious flaw, there are numerous others. For example, unlike today, when the United States schedules many national holidays to provide three-day weekends, in 1947 they were quite rare. But July 4, 1947, fell on a Friday, providing a three-day weekend. Major Marcel recalled that he was at the base, having lunch at the officers' club, when he received a call from the sheriff's office. If DuBose's recollections were correct, Marcel would have been working at the base over the long holiday weekend. It is known that Marcel did not return from the Brazel ranch until Tuesday morning, July 8. Neither he, nor Capt. Sheridan Cavitt, who reportedly accompanied Marcel, ever reported spending *two days and nights* on the ranch.

Perhaps the most important anomaly in DuBose's recollections is the question of how Gen. McMullen could have learned of the Brazel ranch debris on Sunday, July 6. Sheriff Wilcox did not learn of Brazel's finding until Monday, July 7, and he properly notified RAAF officials, not the Pentagon. If RAAF commander Blanchard had notified the Pentagon on (or before) Sunday, July 6, certainly he would have been warned to keep the debris under wraps, as DuBose claims that he was warned. And yet two days later, on July 8, RAAF's public information officer, Lt. Walter Haut, put out a press release announcing recovery of a flying disc, later claiming he did so on orders from Blanchard.

According to Schmitt's April 1991 *MUFON UFO Journal* article, when DuBose was asked if he had ever seen the authentic debris from the Brazel ranch, he responded: "Never. I only saw the container and the container was a plastic bag that I would say weighs [*sic*] 15 to 20 pounds. It was sealed. Lead seal around the top." But shortly after DuBose was interviewed by Schmitt and Friedman, he was interviewed by Jaime Shandera, Moore's partner, who reported sharply different results in an article published in the January 1991 issue of the *MUFON UFO Journal*. Shandera's initial interview was by telephone but he subsequently visited DuBose in Florida. After referring to the Randle and Schmitt claim that the debris photographed in Ramey's office was bogus, Shandera asked DuBose: "So what you're saying is that the material in General Ramey's office was the actual debris brought in from Roswell?" DuBose responded: "That's absolutely right," according to Shandera's article.

When Shandera asked: "What happened to the material (which was photographed) in Gen. Ramey's office?" DuBose replied: "Well, Gen. McMullen in Washington, he ordered me by telephone to take that debris in Roger's [Ramey's] office and put it in a container, lock it, and send it to him in Washington by courier." Shandera responded: "Let me get this straight—Gen. McMullen ordered you personally to take the debris in Gen. Ramey's office and lock it in a container and send it to him by courier?" DuBose responded: "That's exactly right. . . . I put the debris in a heavy mail pouch, sealed it and locked it. I then sealed it to the wrist of [Col.] Al Clark and escorted him to a B-25 out on the runway and sent him to Gen. McMullen in Washington," according to Shandera.

By the time that Schmitt and Friedman had interviewed DuBose in Florida, they had obtained good-quality prints of the photos that Johnson had taken in Ramey's office. *But apparently they never showed these photos to DuBose to help refresh his memory.* So Shandera sent DuBose a copy of an article which he had written for a newsletter published by Moore, which included Ramey office photos. In the *MUFON UFO Journal* article, Shandera reported that when he later asked DuBose if he had had a chance to read the article and look at the photos, DuBose reportedly replied: "Yes, and I studied the pictures very carefully." Shandera then asked: "Do you recognize that material?" DuBose replied: "Oh yes. That's the material that Marcel brought to Ft. Worth from Roswell."

Later, when Shandera visited Florida, he told DuBose that he had then recently interviewed meteorologist Irving Newton, whom Ramey had summoned to examine the debris and who had confirmed it was the remnants from a weather balloon and a radar target. (One of reporter Johnson's photos showed Newton examining the debris.) When Shandera told DuBose that Newton had confirmed finding remnants of a weather balloon on the floor of Ramey's office, DuBose responded: "No Goddamn weather balloon was ever in that room." DuBose admitted he could not recall whether Gen. McMullen or someone else had suggested that the debris be identified as the remnants of a weather balloon and a radar target. But DuBose added: "We had to have a coverup. This was getting out of hand and we had to stop these headlines. It was used to quiet the press. . . ."

The Schmitt article in the April 1991 issue of *IUR* responded to some issues raised by Shandera's earlier article in the *MUFON UFO Journal*. Schmitt indicated that he had recently asked DuBose if he had *ever* seen any of the real Brazel ranch debris and that he had answered with "a resounding NO!!!" Schmitt said he then asked "if the debris on Ramey's floor was the debris from Roswell," to which DuBose replied: "No."

If the debris photographed on the floor of Ramey's office was *not* the authentic debris brought to Fort Worth by Marcel, where could Ramey have obtained the remnants of a weather balloon that had been exposed to desert sun and heat for several weeks? There would be no reason to store such useless debris. So far as is known, the meteorological office at the Fort Worth Army Air Field was not yet outfitted for radar tracking of weather balloons, and so it would not have any radar targets.

Even if Ramey had been instructed to substitute bogus debris, his options were severely constrained because the substitute would need to match the description that would be given by rancher Brazel several hours later in the offices of the *Roswell Daily Record*, and would be offered years later by Brazel's children, and by Marcel and his son. In Schmitt's April 1991 article, he briefly admitted that DuBose "didn't know where Ramey got the debris displayed on his floor." If Ramey had needed to find bogus debris, he would have given that task to Chief of Staff DuBose.

Schmitt added: "He [DuBose] just knew that it wasn't from Roswell, *and that's the important point*" (emphasis added).

12.

New Witnesses,
New Crash Scenario

In early September 1990, Stanton Friedman severed his long association with William Moore. One reason, according to Friedman,
was his objection to Moore's efforts to convince Avon Books not
to publish the Randle/Schmitt book *UFO Crash at Roswell*. For
more than a year prior to Friedman's action, he had been collaborating with Randle and Schmitt in a joint Roswell research effort.
Also, Friedman had long been distressed by the fact that he
believed the 1980 Berlitz/Moore book had not given him adequate
credit for his research effort.

But by the time the Randle/Schmitt book was published in
mid-1991, Friedman had broken with them also and was writing
his own Roswell book, with coauthor Don Berliner. Not surprising, Friedman authored a very critical review of the Randle and
Schmitt book which was published in the September 1991 issue of
the *MUFON UFO Journal*. (By this time Friedman had been
named MUFON's Director of Special Investigations.) Friedman
faulted the Randle and Schmitt book for trying to shift the site of
Barney Barnett's crashed saucer from the Plains of San Agustin to

the Brazel ranch, roughly 150 miles to the east. Friedman reported that the diary of Barney's wife, Ruth, had been located by her niece. The diary showed that Barnett's travels for his employer had not taken him to within 100 miles of the Brazel ranch in early July 1947.

Friedman also sharply criticized Randle and Schmitt for their doubts about the veracity of Gerald Anderson's tale of his crashed-saucer encounter on the Plains of San Agustin. And Friedman criticized Randle and Schmitt for accepting Dr. Buskirk's story that he was in Arizona and not on the Plains of San Agustin, as Anderson claimed. Friedman's harsh four-page review concluded: "I hope the Paragon hard-cover book by Don Berliner and I [sic] about what happened will be more accurate, better reasoned and less easily rejected. It will certainly include details *of the polygraph test of Gerald Anderson, on July 24, which he passed with flying colors*" (emphasis added).

Sometime prior to the time the Friedman/Berliner manuscript went to the printer in early 1992, Friedman had learned of the possibility that Anderson had taken a course in Anthropology under Buskirk. And Friedman knew that Anderson had instructed Albuquerque school officials *not* to release his school records. *But there was no mention in the Friedman/Berliner book of questions about the veracity of Anderson's story, or his efforts to obstruct determination of whether he had been a student under Buskirk.*

The Friedman/Berliner book did mention the alleged "Uncle Ted's diary" pages that Friedman (allegedly) received from Anderson's cousin. Their book cryptically reported: "Forensic examination of the journal [diary] revealed that it was written no earlier than about 1970." But the book did not explain to the reader the critical importance of the 1970 date. Nine months after the Friedman/Berliner book was published, hypnotherapist John Carpenter, in his article in the March 1993 *MUFON UFO Journal*, admitted that Anderson had resorted to falsehood, trickery, and counterfeiting of records, as reported in chapter 9.

The discovery of the diary of Barnett's wife, showing that

Barnett's (alleged) crashed-saucer encounter could not possibly have occurred near the Brazel ranch, posed a quandary for Randle and Schmitt. They were eager to accept mortician Dennis's nurse/ET autopsy story because it ruled out any possible prosaic explanation for the Brazel ranch debris. But if the bodies had been recovered from the Plains of San Agustin, they would have been taken to the much closer air base at Albuquerque rather than to Roswell.

In early 1993, Randle and Schmitt discovered a new "firsthand witness," Jim Ragsdale, who reported that he and his girlfriend—now deceased—had seen a UFO crash one night in early July 1947. Ragsdale claimed that early the next morning they had driven to the crash site where they had seen what appeared to be several ET bodies. When a military recovery party arrived, Ragsdale said he and his girlfriend had quickly departed. The new Ragsdale "impact site" was roughly *35 miles north of Roswell* so the ET bodies would have been brought to RAAF, seemingly confirming the Dennis nurse/ET autopsy story.

The new crashed-saucer scenario, based on Ragsdale's story and other "new witnesses," prompted Randle and Schmitt to start work on a second book that would be published in March 1994: *The Truth About the UFO Crash at Roswell.* Randle and Schmitt provided a preview of their new UFO crash scenario in an article published in the January/February 1994 issue of *International UFO Reporter (IUR)*, published by CUFOS. The *IUR* article concluded:

> Skeptics of UFO crash stories . . . have clamored for one, first-hand witness to the crash of a nonterrestrial object, with bodies, who would sign an affidavit and whose story checks out. *There is such a witness now in the person of Jim Ragsdale*, who has lived in Roswell for many years and has been telling his crash story, completely at odds with the [original Haut] press release and Brazel story, since soon after the event. *Ragsdale has, indeed, signed an affidavit*, and with his public accounting of what he witnessed, the case for Roswell becomes that much stronger. (Emphasis added)

Ragsdale was first interviewed in Roswell on January 26, 1993, by Don Schmitt, who covertly recorded the interview to assure an accurate account of Ragsdale's story. Ragsdale was unsure whether the incident had occurred on Friday night, July 4, or the following night, but he was sure it was during the three-day holiday. Based on that interview, Schmitt typed a brief affidavit which Ragsdale signed the next day in the presence of Max Littell who was a notary public. The affidavit read:

> On a night during July, 1947, I, James Ragsdale, was in the company of a woman in an area *approximately forty (40) miles northwest of Roswell*, New Mexico, during a severe lightning storm. I and my companion observed a bright flash and what appeared a bright light source moving toward the southeast. Later, *at sunrise*, driving in that direction, I and my companion came upon a ravine near a bluff that was covered with pieces of unusual wreckage, remains of a damaged craft and a number of smaller bodied beings *outside* the craft. While observing the scene, I and my companion watched as a military convoy arrived and secured the scene. As a result of the convoy's appearance we quickly fled the area. I hereby swear the afore- mentioned account is accurate and true to the best of my knowl- edge and recollection. (Emphasis added)

In the *IUR* article, Randle and Schmitt now proposed a new and drastically different Roswell crashed-saucer scenario—a pre- view of the one that would be featured in their new book. Randle and Schmitt admitted: "Placing the crash on July 2 has always been difficult to square with other known events, such as Mac Brazel's actions. Brazel . . . took the debris to Roswell on *Sunday, July 6*." (They ignored published accounts by Brazel, Marcel, and Sheriff Wilcox that Brazel came to Roswell on *Monday, July 7*.) The article added: "If the crash happened late in the evening of the 2nd and he found the debris the next day, which seems very likely, why did he wait three days to report his find?" (Brazel himself said he first discovered the debris on June 14, and Marcel—in

Ramey's office on July 8—said Brazel had found the debris three weeks earlier.)

In the *IUR* article, Randle and Schmitt revealed that "our colleagues at CUFOS and we have never been completely comfortable with this three day delay." Randle and Schmitt reported that they had discovered new witnesses and information which "firmly fixes the date of the crash as July 4 [Friday], and it also *proves* that the main body of the object came down far from the Foster [Brazel] ranch, but not far from Highway 285 [which runs north from Roswell to Vaughn]." According to this new scenario, the UFO seemingly had suffered a midair explosion that dropped debris on Brazel's ranch but it had managed to fly about 40 miles south before crashing into a small ravine about 35 miles north of Roswell. (This new Randle/Schmitt/Ragsdale "impact site" was officially "unveiled" on March 25, 1994, following a press conference for the new Randle and Schmitt book in Roswell, which I attended. The site, which I visited along with several TV crews and other media, is located approximately 30 miles north of Roswell and six miles west of Highway 285.)

For Randle and Schmitt, this new "impact site" resolved a number of previous discrepancies (which Randle and Schmitt's first book and the Friedman/Berliner book had failed to mention). The July 8, 1947 edition of the *Roswell Daily Record,* which carried Lt. Haut's announcement about recovery of a flying disc, also reported that Mr. and Mrs. Dan Wilmot said they had seen a UFO the previous Wednesday, July 2, which had been headed in the general direction of the Brazel ranch. "Based on this sighting alone," Randle and Schmitt wrote in *IUR*, "all investigators [previously] have reasonably assumed that the Wilmots saw the Roswell object before it crashed and that the crash occurred on July 2." (This despite the fact that Brazel said he first found the debris on *June 14.*)

The July 2 crash date also seemed to be substantiated, Randle and Schmitt noted, by the recent recollections of Roswell resident William Woody. Woody recalled that he and his father had seen what they then believed to be a meteor-fireball on the night of July 2—although they never reported the sighting to the local newspapers. However, according to Woody's recollection the object was headed *south*—in the *opposite direction* of the Wilmots' UFO. Woody recalled that the object seemed to crash north of Roswell.

Randle and Schmitt reported they had recently discovered "new eyewitnesses" whose statements indicated that July 2 was *not* the correct date for the UFO crash. One, E. L. Pyles, a corporal who had been stationed at RAAF, said he recalled seeing a bright object flash across the sky shortly before midnight, but he did not recall whether it was on July 3, 4, or 5. The Randle and Schmitt article also cited Ragsdale, who was not sure whether he had seen the UFO crash on the night of July 4 or 5. Schmitt reportedly had discovered a Franciscan nun, who was based at Roswell's St. Mary's Hospital, whose log reported sighting a bright object on the night of July 4.

However, the *IUR* article reported that Randle and Schmitt had been able to fix the UFO crash date as *July 4*, based on "extensive conversations with a former military and intelligence officer who was at Roswell in 1947. *He was involved with the recovery of the object and bodies, and he kept a diary of the events . . . although it doesn't list the time of the crash, his log does note military activity related to the recovery taking place early on the morning of July 5*" (emphasis added). *But curiously, when Randle and Schmitt's* The Truth About the UFO Crash at Roswell *was published two months later, there was no mention of this "former military and intelligence officer" and his (alleged) diary.*

By early 1994, when the *IUR* article was published, Randle and Schmitt knew that Gerald Anderson's "Uncle Ted's diary" had been revealed to be a hoax as a result of forensic laboratory tests conducted in 1991 on the ink used in the diary. One should therefore expect Randle and Schmitt to be cautious in accepting the claim of another forty-plus-year-old diary without subjecting it to forensic tests. *Yet nearly three years after this Randle/Schmitt arti-*

cle was published, such forensic tests or analysis had yet to be conducted on the diary cited in the IUR article, as will be discussed in chapter 25.

While it might seem that Ragsdale's story and new "impact site" near Roswell provided support for mortician Dennis's nurse/ET autopsy story, embellishments that Dennis would later add would make the two men's tales contradictory. And within two years, Ragsdale would sign another sworn statement claiming the UFO impact site was really *55 miles west* of Roswell rather than *35 miles north*. He would make numerous changes and embellishments to his original tale, as will be described in chapter 19.

13.

New Witnesses Become TV Celebrities

Because tens of millions of TV viewers were attracted to watch the "Unsolved Mysteries" show on Roswell in September 1989 and its rebroadcast in early 1990, the crashed-saucer/coverup tale attracted other TV and independent movie producers. Soon other residents and former residents of Roswell became TV celebrities by "recalling" their own (alleged) involvement, or that of other family members or friends. Maj. Marcel had died in 1986 so his son, Dr. Jesse Marcel Jr., became the family's TV spokesman, with his recollections of what had (allegedly) occurred when he was only eleven years old.

Walter Haut, who had been hoisted from the obscurity of retirement, nearly always appeared on the many new TV shows on Roswell. But his account was relatively brief and not very dramatic. Former mortician Glenn Dennis, with his colorful story about the nurse and ET autopsy—and (alleged) threats to keep him from talking—soon emerged as one of the most popular Roswell TV celebrities.

In 1990 the Fund for UFO Research (FUFOR) produced a half-hour-long video called *Recollections of Roswell,* containing inter-views with fifteen "witnesses," which was distributed to members of Congress and offered for sale to the public. In 1992, FUFOR offered an expanded 105-minute-long version with a dozen "new witnesses," including Gerald Anderson and Glenn Dennis. Nearly one-fifth of the video (19 min.) was devoted to Dennis while Anderson appeared for nearly half an hour, describing his (alleged) crashed-saucer encounter on the Plains of San Agustin.

During the early 1990s, a variety of other "new witnesses" made their debut on TV shows dealing with the Roswell Incident, and in a video-documentary called *UFO SECRET: The Roswell Crash* pro-duced by Mark Wolf for New Century Productions, Poway, Califor-nia, and released in early 1993. One popular new witness was Mrs. Frankie Rowe, an attractive woman in her late fifties, who claimed that her father and other members of the Roswell city fire depart-ment had been sent to the UFO crash site. Mrs. Rowe's story did not raise any Randle and Schmitt doubts despite the fact that none of the persons *known* to have visited the Brazel ranch or others who *claim* to have visited the new "impact site" closer to Roswell reported any fire or evidence of burning. If there had been a fire at the crash site, a fire engine and crew could have been dispatched from RAAF, which had its own fire-fighting equipment.

Rowe said she visited her father at the firehouse where she saw some of the debris he (allegedly) had brought back from the "impact site." According to Mrs. Rowe, "when he dropped the material on the table, it *spread out like liquid or quicksilver,*" i.e., mercury. *Rowe is the only person claiming to have seen or han-dled the UFO debris who described it as flowing like a fluid.*

During my visit to Roswell on March 25, 1994, for the official unveiling of the new "impact site" and the new Randle and Schmitt book, I had the opportunity to spend some time with Mrs. Rowe when she drove with me to visit the (alleged) crash site. During our drive, she told me—as she would subsequently relate on many TV shows—that Air Force officers came to her home shortly after her visit to the firehouse to warn her not to ever discuss what she had seen. If she failed to heed their warning, she would be taken out into the desert and killed. Mrs. Rowe's account of the incident was so dramatic that I asked if, in her youth, she had aspired to become a movie actress. She responded: "Yes. How did you know?"

Another new witness, first reported in Randle and Schmitt's second book, was Roy Musser who, as a civilian contractor, was said to have been painting the Roswell Army Air Field hospital in 1947 when "he saw the one creature [ET] arrive. Apparently uninjured, it walked under its own power into the hospital." According to Randle and Schmitt, "The military warned Musser that he was never to mention what he had seen to anyone or both he and his family would be in jeopardy." But a few years later, according to Frankie Rowe, Musser told her father who then told her.

William Woody, who had recalled that he and his father had seen a fast-moving bright light on the night of July 2 which appeared to crash north of Roswell (see chapter 12), said that several days later they drove north on Highway 285 to see if they could find the crashed object. Woody said they saw military personnel guarding a side road headed west—seemingly to prevent unauthorized persons from driving to the "impact site."

If there really had been a UFO crash and the military had wanted to keep unauthorized persons away from the site, *it would be stupid to station military guards alongside Highway 285 who would attract the attention and curiosity of every passing motorist. Nor was there any need to do so* as I discovered when I visited the site which is six miles west of Highway 285 and is *not* even faintly visible from the highway. To reach the site, one turns off onto what even today is a small, obscure road and heads west over slightly rolling desert for 3.9 miles to where, in 1994, there is a deserted ranch house. To reach the "impact site," which was 2.1 miles further west, we had to transfer to a four-wheel drive vehicle which plodded along a winding, rocky trail—often having to crawl along at the speed of a turtle.

If a UFO had really crashed and the military wanted to bar

unauthorized visitors, military police would have been stationed at this ranch house where they could not be seen by motorists on Highway 285, nearly four miles to the east. If an unauthorized visitor chanced to reach the ranch house, they could not see the crash site from there and could be told to return to Highway 285. But Woody's story of having seen military guards along Highway 285 got him a brief appearance on the Mark Wolf video *UFO SECRET: The Roswell Crash.*

Although nobody ever mentioned ET bodies to Walter Haut for more than thirty years after the incident, many of the new witnesses who emerged in the early 1990s claimed they had seen or heard about ET bodies back in 1947. The number of ETs varied with the witness, for example:

- Frankie Rowe's father: Three ETs, one alive.

- Glenn Dennis: Three ETs, all dead.

- Frank J. Kaufmann: Five ETs, one alive.

- Jim Ragsdale: Three ETs, all dead.

- Anaya Montoya: Four ETs, one alive.

- Mary Bush: One ET, dead.

The different number of ETs reported by different witnesses did not seem significant enough to Randle and Schmitt to prompt them to dismiss the stories told by any of their new witnesses. For Randle and Schmitt, the important thing was that *strange-looking ET bodies (allegedly) had been seen by "many witnesses" which proved that General Ramey's weather balloon/radar target explanation could not possibly be true.*

The most important new witness reported in Randle and Schmitt's second book—even more important than Ragsdale— was *Steve MacKenzie.* "MacKenzie" was really a pseudonym although this was not disclosed in the main body of the book. (It was only briefly mentioned in an appendix note on p. 217.) Steve MacKenzie was really *Frank J. Kaufmann,* who had been characterized as a secondary figure in Randle and Schmitt's first book. (MacKenzie's true identity was first revealed in the May 1994 issue of my *Skeptics UFO Newsletter* [*SUN*].)

In Randle and Schmitt's first book, they reported that Kaufmann had little firsthand knowledge of the crashed saucer: "His friend, a warrant officer named Robert Thomas, had come in on a special flight from Washington, D.C., and seemed to be involved in the retrieval in some fashion. Thomas let Kaufmann know a few things. He talked about the debris field and suggested that there was a search in progress for the [UFO] flight crew. When Thomas talked to Kaufmann, they hadn't found the bodies, but they were looking for them." But in the second book, based on subsequent interviews with Kaufmann, "MacKenzie" emerges as a major figure in the recovery of the crashed saucer and ET bodies. Kaufmann even claimed that he himself saw a live ET walk into the base hospital—and Randle and Schmitt accepted his claim. In an appendix note (p. 220), they write: "We have met with him [MacKenzie] a dozen times and he has always provided interesting and accurate information."

The second book offered the following explanation for trying to hide MacKenzie's true identity in an appendix note (p. 217): "Because of intervention by third parties, a source who had been willing to go on the record withdrew that permission. Although we were under no obligation to change the name, out of courtesy we did so. But this shows what happens when others interject themselves into a situation they do not understand."

The person responsible for Kaufmann's reluctance to be identified was Karl T. Pflock (pronounced "Flock"), a longtime pro-UFOlogist who had launched his own full-time investigation into the Roswell Incident in mid-1992, with the hope of finding evidence that an ET craft had crashed there in 1947. Pflock would publish the results of his twenty-one-month investigation in mid-1994 in a report titled *Roswell In Perspective*. As will be detailed in chapter 17, Pflock interviewed many of the same principal witnesses as Randle and Schmitt, including Kaufmann on May 17, 1993.

While Randle and Schmitt eagerly accepted the "Tales of

Kaufmann," as Pflock's report would characterize Kaufmann's claims, Pflock spotted many flaws and inconsistencies. Pflock's skepticism was evident to Kaufmann, who then asked Randle and Schmitt to use a pseudonym and they agreed. When I interviewed Kaufmann in Roswell on March 25, 1994, and mentioned a person in the new Randle and Schmitt book "referred to as MacKenzie," Kaufmann falsely responded: "I don't know MacKenzie."

Several weeks later, Kaufmann made his TV debut on the CBS prime-time show "48-Hours," hosted by CBS News anchor Dan Rather, which also featured interviews with Dennis, Haut, and Mrs. Rowe. Kaufmann's face was "electronically obscured" and no name was given. But clearly the person whom CBS referred to as "a former intelligence official" was Frank J. Kaufmann—a former official of the Roswell Chamber of Commerce. When I interviewed Kaufmann on March 25, I had asked about his rank when he was stationed at RAAF. He replied: "My rank fit the occasion." When Kaufmann left the service in late 1945, he was a master sergeant. (Kaufmann then was employed as a civilian at RAAF until late 1947.)

According to Randle and Schmitt's second book, MacKenzie had received a telephone call on Wednesday, July 2 from Brig. Gen. Martin F. Scanlon, Deputy Commander of the Air Defense Command, then headquartered in Virginia. According to MacKenzie, he was told that a UFO had been detected on a military radar at the White Sands Proving Ground, about 100 miles southwest of Roswell. MacKenzie said he was ordered to go to White Sands to monitor the UFO's movements and "report them directly to the general. MacKenzie could not leave the scope [radar display] unattended for even the shortest of times. In fact . . . he set up a *system of mirrors so that he could see the screen even when he needed to use the latrine*" (emphasis added).

Later, when this latrine-mirrors claim was ridiculed, Randle explained that he had misunderstood and that the mirrors only enabled MacKenzie to observe a red light showing whether the UFO had again been detected by the White Sands radar. In reality, radars of that era had no such red light to indicate a UFO was under surveillance. If a UFO had earlier been spotted by the experienced White Sands radar operators, it is not clear why MacKenzie was needed—*especially since Kaufmann admitted to me that he was not a trained radar operator.*

By a not-so-curious coincidence, Randle and Schmitt report that *both Kaufmann and MacKenzie were in telephone contact with an officer in Washington, D.C., named Robert Thomas.* According to their first book (p. 205), Kaufmann's friend Robert Thomas had flown into Roswell on Tuesday, July 8. But according to their second book, MacKenzie's friend Robert Thomas arrived in Roswell on the afternoon of Friday, July 4. One possible explanation for this four-day discrepancy is that there were really two officers named Robert Thomas, both based in Washington, and both had flown to Roswell. But from information contained in both Randle and Schmitt books, it is clear that there could be only one Robert Thomas—*if there was even one.*

According to the second (1994) Randle and Schmitt book, "complete access to the impact site, the immediate area where the object had crashed, was restricted to *those with the highest [security] clearance and a real need to know*" (emphasis added). Allegedly, MacKenzie was included in this very select group and he provided Randle and Schmitt with details of what had transpired. According to MacKenzie, the crashed craft was *not the familiar circular (saucer) shape.* Instead, according to a sketch which he drew, the craft more closely resembled the USAF's F-117A stealth fighter. MacKenzie's sketch, which is shown in the second book, is falsely claimed to have been provided by "a firsthand witness, a high-ranking army officer stationed at Roswell."

In August 1995, Kaufmann made his debut on British television on a program called "The Roswell Incident" broadcast over UK Channel 4, and he allowed his real name to be used. The host introduced Kaufmann saying he claimed to be "a covert member of a highly secret counterintelligence group, code-named Lion. Tonight, Kaufmann reveals for the first time what he says is the true story of the Roswell incident." Kaufmann claimed that his military party had discovered the crashed object "late at night"—presumably on July 4. According to Kaufmann, "we saw this glow of light, kind of a halo of light, kind of beaming out. We got to, I guess, maybe about 200 yards, maybe 300 yards from where it was. *And we knew right then and there it wasn't a plane. It wasn't a missile. It was kind of a strange-looking craft embedded in the arroya.*" Kaufmann said the craft had broken open "and one body was thrown up against the wall of the arroya. The other one was half in and half out of the craft. And when we got in close we noticed that there were three other [bodies] inside the craft. Then we later went back to the base to have a truck, a flatbed, and a crane . . . come out to the site to clear everything off."

Kaufmann's British TV remarks confirmed suspicions that it was he who first "located" the new "impact site" 35 miles north of Roswell which formed the cornerstone of the new Randle/ Schmitt crashed-saucer scenario. The TV-show host said: "Frank Kaufmann provided us with what he claims is a copy of his official report on the Roswell Incident—*a Top Secret document containing observations and sketches of what he saw at the time.*" Kaufmann said that because the ET bodies had begun to deteriorate, "We were in a hurry and got them out to the base hospital. They called the [Ballard] mortuary to find out if there was anything they could preserve the bodies with." This set the stage for a TV interview with Glenn Dennis, whose nurse/ET autopsy story seemed to confirm Kaufmann's story.

British TV viewers were *not* reminded that Kaufmann said he saw *five* ET bodies, while Dennis reported only *three*. Nor were viewers told that, according to Kaufmann, the ET bodies had been taken to the RAAF base hospital on Saturday, July 5. But according to Dennis, it was not until several days later that he (allegedly) received several telephone calls from the base mortuary officer inquiring about how to recover and preserve bodies that had been exposed to the elements. It would seem to British TV viewers that Kaufmann's story was confirmed by Dennis when in reality they contradicted one another.

14.

GAO Launches Roswell Investigation

Karl T. Pflock, whom Randle and Schmitt blamed for Kaufmann's reluctance to be identified, was indirectly responsible
for a Roswell investigation launched in early 1994 by the General
Accounting Office (GAO), the investigative agency for the U.S.
Congress. The GAO investigation was officially requested by
Republican Congressman Steven Schiff of New Mexico, but one
of his senior staff members—Mary Martinek—is Pflock's wife.

Pflock, who acknowledges a "virtually lifelong interest in
UFOs," graduated from San Jose State University in 1964. In 1966
he moved to the Washington, D.C., area to work for the CIA. A
year earlier, Pflock had joined the nation's largest and then most
prominent pro-UFO organization, NICAP (National Investigations
Committee on Aerial Phenomena). When Pflock moved to Washington, where NICAP had its headquarters, he became active in
investigating UFO reports and was named chairman of NICAP's
National Capital Area Subcommittee. After leaving the CIA in the
early 1970s, Pflock worked as a congressional staffer, including the
House Committee on Armed Services. In mid-1985, during the

Reagan administration, Pflock was appointed Deputy Assistant Secretary of Defense for Operational Test and Evaluation, a high Pentagon post which he held for nearly four years. After this he went to work for a prominent consulting company. In 1992, Pflock "retired" to become a freelance writer and pursue his long-standing interest in UFOs, initially focusing on the Roswell Incident.

In the late summer of 1992, Pflock arranged for members of Congressman Schiff's staff and the staff of the Government Operations Committee, of which Schiff was a member, to be briefed on the Roswell crashed-saucer case. Around this time, the Fund for UFO Research (FUFOR), with headquarters near Washington, agreed to provide financial support for Pflock's Roswell investigation.

On March 11, 1993, Schiff sent a letter to Defense Secretary Les Aspin asking him to investigate the Roswell Incident and provide a briefing for Schiff and his staff. Aspin's office sent Schiff's letter to the Pentagon's Legislative Affairs Office, whose function is to respond to voluminous inquiries from members of Congress. Because the USAF had been responsible for UFO investigations until it shut down its Project Blue Book operation in late 1969, Schiff's letter landed on the desk of a USAF officer, Lt. Col. Larry Shockley. When Shockley learned that all of the Project Blue Book UFO files had been declassified and turned over to the National Archives in the mid-1970s, he replied to Schiff on March 31, 1993, suggesting that he contact the National Archives. Shockley, not being familiar with the Roswell Incident, did not know that it had occurred six months *before* the USAF had created an office to investigate UFO reports. When Schiff's office made inquiry to the National Archives, it responded that no Roswell files could be found. This prompted another Schiff letter to Defense Secretary Aspin on May 10, which brought a response from Aspin's executive assistant which again referred Schiff to the National Archives—greatly angering the congressman.

In October 1993, top GAO officials visited Schiff to discuss their upcoming budget request because he was a member of the Government Operations Committee which funds GAO activities.

During their visit, Schiff mentioned the "runaround" he thought he had gotten from the Pentagon and suggested that the GAO might be of assistance. Schiff knew that a recent GAO investigation had revealed that the Atomic Energy Committee had conducted a dozen secret experiments between 1948 and 1952 in which unsuspecting citizens had been subjected to nuclear radiation to assess the biological effects of nuclear weapons.

The GAO officials agreed to consider Schiff's requested Roswell investigation. But subsequent discussions at GAO headquarters raised some questions about the agency's involvement in so unusual an issue. In early 1994, Schiff agreed to a GAO suggestion that the objective of its investigation would be to "determine the [Defense Department's] requirements for reporting air accidents *similar to the crash near Roswell and identify [i.e., search for] any government records concerning the Roswell crash*" (emphasis added).

GAO's Roswell investigation got under way in February 1994 —shortly before Randle and Schmitt's second book was published. Schiff designated Mary Martinek—Pflock's wife—to serve as his liaison contact with GAO for its Roswell investigation. When I interviewed Martinek on January 10, 1994, she told me: "The Congressman did not ask the GAO to look into crashed saucers. The Congressman asked the GAO specifically—and the Department of Defense—to provide him with an explanation of what actually happened in Roswell in 1947." Although Schiff's congressional district was centered in Albuquerque and did not include Roswell, Martinek spoke of "constituent concerns." She added: "They would very much like to know what happened and why their lives were disrupted and would like to have a final answer. The Congressman wants the Government to explain what came down. Why, if something came down, if nothing came down, exactly what did happen. *Why was it necessary for the Government to take these extraordinary measures to coverup . . .*" (emphasis added).

GAO's plans to launch a Roswell investigation at Schiff's request were first disclosed in the January 1994 issue of my *Skeptics UFO Newsletter* (*SUN*) and in an article in the January 13 edition of the *Albuquerque Journal,* written by Steve Brewer who had called me the previous day to discuss the Roswell case. Brewer, who then interviewed Schiff for his article, quoted him as saying: "I would not ask for an investigation of something I was just curious about. *The issue is whether the government is being forthright with the American people, and that is a serious issue to me*" (emphasis added).

A follow-on story by Brewer the next day began:

> Rep. Steve Schiff says his investigation into the 1947 recovery of a mysterious object in New Mexico was prompted by letters from constituents, not by his aide's UFO-hunting husband. Placitus [N.M.] resident Karl Pflock, who's married to Schiff's district director, Mary Martinek, has worked vigorously for nearly a year investigating the so-called "Roswell Incident" under a grant from the Fund for UFO Research [FUFOR] in Washington, D.C.

GAO's Roswell investigation also was the subject of a feature article in the January 14 edition of the *Washington Post,* which carried the headline: "GAO TURNS TO ALIEN TURF IN PROBE: Bodies of Space Voyagers Said to Have Disappeared in 1947." The article, by reporter William Claiborne, quoted Schiff as saying: "Generally, I'm a skeptic on UFOs and alien beings, but there are indications from the run-around that I got that whatever it was *it wasn't a balloon. Apparently, it's another government cover-up*" (emphasis added).

On February 8, 1994, GAO's Richard Davis, Director for National Security Analysis, wrote to Defense Secretary William Perry (who had replaced Aspin) to inform him of GAO's Roswell investigation. Davis said that the investigation would be headed by Gary Weeter, Assistant Director for National Security Analysis. By the time that the Defense Secretary was formally notified of the GAO investigation, the USAF already had launched its own investigation, prompted by the January 14 article in the *Washington Post.*

The USAF's Roswell investigation would be headed by Col. Richard L. Weaver, Director of Security and Special Program

Oversight for the Secretary of the Air Force, Ms. Sheila E. Widnall. This was an excellent choice because one major function of Weaver's office (SAF/AAZ) is to monitor all USAF highly classified ("Black") programs that could not be discussed publicly in open congressional hearings. This meant that Weaver and his staff held the highest security clearances. If an ET craft had been recovered in New Mexico in 1947, it would have prompted extensive USAF research programs to learn more about the craft's construction and propulsion system. If such programs were ongoing, Weaver's office would know about them. If UFO research efforts had earlier been terminated, members of Weaver's staff had sufficiently high military clearances to gain access to the records.

During the next few months, Weaver and associates would search many USAF archives and interview surviving firsthand witnesses. *To assure that such witnesses would be free to divulge everything they knew about the Roswell Incident, they were granted freedom from any previous security oath by the Secretary of the Air Force or other top USAF official.*

By late July 1994, the USAF had completed its rigorous investigation and prepared a report for Secretary Widnall, which was made public on September 8, 1994. The USAF report would disclose what had really "crashed" on the Brazel ranch in 1947—a 600-foot-long train of twenty-three weather balloons and a cluster of radar targets which were being tested for a then "Top Secret" mission called Project Mogul. The USAF had even located the scientist, *Charles B. Moore,* who had launched the balloon train on June 4, 1947. He was now a retired professor who was living in Socorro, New Mexico.

Ironically, two months before the USAF report was released, the Project Mogul "connection" to the Brazel ranch debris had been revealed by Karl Pflock in his report *Roswell In Perspective.* But the person who had first discovered the Project Mogul connection several years earlier was a painstaking UFO researcher named Robert G. Todd, of Ardmore, Pennsylvania.

15.

The Top Secret Project Mogul

While the development of the atomic bomb had hastened the end of the war with Japan, it had opened a "Pandora's box" for the United States. The Soviet Union could be expected to also develop nuclear weapons to further its postwar expansionist ambitions and this would make the United States vulnerable to nuclear attack. Furthermore, because of the USSR's closed society and vast land-mass, it would be difficult if not impossible for the United States and its Western allies to determine when the Soviets had mastered the complex technology of nuclear weapons and might be ready to start World War III. Thus, it became urgent for the United States to find means to determine when the USSR successfully tested its first nuclear weapon.

A novel technique that might be able to detect the Soviet nuclear tests was suggested by Dr. Maurice Ewing, a Columbia University geophysicist, in a five-page memo submitted to Gen. Carl A. Spaatz, Commanding General of the Army Air Forces. The report, classified "Secret," was titled: "Long Range Sound Transmission in the Atmosphere." (Ewing's undated report is believed to have been written in late 1945.) Dr. Ewing noted that there was a "sound channel [i.e., duct] in the atmosphere at a height of about 45,000 ft., and if both the sound source and the receiver are located at this altitude, we may expect extraordinary ranges. . . ." Thus, if sensitive microphones could be flown at an altitude of about 45,000 feet, they might be able to detect the sound generated by a Soviet nuclear explosion. However, if the Soviets learned that the United States was using this technique, they could test their early nuclear weapons underground to muffle the sound.

For this reason, Ewing cautioned that the technique's potential usefulness "depends greatly upon secrecy and that the investigation [of its feasibility] should be started in a quiet way, *restricting knowledge of the purpose of the work to the smallest possible group*" (emphasis added). Because no aircraft of that era could fly at an altitude of 45,000 feet, the logical means of carrying sensitive microphones to this height and remaining there for an extended period would be helium/hydrogen-filled balloons. The technical challenge would be to devise means to enable the balloons to rise to around 45,000 feet *to level off and maintain themselves at constant altitude by dropping ballast.*

By mid-1946, the AAF had decided to investigate the feasibility of Dr. Ewing's idea under a program called Project Mogul, which was given an extremely high security classification: "Top Secret, Priority 1A." In November 1946, the AAF awarded a contract to New York University's Research Division "to develop and fly constant-level instrument-carrying balloons." Most universities do not like to work on highly classified military projects because of their constraints on open discussion of scientific/technical accomplishments. For this reason, and because many elements of the "constant-level instrument-carrying balloons" would use "open" techniques, the New York University Balloon Project was unclassified, as were its periodic progress reports to the AAF's Watson Laboratories, in Red Bank, New Jersey, which initially managed the program. *But the intended application was classified "Top Secret" and thus limited to a few key military personnel with a "need-to-know."*

The first UFOlogist to discover a possible connection between Project Mogul and the Brazel ranch debris was Robert G. Todd of Ardmore, Pennsylvania, a sharp-eyed, painstaking researcher. Todd's use of the Freedom of Information Act (FOIA) requests had been responsible for public disclosure of the USAF-Navy "Top Secret" intelligence report of December 10, 1948, which indicated that the prevailing Pentagon view in late 1948 was that UFOs probably were covert Soviet spy vehicles. (See chapter 7.)

In the fall of 1990, as Todd recently recalled for me, he was reviewing copies of UFO-related documents that had been released by the Federal Bureau of Investigation (FBI) in the mid-1970s (in response to an FOIA request by Dr. Bruce S. Maccabee, a longtime pro-UFOlogist). Todd spotted a brief reference to a "Top Secret Project Mogul" which aroused his curiosity. It appeared in an FBI report on its investigation of "UFO crash debris," turned in by a farmer near Danforth, Illinois, in August 1947. The FBI memo indicated that when one of its agents had shown the debris to a Mrs. Francis Whedon, a high-ranking civilian Army employee, she said that it appeared to be something used in Project Mogul. But she declined to discuss Project Mogul because it was classified Top Secret. (Later USAF analysis showed the Danforth "UFO crash-debris" was a hoax.)

This brief reference prompted Todd to make an FOIA request to the Air Force Historical Agency, at Maxwell AFB, Alabama, in the fall of 1990 which located a cryptic reference to Project Mogul in the papers of Gen. Curtis LeMay. (Project Mogul had been declassified in the early 1970s.) Todd obtained a microfilm copy which linked Project Mogul to Watson Laboratories. Further painstaking research finally linked Project Mogul to the New York University (NYU) constant-altitude balloon project. Todd discovered that in May 1947, the NYU project had shifted its balloon-launch experiments from the east coast to the Alamogordo Army Air Field in New Mexico—located about 90 miles southwest of the Brazel ranch. As a result of Todd's research effort, he learned that the project engineer for the NYU balloon experiments at

Alamogordo was *Charles B. Moore*, who later had become a professor of physics at the New Mexico Institute of Mining and Technology in Socorro.

Professor Moore had been interviewed by author William L. Moore (no relation) in the late 1970s for his book *The Roswell Incident.* Author Moore had asked Prof. Moore if he believed any of the NYU balloon experiments might explain the Brazel ranch debris. The Berlitz/Moore book quoted Prof. Moore as saying: *"Based on the [debris] description you just gave me,* I can definitely rule this out. There wasn't a balloon in use back in '47 . . . that could have produced debris over such a large area or *torn up the ground* in any way . . . [as author Moore erroneously claimed]"* (emphasis added). The Berlitz/Moore book published a sketch of one train of balloons which had been launched by NYU scientists on July 7. Its caption included the following: "Although these balloons were frequently mistaken for UFOs while aloft, it is difficult to imagine how they could be mistaken for one while on the ground."

When Todd located Prof. Moore and began to correspond with him in the spring of 1992, he discovered that Moore had *never seen Brazel's original description of the debris* as reported in the July 9, 1947 edition of the *Roswell Daily Record*! Author William Moore had provided Prof. Moore with *none* of Maj. Marcel's thirty-two-year-old recollections of the Brazel ranch debris, obtained in 1979. Brazel's description, given only a few hours after he, Marcel, and Cavitt had collected the debris, *was not published in the Berlitz/Moore book.*

When Todd sent Prof. Moore a copy of the Roswell newspaper article, and Moore read Brazel's description—especially his mention that "considerable Scotch tape and some tape with flowers printed upon it had been used in the construction"—it struck a strong chord in Moore's memory. He recalled that the radar targets employed in the NYU balloon experiments used Scotch tape to reinforce the fragile kitelike structure. *More important, that these specific radar targets had been fabricated by a New York City toy manufacturer who used tape with colored flowers and symbols which had originally been acquired for making children's toys.* (This would explain the symbols that Maj. Marcel in 1979, and later his son, Dr. Marcel, would characterize as "hieroglyphics.")

By not publishing Brazel's July 8 account, the Berlitz/Moore book tried to coverup the fact that he had first discovered the unusual debris on June 14. This enabled the Berlitz/Moore book to falsely claim that the UFO had crashed on the night of July 2, based on the report by Roswell's Dan Wilmot that he and his wife had seen a glowing object headed northwest (in the general direction of the Brazel ranch) shortly before 10 P.M. on the night of July 2. During William Moore's 1979 interview with Prof. Moore, the latter knew that the NYU team had not launched any balloons on the night of July 2, which further seemed to rule out any NYU project connection to the Brazel ranch debris.

After reading Brazel's July 8, 1947 description, and learning that he had first discovered the debris on June 14, Prof. Moore went through his own records of the NYU experiments. These records showed that NYU had launched a 600-foot-long train of some twenty-three weather balloons, three radar targets, and other instruments on *June 4, 1947.* Further, that this train of balloons, radar targets, and instruments *had been tracked by ground and later airborne radar to within about 17 miles of the Brazel ranch* before radar contact was lost. Also, that the debris from this June 4 launch had never been found, unlike many other NYU launches. (See figure 4.)

But for an ironic coincidence, Moore and his NYU teammates almost certainly would have at least suspected that the "flying disc" reported in Lt. Haut's press release might be debris from their June 4 launch. On the *morning of July 8—several hours before Lt. Haut distributed his famous "flying disc recovered" press release*—Moore and his associates had departed Alamogordo for a long flight back to the East Coast. By the time they arrived, the news media were reporting Gen. Ramey's explanation that the debris was from a weather balloon and radar target.

If Haut's press release had identified the location where the debris had been found, this might have prompted Moore and others to associate the debris with their June 4 launch, and to seek the opportunity to examine the debris. Instead, some forty-five years would elapse before Prof. Moore would learn, thanks to Robert Todd, of the NYU involvement in the famous Roswell crashed-saucer incident. And forty-five years would elapse before an explanation would emerge for the "hieroglyphics" recalled by Maj. Marcel and his son.

Prof. Moore's description of the colored flowers and symbols imprinted on the tape dovetails closely with the 1979 recollections of Brazel's daughter, Bessie, who helped him collect the debris on Sunday, July 6. (She was fourteen years old at the time.) As reported in the Berlitz/Moore book, her 1979 description of the debris was the following: "There was what appeared to be pieces of heavily waxed paper and a sort of aluminum-like foil. . . . Some of the metal-foil pieces *had a sort of tape stuck to them*, and when they were held up to the light *they showed what looked like pastel [colored] flowers or designs . . .*" (emphasis added). This is remarkably similar to Marcel's recollections when he was interviewed in May 1979 for the *UFOs Are Real* movie. He said the symbols were "pink and purple—lavender was actually what it was." (See figure 8.)

During that 1979 interview, Marcel recalled that "the fragments were strewn all over an area about three-quarters of a mile long and several hundred feet wide." A long, narrow field of debris is what would be expected when one or several of the twenty-three weather balloons in the NYU Flight #4 sprang a leak or exploded at high altitude, causing the 600-foot-long balloon train to descend. Based on debris recovered from other NYU balloon flights, Prof. Moore offered the following logical scenario in his letter of September 25, 1995, to me:

> The standard weather balloons used in this flight did not "crash." Instead they probably descended slowly to Earth after

some of the neoprene balloons lifting the train burst as a result of prolonged exposure to sunlight. When the bottom part of the balloon train touched the ground, the upper portion of the train was [still] held aloft by the remaining balloons which were probably blown downwind by the breezes at the surface. A landing like this usually caused the equipment at the bottom of the train [including the radar targets] to be dragged through the underbrush and to be ripped off when any of it snagged in the shrubbery.

Often, after the equipment was ripped off as a result of wind forces, the upper part of the train had enough lift that it would rise again and float downwind until another balloon burst from degradation in the sunlight, whereupon the descent, dragging and equipment-shedding sequence would be repeated. . . .

From Brazel's description of the debris, it appears to me that he found only a portion of the equipment carried on that flight: he picked up broken pieces of several radar targets and fragments of burst balloons. Absent from his description was any mention of the sonobuoy microphone, the pressure switches [used to maintain constant altitude], the boxes of batteries and the tubes holding the ballast; these probably were broken away from the flight train in an earlier touchdown before the target remnants were deposited on the Foster [Brazel] Ranch. . . .

This is an added irony of the Roswell Incident. If only one of these other objects had been found by Brazel, Marcel, or Cavitt, it would clearly have identified the debris as being the remnants from something that had been manufactured in the United States. If, as has been erroneously claimed by some "witnesses," the RAAF had launched a massive search effort of the surrounding area, one of these devices, or its remnants, might have been found to correctly identify the "flying disc."

In Marcel's May 1979 interview, he recalled that the long path of debris stretched in a northeast-southwest direction, and that from the concentration of debris, the object appeared to have been moving from northeast to southwest. More probably, considering that NYU Flight #4 had been launched from Alamogordo, which is southwest of the Brazel ranch, the balloon train was moving in the opposite direction. But Marcel's and Cavitt's primary objective on July 8, 1947, had been to promptly recover the debris and return it to RAAF—*not* to try to determine the direction in which the object. had been moving when it touched down.

16.

The USAF's Roswell Report

A twenty-three-page report that summarized the objectives and the results of the USAF's six-month Roswell investigation was released to the media on September 8, 1994, nearly a year before the GAO's (General Accounting Office) Roswell report would be made public. The document, signed by Col. Richard L. Weaver who had directed the effort, is sometimes called the "Weaver Report" although its official title was: "Report of Air Force Research Regarding the 'Roswell Incident.' " The report referenced thirty-three "attachments," which included sworn affidavits from two key firsthand witnesses—the only ones still alive. These and other very detailed documents dealing with Project Mogul would later become available to the public in a 2¼ in.-thick report published in 1995 by the U.S. Government Printing Office, titled: "The Roswell Report: Fact versus Fiction in the New Mexico Desert."

The USAF's priority effort was spurred in part by GAO's authoritative role as Congress's investigative agency. GAO's investigations of controversial Pentagon programs can determine whether they get congressional funding. Additionally, the USAF was sensitive to Congressman Schiff's public accusation that it had given him a "runaround" in response to his earlier requests for an explanation of the "Roswell Incident." Top Pentagon and USAF officials recognized that if they failed to conduct a rigorous investigation, and if GAO investigators turned up evidence of a recovered crashed saucer—perhaps in the minutes of National Security Council meetings—this would seriously damage the credibility of defense officials seeking congressional approval for major new programs.

Only two of the firsthand witnesses were still alive in 1994: Sheridan Cavitt, who Marcel recalled in 1979 had accompanied him to the Brazel ranch to recover the debris; and Irving Newton, who had been called to Gen. Ramey's office to help identify the debris. (Col. DuBose had since died.) Cavitt was interviewed by Col. Weaver on May 24, 1994, and Newton was interviewed by Lt. Col. Joseph V. Rogan on July 21, 1994. Both signed sworn statements which were among the attachments to the USAF's September 8 (Weaver) report.

Newton's statement is especially important because it counters popular claims that the material photographed in Gen. Ramey's office was *not* the authentic debris recovered from the Brazel ranch. Newton's affidavit states: "While I was examining the debris, Major Marcel was picking up pieces of the [radar] target sticks and trying to convince me that some notations on the sticks were alien writings. There were figures on the sticks [which were] lavender or pink in color, appeared to be weather-faded markings with no rhyme or reason." If the material photographed in Ramey's office was a bogus substitute, the key question is where could he have obtained a radar target so quickly. The only nearby source would have been the Fort Worth Army Air Field's own meteorological office. But in Newton's affidavit he said: *"We did not use them [balloon-borne radar targets] at Fort Worth"* (emphasis added).

Cavitt's sworn statement said that he had studied the photos of the debris taken in Ramey's office

... and it appears to be the same type material that we picked up from the ranch land. . . . There was no secretive effort or heightened security regarding this incident or any unusual expenditure of manpower at the base to deal with it. . . . I have never been sworn to any form of secrecy by anyone concerning this matter and I have received authorization from the Secretary of the Air Force to discuss with Colonel Weaver any information of a classified nature that I may have concerning it. . . . My bottom line is that this whole incident was no big deal and it certainly did not involve anything extraterrestrial.

The USAF search for Roswell-related documents involved many different archives, including those of the Air Force Intelligence Agency, in San Antonio, Texas, and the National Air Intelligence Center, at Wright-Patterson AFB near Dayton, Ohio, where the Roswell debris (allegedly) had been sent for analysis. The USAF report noted that the law requires the Secretary of Defense to periodically report to Congress on all highly secret programs, referred to as Special Access Programs (SAPs). The report added that "SAF/AAZ, the Central Office for all Air Force SAPs, has knowledge of and security oversight over all SAPs. *SAF/AAZ categorically stated that no such Special Access Program(s) exists that pertain to extraterrestrial spacecraft/aliens*" (emphasis added).
   The report added:

Likewise, the Secretary of the Air Force and the Chief of Staff, who head the Special Program Oversight Committee which oversees *all* sensitive programs in the Air Force, *had no knowledge of the existence of any such program involving, or relating to the events at Roswell or the alleged technology that supposedly resulted therefrom.* Besides the obvious irregularity and illegality of keeping such information from the most senior Air Force officials, it would be illogical, since these officials are responsible for obtaining funding for operations, research, development and security. Without funding such a program, operation, or organization *could not exist. Even to keep such a fact "covered-up" in some sort of passive "caretaker status" would involve money. More importantly, it would involve people and create paperwork.* (Emphasis added)

If the Pentagon in 1947 had recovered a crashed saucer which used very advanced materials and propulsion, it would have launched a vast research effort to analyze and try to replicate the very advanced ET technology. Over the subsequent forty-seven years this would have resulted in many tens of thousands of memoranda, letters, and reports. If debris from a crashed saucer had been recovered in 1947, it would certainly have been sent to Wright Field (now Wright-Patterson Air Force Base) near Dayton, Ohio, which was the AAF's center of technical expertise, and turned over to what is now called the National Air Intelligence Center (NAIC).

In response to the GAO request, NAIC historian Bruce Ashcroft conducted an "electronic search" of *several million pages of documents,* looking for any reference to "Roswell," or the presence of flying saucers or aliens that had been sent to Wright Field. *The search turned up nothing.* Ashcroft then visited the Air Force's Historical Research Agency in Alabama and conducted an electronic search of several million pages of documents stored there. His effort included a search of the minutes of periodic meetings of top Air Force commanders, including once-"Top Secret" portions dealing with intelligence, research, and design. Ashcroft found no reference to Roswell or to extraterrestrial vehicles—nor to any research or development programs which would have been triggered by the recovery of an ET craft.

If the USAF investigation had discovered *only one document, memo, or letter that even cryptically referred to recovery of a UFO or an ET craft, it would have provided a "smoking gun" to confirm the Roswell crashed-saucer tale, but no such document was ever found.*

Shortly after the USAF launched its Roswell investigation, on February 28, 1994, its researchers did discover a letter which referred to the NYU balloon tests at Alamogordo during mid-1947. Shortly afterward, a letter dated July 8, 1946, was discovered which mentioned a "Top Secret" Project Mogul. Also located by USAF investigators were letters dated September 9 and 10, 1947, which were classified "Top Secret" and referred to Project Mogul tests planned to be conducted in Alaska. USAF investigators, as with Robert Todd and Karl Pflock before them, found the NYU/Project Mogul trail led to Charles B. Moore and on June 8, 1994, he was visited by Col. Jeffrey Butler and 1st Lt. James McAndrew. Thanks to the 1992 efforts of Todd, Moore had by this time retrieved his records of the NYU project to refresh his memory.

Moore's lengthy sworn statement of June 8, 1994, contained in the USAF report, included the following: "On review of the photos in the Randle/Schmitt book [taken in Gen. Ramey's office], the material looks like one of our balloon and target assemblies. The wooden beams were made of balsa wood *that had been coated in an Elmers-like glue* [to strengthen them]" (emphasis added). Moore also said: "I have a specific recollection of reinforcing tape applied to the seams of the reflectors *that had some symbols such as arcs, flowers, circles and diamonds. These were pinkish in color*" (emphasis added).

The USAF investigators wisely did not try to respond to every claim made by every (alleged) witness cited in the books by Berlitz/Moore, Randle/Schmitt, and Friedman/Berliner. More than forty years earlier, the USAF's Project Blue Book had investigated the claim of a Florida Scoutmaster that he and a group of Boy Scouts had had a close encounter with a UFO. When the USAF subsequently made public the result of its investigation, which indicated that the incident was a hoax, the Scoutmaster's influential congressman sharply criticized the USAF and defended his constituent.

Because Congressman Schiff said his request for a GAO investigation was prompted by claims made by some of his constituents, any USAF challenge to their veracity would almost certainly anger Schiff. However, the veracity of a number of Randle and Schmitt's key "witnesses" would be challenged by Roswell researcher Karl Pflock in his *Roswell In Perspective* report, as will be described in chapter 17.

However, the USAF/Weaver report did cite, and demolish, one false "coverup" claim made in Randle and Schmitt's first book, *UFO Crash at Roswell.* In the book, Schmitt reported that he had tried without success to locate eleven persons known to have been stationed at RAAF in July 1947. Randle and Schmitt asked: "Why does neither the Defense Department nor the Veteran's Administration have records for any of these men when we can document that each served at Roswell Army Air Field?" This was a serious coverup charge which could readily be checked by a USAF investigator who contacted the National [military] Personnel Records Center in St. Louis. The USAF report stated: "Using only the names (since the authors did not list the serial numbers), the researcher quickly found records readily identifiable with *eight* of these persons. The other three had such common names that there could have been multiple possibilities." (Schmitt would shortly be caught spinning tall tales about his work and academic background, as will be reported in chapter 20.)

The USAF report concluded:

> The Air Force research did not locate or develop any information that the "Roswell Incident" was a UFO event. All available official materials, although they do not address Roswell per se, indicate that the most likely source of the wreckage recovered from the Brazel Ranch was from one of the Project Mogul balloon trains. Although that project was TOP SECRET at the time, there was also no specific indication found to indicate an official pre-planned cover story was in place to explain an event such as that which ultimately happened.
>
> It appears that the identification [by Gen. Ramey] of the wreckage as being part of a weather balloon device, as reported in the newspapers at the time, was based on the fact *that there was no physical difference in the radar targets and neoprene balloons (other than the numbers and configuration) between*

Mogul balloons and normal weather balloons.... Likewise, there was *no* indication in official records from the [1947] period that *there was heightened military operational or security activity which should have been generated if this was, in fact, the first recovery of materials and/or persons from another world.* (Emphasis added)

When the GAO's report of its lengthy Roswell investigation was issued nearly a year later, in mid-1995, the GAO would not challenge or question any of these USAF findings.

17.

Pflock's Roswell Perspective

Approximately two months *before* the USAF released its Roswell report, the Fund for UFO Research (FUFOR) published a 189-page report by Karl Pflock, based on his nearly two-year Roswell investigation. Pflock's report, titled *Roswell In Perspective,* would generate much controversy among UFOlogists and within FUFOR. Its front cover carried the following disclaimer: "The conclusions, opinions, and ideas expressed herein are those of the author and do not necessarily represent the views of the Fund for UFO Research, its officers, or its board members."

In the concluding portion of the report, Pflock wrote: *"It is all but certain that at least the great majority if not all of what was found at the debris field on the Foster [Brazel] ranch was the wreckage of a huge balloon and instrumentation array launched from Alamogordo AAF as part of the 'crash' Top Secret, highly sensitive Project Mogul"* (emphasis added). This was a remarkable admission for Pflock who had devoted nearly two years to investigating what he clearly hoped would provide impressive evidence that some UFOs were ET craft.

Based on Pflock's interviews with a number of Randle and Schmitt's key witnesses, his report detailed major inconsistencies in witness tales which challenged their veracity. These witnesses included Frank J. Kaufmann, Jim Ragsdale, and Mrs. Frankie Rowe, among others. But Pflock *did* endorse one key witness whose tale also was endorsed by Randle/Schmitt and Friedman/Berliner: *former mortician Glenn Dennis.* This despite knowledge that Dennis clearly had violated his "sacred oath" to never reveal the (alleged) nurse's secret, and inconsistencies in his tale. (Within a year after *Roswell In Perspective* was published, Pflock would learn that Dennis had lied in his December 9, 1991 interview with me, when he claimed not to have given the ET sketches to Randle and Schmitt, as reported in chapter 9.)

A curious new development had occurred during Pflock's telephone conversation with Dennis on March 30, 1994, as the report was being readied for publication. Dennis told Pflock of a recent "flash recall" which conflicted with the well-established chronology of events. Pflock included this new Dennis claim in the report appendix under the headline, "An Important New Development." Pflock noted that previously Dennis said he could not recall the exact date of his (alleged) meeting with the nurse in the hospital and his lunch the next day when she told him of the alien autopsy and gave him the ET sketches. But Dennis told Pflock that after hearing Randle and Schmitt describe their new "impact site" scenario he had a "blinding flash of recall" that now established the precise date.

Pflock wrote:

Dennis is absolutely certain it was the *afternoon of Monday, July 7, when he received the calls [from the mortuary officer]* about body preservation and caskets. . . . The next day, Tuesday, July 8, . . . just before noon Dennis met with the nurse, who fearfully told him the story of the strange bodies. *How can Dennis be so certain about the dates? Late in the afternoon of the day he met with the nurse . . . he picked up the* Roswell

Daily Record *as it was delivered to the Ballard Funeral Home. Emblazoned across the top of the front page was this headline: RAAF CAPTURES FLYING SAUCER ON RANCH IN THE ROSWELL REGION. The date on the masthead was, of course, Tuesday, July 8, 1947.* (Emphasis added)

According to this Dennis "flash recall," the alien autopsy was already taking place on the afternoon of Monday, July 7, when Marcel and Cavitt are known to have been driving north to Brazel's ranch to recover the debris. If strange creature bodies were undergoing autopsy on the afternoon of July 7, they could not possibly have come from the Brazel ranch. While Pflock rejected the new Randle/Schmitt "impact site" 35 miles north of Roswell, he failed to suggest any alternative location for recovery of alleged ET bodies.

Pflock wrote that "it is reasonable to conclude that there were human-like but strange or strangely disfigured bodies at Roswell Army Air Field sometime before and probably until the afternoon of July 9, 1947." Further, "the bodies and wreckage [reported by Dennis] resulted from Something Else [*sic*], knowledge of which Army Air Force officials were very concerned to keep closely held. . . . *That Something Else may have been the crash of an alien spacecraft*" (emphasis added).

Pflock speculated that a "Something Else" craft (with crew) might have collided with the Project Mogul balloon train, causing both to crash, or that the "Something Else" craft accident was quite unrelated to the Project Mogul descent. *But Dennis's "flash recall" and his other statements contradict both of Pflock's suggested scenarios.* If strange creature bodies were at the RAAF base hospital undergoing autopsy on the afternoon of Monday, July 7, then the crash of "Something Else" must necessarily have been discovered *no later than the early morning of July 7.* If so, then certainly both Marcel and Cavitt would have been at the crash site of "Something Else"—much too busy for *both* of them to drive with Brazel to his ranch to recover some unusual debris.

If "Something Else" was an ET craft with alien bodies which was discovered by Monday morning, almost certainly RAAF commander Blanchard would have notified Gen. Ramey that morning, who would in turn have promptly notified Pentagon officials. If "Something Else" was an ET craft—which might be the precursor of an ET attack—Blanchard would have been informed by early Monday afternoon to keep the incident under wraps. And Lt. Haut would never have put out his famous "flying disc" press release the following day, around noon.

After Pflock had interviewed Prof. Moore in May of 1993 and Brazel's daughter several months later and wisely concluded that the Brazel ranch debris was from a NYU balloon flight, Pflock faced a very difficult decision. He knew that his mid-1992 action in arranging for a Roswell briefing for the staff of Congressman Schiff had sparked his interest in Roswell. This had prompted Schiff's letters to Defense Secretary Aspin, which in turn led to the GAO investigation launched in early 1994. News of the GAO investigation had resulted in widespread media publicity for Schiff, who would be running for reelection a few months later. For Pflock now to publicly admit in *Roswell In Perspective* that the Brazel ranch debris probably was from a Project Mogul balloon flight would itself be a courageous and commendable act.

But if Pflock also admitted that this *completely explained* the Roswell Incident and that there had been *no* USAF coverup, this could be embarrassing to Schiff and might hurt his chances in the upcoming November election.

Fortunately, when news of the GAO Roswell investigation broke in early 1994 and Schiff was widely interviewed by the media, he had taken a cautious, if sometimes contradictory, stance on the Roswell Incident. For example, the article in the January 14, 1994 edition of the *Albuquerque Journal* reported: "Schiff said Thursday he doesn't believe a UFO was recovered at the ranch." Schiff was quoted as saying: "I think, first of all, it could be a weather balloon. . . . But because of the government's obvious disinterest in giving me the information, that leads me to think it might've been something else. If I had to guess, I would say some kind of military experiment."

The article in the January 14, 1994 edition of the *Washington Post* quoted Schiff as saying: "Generally, I'm a skeptic on UFOs and alien beings, but there are indications from the run-around that I got that whatever it was, *it wasn't a balloon. Apparently, it's another government cover-up*" (emphasis added).

Pflock's belief that Dennis was truthfully trying to recall the nurse/autopsy incident prompted Pflock to conclude that this was evidence of a government coverup—which would support Schiff's widely stated view. Pflock wrote in his report: "I am personally convinced there were bodies and that they were either alien entities or humans or other earthly creatures who had undergone something horrible." Perhaps, he suggested, these were human crew members of a very risky AAF experiment whose tragic results the government wanted to keep secret.

In suggesting the possibility that the bodies might be human, Pflock chose to ignore Dennis's sworn statement. According to Dennis, the nurse "told me the doctors [performing the autopsy] said: 'This isn't anything we've ever seen before; there's nothing in medical textbooks like this.'" Additionally, according to Dennis's recreation of the (alleged) nurse's creature sketches, the creatures had *no thumbs* and there were *small suction cups on the tips of their four elongated fingers*.

Roswell In Perspective received a very perceptive, and generally favorable, review in the July 1994 issue of the *MUFON UFO Journal*, written by its editor, Dennis Stacy. He characterized the report as

> a model of how any thorough, objective UFO case investigation should be conducted, which is to let the chips fall where they may. . . . In the process, Pflock shatters several shibboleths or nuggets of accepted wisdom surrounding long ago events reported at or near Roswell, N.M., in the summer of 1947, while leaving one or two relatively intact.

The Ramey press conference in Fort Worth on the afternoon of July 8, 1947, for example, which claimed the wreckage retrieved from the Foster ranch was that of an ordinary weather balloon, really was a deliberate cover-up. What was being covered-up in all probability, however, was a balloon of another type, belonging to the supersecret Project Mogul. . . .*

Stacy wrote,

In fact, Pflock's overall case for Project Mogul is so persuasive that one can only wonder how critics will respond. My own prediction is that a number of attempts will be made to shoot the messenger, rather than the message, primarily by drawing attention to Pflock's past involvement with numerous government agencies, including a stint with both the Central Intelligence Agency and the Department of Defense. . . . [Stacy's prediction proved accurate.]
    I should also note that Pflock is not wholly dismissive of *everything* revolving round [sic] Roswell and claims of government coverup; in fact, he maintains that bodies of some kind probably *were* recovered near Roswell, based primarily on the testimony of mortician Glenn Dennis. The author's arguments in this area aren't wholly convincing. . . .

Although *Roswell In Perspective* had been published by the Fund for UFO Research with the aforementioned disclaimer on the cover, and FUFOR had funded roughly half of Pflock's research, the report generated sharp controversy within FUFOR's board of directors. Pflock had strong support from board member

---

*Pflock later discovered that he had erred in attributing the Brazel ranch debris to an NYU launch on July 3 which did use a new type of giant-size balloon made of polyethylene. The correct, June 4, launch used twenty-three ordinary weather balloons, as reported in chapter 15. If Gen. Ramey had been aware of Project Mogul, which is unlikely because it was a research effort, and if he had recognized that the debris was from a Project Mogul test, he would certainly have sent the debris to Moore et al. But this was not done.

Fred Whiting. But another board member, longtime pro-UFOlogist Don Berliner, who coauthored a Roswell crashed-saucer book with Friedman, was extremely displeased with *Roswell In Perspective.* Berliner had a close relationship with FUFOR's chairman, Richard Hall, dating back more than thirty years to when Hall was deputy director of NICAP (National Investigations Committee on Aerial Phenomena).

Approximately two months after *Roswell In Perspective* was published, the USAF (Weaver) Roswell report would be released with its Project Mogul explanation. Now FUFOR could sharply challenge the Project Mogul explanation proposed by its favorite target, the USAF, rather than criticize pro-UFOlogist Karl Pflock.

18.

Reactions to the USAF's Roswell Report

A favorable summary-review of the USAF's Roswell report was featured on the front page of the Sunday, September 18, 1994 edition of the *New York Times*, under a headline that read: "Wreckage in the Desert Was Odd but Not Alien." The lengthy article, which continued on page 40, was authored by a respected *Times* reporter, William J. Broad. The only negative comment, at the end of the article, came from Walter Haut who was quoted as saying: "It's a bunch of pap. All they've done is given us a different kind of balloon. Then it was weather, and now it's Mogul. . . ." Haut's comment revealed that he had not carefully read the USAF report. The Associated Press wire service also carried a favorable but shorter review on September 9 which was published in a number of client newspapers. It also included a critical comment by Haut.

Albuquerque Tribune reporter Karen MacPherson obtained the reaction of Congressman Schiff to the USAF report for an article published in the newspaper's September 17 edition. Schiff was quoted as saying: "This [Project Mogul] could well be the correct explanation. It does explain certain actions that were taken at the time. But I think the biggest problem is that they provide this explanation after insisting over and over, up through last year, that they had no information." (As explained in the USAF's report, its investigators did not discover the Project Mogul connection until the spring of 1994, shortly after launching its GAO-requested Roswell investigation.)

The favorable *New York Times* and Associated Press reviews prompted the Fund for UFO Research to issue a press release which was headlined: "Air Force Still Trivializes UFOs." FUFOR's release began:

> The U.S. Air Force has once again dismissed a major UFO case by ignoring all evidence which conflicts with its conclusion. In a report issued Sept. 8, the 1947 "Roswell Incident" has been blamed on an experimental balloon [note singular], despite the testimony of first-hand witnesses who describe totally un-balloonlike materials. . . . One of the main sources quoted in the report, Prof. Charles Moore, states that the material from such balloons, after being in the sun for a few days, would "almost look like dark grey or black flakes or ashes. . . ." How this could have been the "shiny," "metallic" and "indestructible" materials described by witnesses is hard to fathom.

If the person who wrote this FUFOR press release had carefully read the USAF report or Pflock's report—which FUFOR itself had recently published—they would have known that the shiny, metallic material was from the radar target, not a balloon.

The press release concluded: "The Fund for UFO Research challenges the Air Force *to produce a balloon of the type flown in early July, 1947,* and ask the surviving witnesses if that is what they saw" (emphasis added). FUFOR ignored the fact that photos of the debris which had been taken in Gen. Ramey's office had been examined and "endorsed" both by Prof. Moore and Sheridan Cavitt. Earlier, Roswell researcher Todd had sent copies of the Ramey office photos to Brazel's daughter, Bessie, for her examination. She responded: "The debris shown [in the photos] does look like the debris we picked up."

Among the pro-UFO groups the reaction of the Hynek Center for UFO Studies (CUFOS) was the most interesting because of its strong vested interest in the Roswell Incident. In 1988, Don Schmitt—then CUFOS's director of special investigations and a member of its board of directors—had joined with Kevin Randle on a new Roswell investigation, partially funded by CUFOS. In mid-September 1989, a CUFOS team had visited the Brazel ranch in the hope of finding some of the original debris—without success. The March/April 1991 issue of the CUFOS *International UFO Reporter* (*IUR*) said the then soon-to-be-published first Randle/Schmitt book "records *the most thoroughly investigated, the most completely documented event in the history of ufology. The Roswell Incident is, of course, the most important case of all*" (emphasis added). The article by Jerome Clark, a longtime pro-UFOlogist and UFO historian, predicted that the "heretofore un-killable canard, that UFO research has made no progress in four decades, [will be] disposed of once and for all."

In the July/August 1993 issue of *IUR*, barely a year before the USAF report was released, Clark wrote: "So far no credible non-UFO explanation has emerged, the best efforts of would-be debunkers notwithstanding. *The Roswell Incident is surely the most important case in UFO history*" (emphasis added).

The USAF report, which challenged Clark's claims, was reviewed in the September/October 1994 issue of *IUR* in an article authored by CUFOS's scientific director, Mark Rodeghier, and Mark Chesney, a research associate. *IUR* provided its readers with the report's Executive Summary and offered the following commentary:

> There are two important points to note immediately. It is clear from this summary that the Air Force couldn't find any physical evidence that proves or documentation that clearly states that a balloon from Project Mogul was recovered by rancher Mac Brazel or officers of the 509th Bomb Group. Second, the Air Force has no Mogul balloon material from 1947 to show to witnesses to provide a positive identification; given the many years

since the project ended, it is not surprising that no material can be located. Still, without such confirmation, the Air Force explanation relies upon inference from verbal testimony, not solid, hard evidence.

Rodeghier and Chesney criticized the USAF for not interviewing "the many persons who have been identified as firsthand or secondhand Roswell witnesses," such as mortician Glenn Dennis. The *IUR* review added:

What makes the Air Force report inferior to the best Roswell investigations is its refusal to use all the available testimony, especially their star witnesses. If, as the Air Force claims, time makes memories hazy, then you would expect them to use statements from Charles Moore from around 1980 rather than 1994. ... Air Force completely ignores the following key statement Charles Moore gave to Bill Moore in 1980: "Based on the description that you just gave me, I can rule this out [that Roswell could be a weather or other scientific balloon]. ..."*

The *IUR* review concluded:

The Air Force report has not halted the GAO investigation or reduced the resolve of Rep. Schiff, who told CUFOS that he is determined to continue his efforts at learning the truth about Roswell. We thank and applaud him for his resolve and political courage. In this article we have criticized the Air Force report without [sic] resorting to much of the evidence collected over the past 15 years. *When that information is brought to bear, the superficial nature and inherent bias of the report are even more apparent."* (Emphasis added)

---

*As explained in chapter 15, Prof. Moore was not aware of rancher Brazel's original description of the debris until mid-1992 when researcher Robert Todd sent him a copy of the Brazel interview published in the *Roswell Daily Record* on July 9, 1947, which author Moore had withheld from Prof. Moore.

The next issue of *IUR* (November/December 1994) featured a curious commentary on the USAF report by Karl Pflock. He characterized the Weaver report as "a victory for UFO research, U.S. Rep. Steven H. Schiff (R-New Mexico) and the American people. *We have won the first battle in the struggle to pry loose Roswell-related information which the U.S. government has in its possession, a significant step toward full government accountability and public discourse of the whole truth about this important case*" (emphasis added).

Pflock continued:

> In July 1947 the then Army Air Force concocted a cover story— or, more correctly, cover stories—to squelch press and public excitement engendered by the startling announcement from Roswell Army Air Field that it had captured one of the mysterious flying saucers. There was a mistake, the story went, the "saucer" was only a weather balloon and its radar target. What was the Air Force covering up? There are those of us who have concluded from analysis of the currently available evidence that it was almost certainly a Top Secret Air Force research project called Mogul (of course there is more to the Roswell story—*a little matter of strange bodies*—about which more below). Others believe it was what the original announcement said it was, a crashed flying saucer.
>
> Whatever the case may ultimately prove to be, the *fact remains that the Air Force lied about Roswell in 1947*. Given national-security considerations at the time, the lie was justifiable. . . . (Emphasis added)

At the time that Pflock wrote his *IUR* article, he (apparently) still believed that the Brazel ranch debris had come from NYU Flight #9, launched July 3, which used a single, giant polyethylene (plastic) balloon. Later he would concede that the debris was from Flight #4, launched June 4, which used twenty-three weather balloons. Thus, Gen. Ramey did *not* lie when he and weather officer Newton identified the debris as being from a weather balloon and a radar target.

Pflock conceded that

> even with the remarkably Mogul-consistent testimony of not
> fewer than 15 Roswell-Incident witnesses (14 firsthand), even
> with the seemingly supportive analysis of the photographs taken
> in Ramey's office (Weaver Report, pp. 20–21 and Attachment
> 33), we still do not have *proof positive* that Mogul is the answer
> to what was found in Brazil's debris field. . . . The case for
> Mogul, though substantial, is purely circumstantial and in some
> important respects anecdotal and dependent upon decades-old
> memories. *But so, too, is the case for Brazel's find being extra-*
> *terrestrial spacecraft wreckage, which is also anecdotal and far*
> *more tenuous than its early rival.* (Emphasis added)

Pflock continued:

> The Air Force's all-out effort on Mogul contrasts starkly with its
> less than half-hearted attempt to get at the truth about *the bod-*
> *ies.* . . . [T]he Air Force failed to do their duties in responding to
> Congressional direction. Weaver and his research team were
> supposed to have conducted a no-stone-unturned search for any
> and all Roswell-related documents—*including those that may*
> *have dealt with bodies.* . . . They did not do so, and in their arro-
> gance they attempt to justify it with the sorts of excuses most of
> us gave up in grade school. In an odd way this Air Force failure
> is another victory for us. *It highlights for priority consideration*
> *a very important question among the many the GAO will pursue*
> *as it independently checks the Air Force claims and findings*
> [emphasis added]. . . .
>   In fact, the report and its attachments are only what the Air
> Force has chosen to "volunteer" for GAO consideration in the
> vain hope the Congressional bloodhounds will be satisfied that
> is all there is to be found. Speaking from experience [as a for-
> mer Congressional staffer and Pentagon official], I can assure
> you such tactics do *not* work with the GAO. The material
> offered by the Air Force will be scrutinized thoroughly, with
> nothing taken on faith. Moreover, the GAO will pursue its own
> hands-on review of Air Force records, paying particular atten-

tion to such "oversights" as the bodies issue and, it is hoped, the reasons for the Air Force's failure to interview retired Air Force Brig. Gen. Arthur E. Exon.*

Pflock's *IUR* article concluded: "The last word on the Congressional-GAO probe of Roswell has yet to be written. When it is, I think there will be surprises for all of us—especially good Col. Weaver." Pflock's prediction would prove to be only partially correct. When the GAO Roswell report was issued the following July, there would indeed be surprises for Pflock, Schiff, and CUFOS—*but not for Col. Weaver*. (Highlights of the GAO report will be described in chapter 21.)

---

*This criticism of the USAF for failing to interview Exon is surprising in view of Pflock's own interview with him, as reported in *Roswell In Perspective* (p. 30). Exon, who in July 1947 was a lieutenant colonel taking a course in industrial administration at Wright Field, had been cited in Randle and Schmitt's first book as a key witness. According to Randle/Schmitt, Exon "was there when the wreckage from the Roswell crash came in. . . . He knew that it was brought in and knew where it was sent." But when Pflock interviewed Exon on September 30, 1992, he admitted that "what he had told Randle and Schmitt about debris and bodies at Wright Field was *nothing more than rumors he had heard* [emphasis added]," as reported in *Roswell In Perspective*.

19.

Key Witness Changes Crashed-Saucer Tale

Roswell-researcher/author Kevin Randle initially seemed to have had ambivalent feelings about the Project Mogul explanation for the Brazel ranch debris. On July 6, 1994, after he had read Karl Pflock's *Roswell In Perspective* report, Randle wrote him a brief note which characterized the report as "an impressive work." Randle said the report "certainly supports the theory that a Mogul balloon was responsible for the Brazel ranch find." Randle added: "The array of testimony and evidence does seem to lead to that conclusion." But on September 7, when Randle was interviewed on New York City radio station WBAI, he said: "There's absolutely no evidence that Project Mogul was responsible for what was found on the [Brazel] ranch." Randle added: "Nor does it explain the 'impact site' some 35 miles from the ranch."

When Randle later spoke at a UFO conference in Pensacola, Florida, on October 16, he again challenged the Project Mogul explanation. But he added that because there were "two distinct sites," one 35 miles north of Roswell and the other on the Brazel

144

ranch, as Randle and Schmitt claimed in *The Truth About the UFO Crash at Roswell,* "we could . . . give [concede] the Air Force Project Mogul on the Brazel ranch . . . and not damage the Roswell case at all." In other words, even if Project Mogul explained the Brazel ranch debris, it could not possibly explain the crashed UFO and ET bodies at the north-of-Roswell "impact site" reportedly seen by Jim Ragsdale and Frank J. Kaufmann (Steve MacKenzie).

However, later in Randle's Pensacola talk he candidly revealed that *Ragsdale recently had drastically changed his story and now claimed the "impact site" was about 55 miles west of Roswell, not 35 miles north of the city.* Randle said that Ragsdale's new account "is much more exciting than just seeing bodies in the distance. [See chapter 12.] He's now talking about going down and *trying to pull the helmet off one of the dead aliens and seeing his big black eyes"* (emphasis added). Randle added that Ragsdale's new description of the ET's appearance "is not consistent with what we have learned about what the Aliens looked like." Randle was referring to the more humanlike ET description given by Kaufmann, which in turn differed sharply from the "nurse's sketches" drawn by mortician Glenn Dennis.

Only a couple of months earlier, Randle had authored an article in the *HUFON Report,* a newsletter published by the Houston (Texas) UFO Network, which cited the importance of Ragsdale's *original* version *because it corroborated Kaufmann's claim* of having seen ET bodies. Randle noted that Kaufmann had been "the *first eyewitness link* between the events in Roswell in July 1947 *and alien creatures"* (emphasis added).

In Randle's Pensacola talk he charged that Ragsdale had changed his story "for monetary inducements. In other words, he's getting paid for his story now. . . . We believe the changes were coached by those who want to sell his story." Randle did not then identify those whom he accused of having induced Ragsdale to change his tale, but he was referring to officials of the Roswell International UFO Museum.

On September 10, 1994, Secretary-Treasurer Littell had con-

firmed in writing an agreement with Ragsdale whereby the museum would gain exclusive rights to exploit his crashed-saucer story and new crash site which would be named "The Jim Ragsdale Impact Site." In return, Ragsdale would receive 25 percent of the gross income. (Later, when it was learned thàt Ragsdale's cancer would soon be fatal, the agreement was revised so that 50 percent of the profits would go into a trust fund for his seven grandchildren.) By the summer of 1996, Littell's Roswell museum would be selling for $14.95 a handsome 42-page booklet titled "The Jim Ragsdale Story," and a one-hour video with the same title priced at $29.50. The museum also would sell T-shirts which showed the new Jim Ragsdale Impact Site, priced at $13.95.

Randle and Schmitt had first publicly revealed the location of their new "impact site" 35 miles north of Roswell in their article in the January/February 1994 issue of *IUR*, several weeks before publication of their second book. The then new Randle and Schmitt "impact site," which would be officially unveiled and visited by TV and other news media during the March 25, 1994 press conference in Roswell for their second book, was located on a ranch now owned by Miller ("Hub") Corn.

In early 1994, several months before the new "impact site" was unveiled, Corn later told me, he had been invited to meet with Littell, Haut, and Dennis at their Roswell museum, to discuss whether Corn would be interested in selling the "impact site." Corn said he was not interested in selling, but several weeks later he returned with a counterproposal under which the museum could sell bus tours to the "impact site" and they would split the profits. Museum officials declined Corn's offer. Several months later, museum officials struck a deal with Ragsdale to exploit his "impact site," 55 miles west of Roswell, located on government-owned land. (Corn then erected a large sign near Highway 285 to attract tourists to visit his "impact site" for a charge of $15.)

Ragsdale signed a new affidavit on April 15, 1995, providing new details about his (alleged) experience with the crashed saucer, some of which flatly contradicted his earlier sworn statement of January 27, 1993:

- In the new Ragsdale affidavit, he claimed that shortly after the crash—around midnight—he and his girlfriend searched for *and found* the crashed saucer in darkness, whereas in the first affidavit Ragsdale said they had waited for daybreak.

- In the new affidavit, Ragsdale reported: "When we looked *into the craft, we saw four bodies . . .*" (emphasis added). In the previous sworn statement, Ragsdale said they saw "a number of small bodied beings *outside* the craft" (emphasis added).

- In the first affidavit, Ragsdale said he had not gotten close enough to tell whether they were "bodies or dummies." But in his second affidavit, Ragsdale claimed: "They were dressed in a silver type uniform and wearing a tight helmet. . . . I tried to remove one of the helmets, but was unable to do so."

- In Ragsdale's original affidavit he said: "While observing the scene, I and my companion watched as a military convoy arrived and secured the scene. As a result of the convoy's appearance we quickly fled the area." And in Ragsdale's tape-recorded January 26, 1993 interview with Schmitt, he described the convoy and said it included "two or three six by six Army trucks, a wrecker. . . . And leading the pack was a 1947 Ford car. . . ." But in Ragsdale's second affidavit he reported: "We heard what we believed was [*sic*] trucks and heavy equipment coming our way, so we left *and were not there when whatever it was arrived*" (emphasis added).

In the later affidavit and also during the January 26, 1993 interview with Schmitt, Ragsdale claimed that he and his girl-friend had "filled two large gunny sacks with the material [crash debris] and it was with us when we left the site." But Ragsdale said he could not provide even one small piece of debris to substantiate his story because all of it (allegedly) had disappeared under mysterious circumstances. His affidavit explained:

> My friend had some of it [UFO debris] in her vehicle when she was killed hitting a bridge, and it was gone when the [car] wreckage was brought into town. My truck and trailer was [*sic*] stolen from my home. Again, the material in the truck, never to be heard from anywhere. My home was broken into, completely ransacked, and all that was taken was the material, a gun and very little else of value.

Although some important details in Ragsdale's second affidavit differed significantly from the story first told to Schmitt on January 26, 1993, and from a second interview conducted by Randle on April 24, 1993, *Ragsdale had not really changed his "impact site" location*. Schmitt and Randle had been too eager to have Ragsdale confirm the Kaufmann "impact site" 35 miles north of Roswell. During both interviews Ragsdale said that he and his girlfriend had driven *west* from Roswell on Highway 48 (Pine Lodge Road), rather than *north* on Highway 285. Randle and Schmitt *assumed* that Ragsdale had circled around and spent the night near the Kaufmann site north of Roswell, despite the lack of roads from Highway 48 to the Kaufmann site.

Because Ragsdale's health did not allow him to visit the Kaufmann "impact site," Schmitt had shown him photos of the north-of-Roswell site, and Ragsdale had responded: "That's the place right there." Yet the relatively barren Kaufmann "impact site" looks far different from the heavily wooded Ragsdale "impact site."

In the 42-page booklet titled "The Jim Ragsdale Story," now sold at the Roswell International UFO Museum, his daughter Judy Lott recalls that her father often took his family for picnics to the "impact site" area. "I remember him telling us of a plane crash in that area. . . . I had no idea it was a UFO crash he was referring to then," according to Lott. "My dad first told me the story of the flying saucer and of its little people in November, 1994." (This was several months *after* Ragsdale accepted Littell's offer.)

While Roswell researcher-author Stanton Friedman agreed with Randle that one or more flying saucers had crashed near Roswell and that the government was involved in a coverup, the two men sharply disagreed on most other details. Randle had played a key role in exposing and discrediting Friedman's star Plains of San Agustin "witness," Gerald F. Anderson (chapter 9), whose tale Friedman had credulously endorsed. Friedman had sharply criticized *UFO Crash at Roswell,* claiming his then up-coming book would be far more accurate. Later it had been embarrassing for Friedman that Randle and Schmitt had been the first to "discover" the new north-of-Roswell "impact site."

Thus it is not surprising that Friedman would endorse the new Ragsdale "impact site" west of Roswell, as he did in an interview in late 1995 for "The Jim Ragsdale Story" video. Friedman offered his assessment based on a personal interview with Ragsdale, arranged by Max Littell. Friedman said: "Over the years I have developed a kind of approach to these things. I learned the hard way *that you need to verify.* I was impressed with his story. . . . I have no reason to doubt it and certainly there wasn't a profit motive here" (emphasis added). Despite Friedman's claim that as a result of his many years spent in investigating UFO reports he had "learned the hard way that you need to verify," *he made no attempt to do so for Ragsdale's story.*

However, William P. Barrett, an experienced Albuquerque journalist researching the Roswell Incident for an article for *Forbes* magazine, did what Friedman failed to do. Barrett visited the Ragsdale "impact site" area and interviewed persons whose families had long lived nearby. As Barrett reported in his article published in the July 15, 1996 issue of *Forbes, not one of them had ever heard of a crashed saucer in the area.* Barrett quoted eighty-two-year-old Dorothy Epps, whose family owned land within half a mile of the Ragsdale impact site since 1909, as saying: "It's all a hoax." *Barrett later told me (in late July 1996) that none of the nearby residents reported that they had ever been interviewed by any Roswell International UFO Museum official to verify Ragsdale's story.*

Barrett's *Forbes* magazine article carried the headline: "Unidentified Flying Dollars" with a lead-in head: "P.T. Barnum Is Alive and Apparently Living in Roswell, N.M." The article began:

> In good old American tradition, Roswell has turned the Unidentified Flying Object mystique into a nice business. The Roswell area now supports three UFO museums, competing UFO landing [impact] sites and a growing UFO summer festival that together are expected to draw 90,000 tourists this year. Entrepreneurial local artists and manufacturers churn out alien dolls and puppets, ceramic miniatures of crash sites, spaceship earrings, UFO hats, T-shirts showing aliens spying on soldiers, and bumper stickers. . . .
>
> City hotel-room tax revenues have risen 36% over four years. Hotel operators say up to one-fifth of their business comes from UFO seekers. By some estimates, the UFO craze pumps more than $5 million a year into this community of 50,000 which badly needs the money—median household income here being 27% below the national average.

Barrett's article included a photo showing Roswell mayor Tom Jennings posing alongside some ET dolls.

Barrett's article prompted me to recall Littell's comment when I interviewed him and Walter Haut on December 7, 1991, as they were preparing to open their Roswell crashed-saucer museum. Littell said:

> The jury is going to be the public and they're gonna decide what they want to believe. We hope 10,000 of 'em come here to find out because while you're here—over this weekend—you're gonna drop 200 or 300 bucks here in town. Alright, times 10,000, is good for our economy.

20.

Schmitt Spins Tall Tales

The June 17–24, 1993 edition of the Milwaukee weekly newspaper *Shepherd Express* carried a lengthy, flattering feature story on the Roswell research conducted by Don Schmitt, who lives in the small town of Hubertus, not far from Milwaukee. The article, authored by Ms. Gillian Sender, quoted Schmitt as saying: "We have six generals telling us that it is true—Roswell happened. We have eight living witnesses describing the recovered bodies, and we have two dozen witnesses describing the [crash-site] material."

In late 1994, Ms. Sender returned for another interview with Schmitt for a feature article that would be published in the *Milwaukee* magazine's February 1995 issue. The article carried the headline: "Out of This World." But the subhead read: "Can a man who stretches the truth about himself be trusted to report accurately about UFOs and extraterrestrial life?" Midway in the article, author Sender challenged Schmitt's claim that he earned his living as a medical illustrator and his claim to having an academic background.

Schmitt did study commercial art at Milwaukee Area Technical College, receiving an associate's degree. He also says he studied at or received degrees from other local universities or colleges, but many of those claims appear to be bogus.

In a 1990 biography he used to promote himself, Schmitt wrote that he has attended the University of Wisconsin-Milwaukee [UWM] and Marquette University, taking classes in criminology, theology and sociology. During an interview—with his parents and fiancee present—he said he is currently "pursuing his doctorate in criminology from Concordia College." Schmitt also said he received a master's degree from UWM and a bachelor of arts degree from Concordia College.

However, the article reported that investigation of these claims revealed that "Schmitt has never been a student at UWM or Marquette and can't be studying for a Ph.D. because Concordia doesn't offer doctorate programs. Schmitt was enrolled at Concordia for two and a half years (he last attended class in 1993), but has yet to earn a bachelor's degree," Ms. Sender wrote. She added: "Schmitt has not returned phone calls about his educational background."

Later in the article, Ms. Sender wrote:

At first glance, the cumulative evidence in Schmitt's books—the testimony, the documentation—looks convincing. . . . But a closer look begs questions. Since some of the key witnesses aren't identified and most of the documentation refers to personal interviews, readers must rely on the author's credibility. And that may be a problem. In addition to his false statements about his educational background, Schmitt embellishes reality. He constantly refers to his books as "bestsellers," but that is certainly stretching the facts since the books have never appeared on any bestseller lists.

Kevin Randle quickly responded to defend his partner. In one open letter sent to many UFO researchers, Randle said: "I've known Don Schmitt since 1988 and have found him to be one of the most honorable, honest, sincere and ethical people I have ever known." Randle suggested that Ms. Sender had misunderstood Schmitt's academic claims. As for her doubts that Schmitt was indeed a medical illustrator, Randle said that if she had asked Schmitt "he could have provided many samples of his work."

The next month's issue of *Milwaukee* magazine carried a brief letter-to-the-editor from an anonymous writer: "I read with interest the 'Portrait' article on Don Schmitt. . . . [Regarding] the question of how Schmitt earns his living . . . he delivers mail out of the Hartford, Wisconsin, post office. . . . If you believe half of what he tells you, you are a prospect for buying a bridge." The letter was followed by a comment by Ms. Sender which said: "I spoke to Don Schmitt on a number of occasions, and he never gave any indication that he worked for the post office. He insisted he earned his living as a medical illustrator. However, Hartford Postmaster Ken Eppler confirms that Schmitt is employed as a full-time carrier. Schmitt has worked at the Hartford Post Office since 1974."

Postmaster Eppler issued a brief statement on March 13 which *seemed* to deny Ms. Sender's comment: "In the letter section of the March, 1995 issue of *Milwaukee* Magazine, it is implied that Donald Schmitt has worked full-time for the U.S. Postal Service since 1974. Not only is this untrue, but I have never made such a statement to *Milwaukee* Magazine or anyone else." Randle distributed a copy of Eppler's statement widely. On the copy he sent me he had added the comment: "What does this say about the credibility of the rest of the article about Don? . . ."

Within three weeks, Randle would learn from a Hartford post office employee that Schmitt was indeed employed there as a full-time rural mail carrier, and that he had started as a *part-time* employee in 1974. On April 18, 1995, Randle wrote to me—and others to whom he had earlier defended Schmitt—to candidly admit his error. Randle said that when the issue first arose he had asked Schmitt for the truth and was told that he did not work at the post office. Randle's letter concluded: "My only excuse is that I believed my friend and he let me down."

Schmitt, who served as Director of Special Investigations for the Hynek Center for UFO Studies as well as being a member of the CUFOS board of directors, soon resigned as Director of Special Investigations as a result of the *Milwaukee* magazine disclosures. But he remained on the CUFOS board. (Later he would resign that position also.)

The sorely strained relations between Randle and Schmitt reached the breaking point in September 1995 as a result of revelations in an article published in the fall issue of *Omni* magazine. The article, authored by longtime pro-UFOlogist Paul McCarthy, was prompted by the nurse/ET-autopsy claim by Glenn Dennis (chapter 8). In the article, titled "The Case of the Vanishing Nurses," McCarthy noted that in Randle and Schmitt's second book the authors claimed that the military records for all the nurses stationed at the Roswell base hospital, whose pictures appeared in the RAAF annual yearbook, had mysteriously disappeared.

McCarthy reported that during an interview, Schmitt said that he had "worked with the Army Nurse Corps Historian's Office at the Department of Defense in an attempt to track the five yearbook nurses who, it was assumed, might have talked to Nurse X [Dennis's ET-autopsy nurse]. . . . He had also checked with such organizations as WWII Flight Nurses Association, the Military Reference Branch of the National Archives. . . . Even the Women in Military Service for America Memorial Foundation in Washington, D.C., had never heard of them." McCarthy quoted Schmitt as saying that "even though we have photographs of these nurses from the yearbook, there are no records on these people." McCarthy added: "The Schmitt-Randle conclusion, communicated emphatically, was plenty clear: *Either Glenn Dennis had fabricated Nurse X, they said, or the government had eliminated all vestiges of actual, and documented life*" (emphasis added).

McCarthy proposed to *Omni* magazine that his article describe Schmitt's rigorous efforts to locate the RAAF nurses as "an example of investigative diligence and the lengths to which UFO researchers would go to uncover witnesses." To McCarthy's surprise, *Omni* suggested a slightly different approach—that he himself try to locate the military records for the RAAF nurses to verify Schmitt's account. This was a challenge because McCarthy then lived in Hawaii and *Omni* was not willing to underwrite travel expense, so his investigation would necessarily have to rely on telephone and letter inquiries. Furthermore, to meet *Omni*'s deadline, McCarthy would have only a few weeks for his own investigation. Not surprisingly, as McCarthy wrote in his article, "I halfheartedly agreed to look for the nurses myself, but didn't have high hopes. Hadn't these guys [Randle and Schmitt] been at it for five years?"

McCarthy's efforts to find records for the five nurses listed in the RAAF yearbook for 1947, and Nurse X (whose name—Naomi Maria Selff—had been provided by Randle), initially were unsuccessful. But when McCarthy contacted the National Personnel Records Center (NPRC) in St. Louis, an archivist found the records for *all five nurses. But there was no record of Glenn Dennis's nurse.* This prompted McCarthy to write: "Amazingly, I had located the records in three days flat, something the Roswell researchers told me they'd been unable to do in five arduous years. But could I find the nurses themselves?"

McCarthy filed an FOIA request to the St. Louis center and within three weeks he had the records for the five nurses. They showed that one of the nurses had died in 1975, a second in 1981, and McCarthy's investigation showed a third had died several years before and a fourth in May 1994. The chief nurse at RAAF, Lt. Col. Rosemary McManus, was more difficult to track down because she had since been twice married. Finally, McCarthy located and talked with McManus, now seventy-eight years old and living in a nursing home.

According to McCarthy, McManus

> had already been approached by two other investigators, possibly Schmitt and an associate, but the names escaped her. . . . *She remembered the other four yearbook nurses, but not Nurse X,*

and not Glenn Dennis himself. What's more, she told me, she
had witnessed nothing to suggest a crash at Roswell or any
unusual goings-on at the base hospital. (Emphasis added)

Naturally, McCarthy was curious to obtain the reactions of Schmitt and Randle. When Schmitt failed to return McCarthy's telephone calls, he talked with Randle who was surprised to learn how easily and quickly McCarthy had located the records for the five nurses. But he suggested that McCarthy pursue the matter with Schmitt who was responsible for the search for the nurses' records. According to McCarthy's *Omni* article: "Weeks passed, and finally Schmitt left an enigmatic message on my [answering] machine. I tried to call him to talk directly but he did not return my calls," prompting McCarthy to again talk with Randle who told him that "Schmitt had the documentation to prove that the [nurses'] records were unavailable when he had requested them in 1990."

When Schmitt finally called McCarthy, Schmitt admitted he'd known about the St. Louis records and had even found and interviewed Lt. Col. Rosemary [McManus] Brown. "I was incredulous," McCarthy wrote, recalling his original intention of featuring Schmitt's fruitless search for the records. Schmitt explained: "It is not that we were putting out misinformation. It is just that we were denying that we found anything." Schmitt went on to explain that he suspected that Lt. Col. Rosemary [McManus] Brown might actually be Nurse X, even though her name was not even similar to the name of the nurse that Dennis had supplied and she did not resemble Dennis's description. Schmitt told McCarthy: "She may or may not know something. . . . That is why we have treated her with kid gloves, and why I haven't publicized the fact that we have found her."

Schmitt's explanation prompted McCarthy to comment: "All well and good, but then why make an issue of the missing nurses [records] in the first place, as if their very absence were proof of a government attempt to perpetrate conspiracy, erase information (and even people), and be sinister in the extreme?"

A more likely explanation for Schmitt not wanting to disclose that he had located the RAAF's chief nurse was that she flatly denied that anyone resembling Dennis's Nurse X was stationed at the base hospital during the summer of 1947.

Further investigation by McCarthy, as reported in his *Omni* article, revealed that Schmitt had not himself conducted the search for the nurses' records but that it had been performed by an associate. When McCarthy tried to learn more about the associate's search efforts and whether he had ever contacted the St. Louis records center, McCarthy came to doubt that Schmitt's research associate had ever contacted the center.

On September 10, 1995, shortly after publication of McCarthy's article in *Omni* magazine, Kevin Randle issued and widely circulated the following "To Whom It May Concern" memo which harshly and candidly criticized his longtime partner:

The "day-job" of Don Schmitt has never been the issue, though some have tried to make it the issue. It was the lies he told about it. When I asked him, repeatedly about it, he told me he didn't work at the Post Office. . . . To compound the lie he had Postmaster Ken Eppler write a letter that he and Schmitt knew was misleading. It was designed to mislead everyone. . . .

When asked about his educational background, he offered more lies. He was working on a Ph.D., he had a masters degree, he had a bachelor degree, he had attended various colleges. All lies. . . . He told tales of drug enforcement work, secret meetings and being in a witness protection program. More lies. . . . I had believed that his lying related only to his personal life. Now I learn that it doesn't. . . . He claimed that he had searched for the Roswell nurses but their records were all missing. That is not even close to the truth. . . .

These lies do not appear in either of the books I wrote about Roswell. Yes, I did the writing. Schmitt would review the rough draft of chapters for the first book and then add his comments. Sometimes I would use what he wrote, if I had verified it. . . . He did contribute one chapter [in *UFO Crash at Roswell*] which was the "Conclusions." In it, he claims that he had searched for

the records of 11 men. He could not find those 11 records. The
Air Force [later] researched the names and found the "missing"
records for most of them. The others were of men with such
common names that no determination could be made. [See
chapter 16.]

I asked for the documentation from Schmitt to prove this
[charge of missing records]. He said he would send it but never
did. . . . I find that he had queried the DoD [Department of
Defense] and the Veterans Administration. What I should have
asked at the time, but didn't was why he hadn't gone to the
Army Record Center in St. Louis to begin the search. . . . So, his
statement about the records was true, they weren't filed with the
DoD or the Veterans Administration, but then, that isn't surprising either. . . .

In the second book [*The Truth About the UFO Crash at
Roswell*], he didn't even bother to make any changes. . . .
Everything I put into the books, I knew to be the truth because
I had researched it myself, or had checked to make sure the documentation existed. [Yet earlier Randle admitted that he had not
himself verified the missing nurses' records allegation which
appeared in their second book.] . . .

That said, let me now point out that I do not believe anything
that Schmitt says and neither should you. . . . I'm not sure he
understands the truth. And this has slipped into his research. HIS
research. . . . When there is corroboration for what he said, when
others had backstopped the work and reported the same things, I
have great confidence. If it is work he claims to have done himself, I have no confidence. The search for the nurses proves that
he will lie about anything. . . . I have said since April [1995] that
we would not work together again because I could not trust his
work. . . . He has destroyed his work and badly damaged mine. I
believed him to be honest, I believed him to be honorable, and I
trusted him to tell me the truth. I was taken in by him.

The fact that Randle could be "taken in" by the tall tales of a
person with whom he had worked so closely for seven years
should have alerted him to the possibility that he might also have

been "taken in" by tall tales told by alleged witnesses he knew only casually. By the spring of 1996, Randle would conclude that he had also been "taken in" by Dennis's nurse/ET-autopsy tale— an admission he would make publicly in his new UFO book, *The Randle Report,* published in May 1997 (New York: M. Evans and Company, Inc.).

21.

The GAO Roswell Report and Schiff's Spin

On July 28, 1995, Congressman Steven Schiff's office issued a two-page press release which carried the headline: "Schiff Receives, Releases Roswell Report." If the press release had accurately conveyed the important findings of the GAO investigation, its subhead should have read: "Rigorous GAO Investigation Finds No Evidence of Crashed-Saucer or Government Coverup." Instead, the subhead to Schiff's release read: "Missing documents leave unanswered questions." The press release, whose inaccurate or false statements are shown below in italics, began:

> Washington: Congressman Steve Schiff today released the General Accounting Office (GAO) report detailing the results of a record audit related to events surrounding a crash in 1947, near Roswell, New Mexico, and the military response. The 20 page report is the result of constituent information requests to Congressman Schiff and the difficulty he had getting answers from the Department of Defense in the now 48-year-old controversy.
>
> Schiff said *important documents*, which may have shed more light on what happened at Roswell, are missing. "The

GAO report states that the outgoing [teletype] messages from Roswell Army Air Field (RAAF) for this period of time were destroyed *without proper authority*." Schiff pointed out that these messages would have shown how military officials in Roswell were explaining to their superiors exactly what happened. "It is my understanding that these outgoing messages were permanent records, *which should never have been destroyed*. The GAO could not identify who destroyed the messages, or why." But Schiff pointed out that the GAO estimates that the messages were destroyed over 40 years ago, making further inquiry about their destruction impractical.

Documents revealed by the report include an FBI teletype and reference in a newsletter style internal forum at RAAF that refer to a "radar tracking device"—a reference to a weather balloon. Even though the *weather balloon story has since been discredited by the US Air Force*, Schiff suggested that the authors of those communications may have been repeating what they were told rather than consciously adding to what some believe is a "coverup." "At least this effort caused the *Air Force to acknowledge that the crashed vehicle was no weather balloon*," Schiff said. "That explanation never fit the fact of *high military security used at the time*." The Air Force in September, 1994 [i.e., USAF/Weaver Roswell report] claimed that the crashed vehicle was a then-classified device to detect evidence of possible Soviet nuclear testing. Schiff also praised the efforts of the GAO, describing their work as "professional, conscientious and thorough." (Emphasis added)

Not surprisingly, as a result of the emphasis in Schiff's press release, most newspaper articles on the GAO report focused on the "missing documents" and all but ignored the fact that the GAO was unable to find *any* evidence of a crashed ET craft or a government coverup. For example, the article in the *Albuquerque Tribune* was headlined: "Some Roswell Incident Records Missing." A report in the Dayton, Ohio, *Daily News* carried the headline: "Military Documents from Roswell Incident Destroyed." And the feature article in the *Roswell Daily Record* was headlined: "GAO: RAAF Messages Destroyed."

The GAO reported that its lengthy search of archives of many agencies had turned up only two Roswell-UFO-related documents. One was a teletype message from the FBI office in Fort Worth to FBI Director Hoover in Washington, on July 8, 1947, based on a telephone report from Eighth Air Force Headquarters that the recovered debris "resembles a high altitude weather balloon with a radar reflector." [See p. 16.] This document, and other UFO related material, had been released by the FBI in the mid-1970s and was first published in 1980 in the Berlitz/Moore book on Roswell.

The only other Roswell-UFO-related document that turned up in the GAO's lengthy investigation was the July 1947 history of the 509th Bomb Group which briefly noted that the RAAF public affairs office "was kept quite busy ... answering inquiries on the 'flying disc,' which was reported to be in [the] possession of the 509th Bomb Group. The object turned out to be a radar tracking balloon." The GAO noted that the RAAF's commanding officer (Col. Blanchard) had signed the history report, thereby certifying it to be a complete and accurate account of RAAF activities in July 1947.

The GAO had even examined the once highly classified minutes of meetings of the National Security Council for 1947–48. If an ET craft had crashed in New Mexico, the incident would be a top priority topic for discussion at subsequent NSC meetings. But there was no mention of Roswell or ET craft in any of the NSC meeting minutes for 1947 or 1948. The GAO cited the highlights of the results of the USAF's own investigation, as detailed in its 1994 report. *The GAO did not challenge the USAF's conclusion that the most likely source for the Brazel ranch debris was from a Project Mogul balloon launch.*

The July 28 press release issued by Schiff's office said the congressman would be available to talk to the media the next day, Saturday, from 10 A.M. until 2 P.M. in his Rayburn Building office. I arrived shortly before 10 and was the first journalist to interview Schiff on the GAO report. (It was our first meeting although Schiff had telephoned me from Albuquerque in early 1994 to ask if I would be willing to meet with him to discuss my views on Roswell. I agreed, but he never called again to schedule a meeting.)

During our July 29 meeting, I mentioned Schiff's 1994 statements to the media that he was inclined to doubt that an ET craft had crashed near Roswell. I then asked if the results of the GAO investigation had "increased your belief that it was not an extraterrestrial craft." Schiff responded: "I think you're centering too much on my beliefs in the matter." Later he commented: "I predict that the GAO report is not going to change anybody's mind. But it did what I wanted it to do. . . . I think GAO did a very competent job . . . they looked in every nook and cranny they could think of."

The "missing/destroyed documents" included outgoing teletype messages from RAAF for the period from October 1946 through December 1949, as well as accounting, administrative records from early 1945 to late 1949. Schiff explained why he believed the missing outgoing RAAF teletype messages were so important. When top AAF officials in the Pentagon first learned that RAAF had announced recovery of one of the mysterious flying disks, they would be eager to obtain more details. Schiff assumed that a top Army Air Force official would have sent a teletype message to RAAF base commander Blanchard and that he would have replied by teletype.

I questioned Schiff's view, and suggested that a curious AAF official in Washington would reach for his telephone and call Blanchard to get a speedy explanation rather than take the time to write out a message and send it to the Pentagon's central teletype room. Schiff responded that he believed that AAF officials would probably have used "both" telephone and teletype. He added: "It is my understanding that outgoing message traffic is a permanent record which shouldn't have been destroyed by anybody." Schiff was wrong, because he had not carefully read the *final/published* version of the GAO report—as will be detailed below.

Inasmuch as Schiff had requested the GAO investigation because he felt the Pentagon had failed to respond properly to his 1993 inquiries, one might have expected him to have carefully read the twenty-three-page USAF Report released in September 1994, describing the results of its extensive Roswell investigation. But based on Schiff's press release, his comments to me, and subsequent statements to the media, it was clear that he had *not* read the USAF report *carefully.*

For example, Schiff's press release claimed that the GAO investigation "caused the Air Force to acknowledge that the crashed vehicle was no weather balloon." Had Schiff read the USAF Report more carefully, he would have known that the USAF's investigation indicated that the Brazel ranch debris resulted from the touchdown of a train of twenty-three weather balloons, three radar-targets, and other instruments that had been launched by an NYU team on June 4, 1947. The USAF Report's conclusion section, p. 21, stated: "It appears that the identification of the wreckage as being part of a weather balloon device [by Gen. Ramey] . . . was based on the fact *that there was no physical difference in the radar targets and neoprene balloons (other than the numbers and configuration) between Mogul balloons and normal weather balloons*" (emphasis added).

Schiff's press release said that the weather balloon explanation (by Gen. Ramey) "never fit the fact of high military security used at the time." When he repeated this allegation during our interview, claiming there had been "an extraordinary degree of security" invoked by RAAF, I pointed out that GAO investigators had not found *any* evidence to support such claims.

Schiff said he strongly believed that "a democratic government has an obligation at all times to be forthcoming with the people about what it is doing—with the sole exception of where there is a legitimate need for classification" for national defense. It was this, he said, that had prompted him to ask the GAO to investigate all government documents relating to the Roswell Incident. But he admitted that he did not expect the GAO report to resolve the all-important question of whether the government had recovered a crashed saucer near Roswell and kept that fact under cover for nearly half a century. He conceded that persons who were disposed to believe that an ET craft had crashed near Roswell "will say: ah ha, the messages are missing." In response to my question, Schiff said he had no intention of seeking congressional hearings on the issue.

At one point in our interview, Schiff said that the GAO had shown him "two drafts" of its Roswell report to enable him "to make any suggestions I might make." It is a standard GAO practice to allow agencies or persons involved in an investigation to see a draft of an intended report to correct any errors of fact and to comment on the GAO's findings. Typically a brief summary of a criticized agency's rebuttal-comments are then included in the final report. Schiff's comment that he had received *two* drafts suggested to me that he had recommended significant changes in the first version. I was curious to learn what changes Schiff had suggested.

So on August 6, 1995, I wrote the congressman "to request that you provide me with copies of these two 'drafts' of the GAO report which you examined together with a list of changes/revisions which you suggested to the GAO." When two weeks passed without any response, I again wrote Schiff and enclosed a copy of my earlier letter. When nearly three months had passed without any response, I decided to "needle" him with a brief item in the November 1995 issue of my *Skeptics UFO Newsletter* (*SUN*), which noted that Schiff had proclaimed his belief that "people have a right to information from their government."

On February 20, 1996, I received a letter from Schiff's press secretary, Barry Bitzer, who accepted the blame for taking so long to respond. Bitzer wrote:

As to memos or letters this office is supposed to have sent the GAO relating to revising a draft of their report, there aren't, and never have been, any. The only input from the Congressman to the GAO during that time was that, when told that the GAO was about to produce a draft report, he asked if they had searched for outbound messages from Roswell Army Air Base. As a 27-year Air Force Reservist, Congressman Schiff thought those messages might contain information relevant to the case. But when he made the suggestion that the GAO look for these messages, he obviously had no idea what would or wouldn't be found in them. Everything thereafter was exclusively between the GAO and the Air Force.

By the time I received Bitzer's February 20 letter, I had obtained a copy of the GAO's next-to-final (second) draft of its Roswell report from a confidential source, as well as other information that prompted me to pose three questions in my February 25 reply to Schiff's press secretary. In Bitzer's reply of March 4, he declined to provide me with copies of early drafts of the GAO report "even if we did have one (which we don't)." His letter raised more questions which led to further correspondence. Finally, on May 1, Bitzer called to try to resolve the matter but he was unsure of the chronology of events, explaining: "We don't keep very detailed records about such things." When Bitzer suggested I contact the GAO officials involved in the Roswell investigation to obtain more precise answers to my questions, I eagerly agreed.

On May 2, I wrote a one-page letter to Richard Davis, GAO's Director for National Security Analysis, seeking corroboration of the chronology of events and posing one question. Davis passed my letter on to Gary Weeter, who had headed GAO's Roswell investigation. Because of Weeter's extended vacation and my own travel it was late June before we first talked by telephone. Because Weeter did not recall one key item, he said he wanted to check his records and would call back, which he did on July 3. These two conversations with Weeter, plus information obtained from other sources, provide revealing insights into the "missing/destroyed" documents issue and Schiff's role in their *even being mentioned in the GAO report*.

- In early June of 1995, the GAO sent Schiff a first-draft copy of its proposed Roswell report for his review and comments.

- On June 14, GAO's Weeter and his deputy, Jack Kriethe, met with Schiff and members of his staff to obtain their comments on the first draft. Because the first draft made no mention of outgoing teletype messages from RAAF, Schiff asked if the GAO had examined them. GAO representatives replied that they had visited the National Personnel Records Center in St. Louis to examine both *incoming and outgoing* teletype messages of RAAF as well as the Fort Worth Army Air Field and the Pentagon, looking for references to the Roswell Incident. They told Schiff that they did not recall finding any *outgoing* messages from RAAF, but had not considered this significant enough to include in their first-draft report. (The reason, Weeter explained to me, was that the GAO had found *incoming* messages to RAAF but *none* dealt with the recovery of a flying disc. Nor had the GAO found any *incoming* messages *from RAAF* in the archival records of the Pentagon or Fort Worth AAF base.) But because of Schiff's keen interest, GAO representatives said they would verify whether the RAAF outgoing messages were missing.

• On June 19, the GAO called the chief archivist at the St. Louis center who confirmed that RAAF's *outgoing* teletype messages for the period from October 1946 through December 1949 had been destroyed, probably in the mid-1950s when 38,000 boxes of old records had been transferred to St. Louis from a previous archive center in Kansas City. The GAO so informed Schiff's office on June 20. Because this seemed so important to Schiff, the GAO prepared a revised (second) draft which included the following:

In our search for records concerning the Roswell crash, we learned that some government records covering RAAF activities have apparently been destroyed and others have not. For example, our investigation indicates that RAAF administrative records (March 1945 through December 1949) and RAAF outgoing messages (October 1946 through December 1949) have been destroyed. These records were listed on the RAAF document disposition register as "permanent" records. *Senior gov-*

ernment records management officials told us that because these were permanent records, they should not have been destroyed. (Emphasis added)

- On July 5, the GAO sent copies of this second draft to the Pentagon and other involved agencies, including the National Personnel Records Center (NPRC) in St. Louis, asking for comments by July 11. Presumably, a copy was also sent to Schiff's office.

- On July 7, at 4:30 P.M., NPRC's chief archivist, W. G. Seibert, sent a fax message to GAO's Weeter and Kriethe, *which challenged the accuracy of GAO's statement that the "missing records" were "permanent records ... [that] should not have been destroyed."* Based on Seibert's comments, *the GAO revised this part of its Roswell report.* The final/published version added:

According to this official [Seibert], the documentation disposition form did not properly indicate the authority under which the disposal action was taken. [However], the Center's Chief Archivist stated that from his personal experience, many of the Air Force organizational records covering this time period were destroyed without entering a citation for the governing disposition authority. Our review of the records control forms showing the destruction of other records—including the outgoing RAAF messages for 1950—supports the Chief Archivist's viewpoint.

Although the final GAO Roswell report is dated July 28, 1995, and Schiff issued his press release on that date, it is not known when his office first received copies of the final report. But the charge prominently made in the press release that the "GAO report states that the outgoing messages from Roswell Army Air Field (RAAF) for this period of time were destroyed *without proper authority*," which was featured in many media accounts, *was erroneous.*

Shortly after the GAO report was released, Schiff was interviewed on August 4 on the popular "Larry King Live" TV show.

At one point in the program Schiff said, "I think the GAO report will further fuel the debate. In other words, there are some missing records that shouldn't be missing. . . . I think they were permanent records and shouldn't be destroyed." To my knowledge, Schiff has never publicly admitted that this widely publicized charge is false.

22.

Reactions to the GAO's Roswell Report

When the GAO began its Roswell investigation in early 1994, its officials knew that if Congressman Schiff's suspicions were correct, this investigation could be the most important in the agency's history. According to UFO-lecturer Stanton Friedman, Roswell was a "Cosmic Watergate," as he characterized it in a briefing of Schiff's staff in August 1992. If the GAO's investigation confirmed Friedman's claim and Schiff's suspicions, it would give him a tremendous boost up the "political ladder," perhaps even taking Schiff as far as the White House.

However, if the GAO investigation failed to confirm Schiff's suspicions, which he had stated in media interviews, this could be embarrassing for him. And Schiff was an influential member of the Government Operations Committee to which the GAO reports. By late spring of 1995, GAO investigators faced the challenging task of writing their Roswell report, knowing that their findings did not support some of Schiff's earlier publicly stated charges. And the USAF (Weaver) report released the previous year had flatly challenged Schiff's suspicions. When the GAO asked Schiff if he wanted its report to include GAO's assessment of the USAF's Project Mogul explanation, the answer was "no."

Following the release of the GAO Roswell report, it was sharply criticized in an article which appeared in the July/August 1995 issue of *International UFO Reporter* (*IUR*), published by the Center for UFO Studies (CUFOS)—which had partially funded Schmitt and Randle's Roswell research. The article, authored by Mark Rodeghier, CUFOS's scientific director, and Mark Chesney, a CUFOS consultant, was headlined: "What the GAO Found: Nothing About Much Ado." The same issue of *IUR* reproduced highlights from the GAO report as well as the "missing documents" press release issued by Schiff's office.

The Rodeghier/Chesney commentary said: "With one exception, the GAO's 16-month investigation turned up nothing whatsoever. Except for two documents which are already known to the UFO community, no new documents concerning the Roswell crash were discovered in any government agency, including the supersecret CIA and National Security Agency (NSA)." If the Brazel ranch debris came from a Project Mogul, the authors asked, "shouldn't there be some record of that event in some government agency beyond the FBI telex and the note in the *Combined History of the 509th Bomb Group*? Yes, absolutely, yet no documents that refer to the Roswell debris as coming from Project Mogul were located, which strikes us as very peculiar. . . ."

If Rodeghier and Chesney had more carefully read the USAF report, they would have learned that because of Project Mogul's "Top Secret" classification in 1947, it was a closely held secret. The possible link between the Brazel ranch debris and Project Mogul was not discovered by USAF investigators until early 1994, shortly after it was discovered by UFO-researchers Robert Todd and Karl Pflock after much research effort.

According to the Rodeghier/Chesney article:

The most intriguing and, perhaps, ominous, finding of the GAO came when it searched the National Personnel Records Center for Roswell Army Air Field records on outgoing message traffic from October 1946 through December 1949. . . . The GAO investigators found that these records were destroyed. . . . The message traffic records would have been especially valuable, since they would have contained communications between officers at Roswell and Fort Worth and Washington concerning the Roswell event. Although it might appear that the missing records are proof of a coverup, the Chief Archivist at the Records Center said that many Air Force organizational records were destroyed from this time period without proper documentation. *Nevertheless, the destroyed records are certainly consistent with the existence of a cover-up.* (Emphasis added)

Rodeghier and Chesney commented: "We find it unthinkable that there are no CIA records on Mogul. Also surprising that there are no CIA records on Roswell. . . . [T]he lack of records on Project Mogul and Roswell again raises the specter of a cover-up at the highest levels of government." If Rodeghier and Chesney had taken time to research the history of the CIA they would have learned that the agency was not created by President Truman until September 18, 1947—two months *after* the Roswell Incident. Furthermore, the CIA had no "need-to-know" about Top Secret USAF research projects such as Project Mogul which never went into operational use.

The Rodeghier/Chesney commentary concluded: "Despite the lack of documentation found by the GAO, its report should be seen as further support for the position of most in the UFO community that something truly extraordinary crashed near Roswell. . . . In our view, the GAO report makes it less likely that Project Mogul was the source of the Roswell debris, since no records were located to support that conjecture." (Because the USAF's investigation located and made public many original records to support the Project Mogul explanation, the GAO did not waste time doing so.)

Further evidence that Rodeghier and Chesney failed to carefully read the USAF's brief 1994 report is found in their final comment: "And since the Air Force has previously stated that the weather balloon explanation is incorrect, that doesn't leave many (if any) terrestrial causes [i.e., explanations] for the debris. That is the fundamental and important upshot of the GAO report, even if the GAO was too timid to say so forthrightly in its report." If Rodeghier and Chesney had examined other GAO reports they would have known that the agency is not "too timid" when its investigators find evidence which warrants exposure and/or criticism.

The *MUFON UFO Journal* reproduced highlights of the GAO report in its September 1995 issue, but did not offer any pro or con commentary on its content. However, the same issue carried a short article by Karl Pflock reporting that his research into Project Blue Book files at the National Archives in June 1995 had turned up USAF documents showing that balloon-borne radar targets, being launched by the Air Weather Service, had generated UFO reports in the late 1940s.

One such incident cited in a letter dated December 12, 1950, said that "one such target was sighted and recovered on a farm in Eastern Maryland. A report was received that a 'flying saucer' or 'disk' had been observed in flight and it had landed in this particular locality. Two OSI [Office of Special Investigations] Agents, FBI Agents and a Maryland State Trooper expended 1½ days in locating the object and interviewing the individual who had sighted the object. This time and expense would undoubtedly have been unnecessary had the target born [sic] a simple stamp to the effect that it was a weather target and that if found it could be retained by the finder. . . ." The letter recommended that a suitable note to this effect be placed on balloon-borne radar targets.

Pflock reported that this recommendation was endorsed in a memo dated January 21, 1951, signed by an official of the Air Weather Service (AWS), and sent to the commander of the USAF's Military Air Transport Service. The memo stated: "(1) All AWS units which use Corner Reflectors [radar targets] will be instructed to indicate on the target that it is a weather target and may be retained by the finder. (2) The [Army] Signal Corps will be requested to have similar information stamped on the radar targets by the manufacturer in the future."

Pflock's article did not comment on the GAO's Roswell report, nor did he publish any follow-up article offering his own views on the report. This is hardly surprising in view of Pflock's own growing belief in the Project Mogul explanation for the Brazel ranch debris, Schiff's press release, and the fact that Pflock's wife, Mary Martinek, was employed as a senior member of Schiff's staff.

Were it not that Schiff would have found it politically embarrassing, the GAO report could have cited hard evidence to show that the Air Force had not recovered a crashed saucer in New Mexico in 1947. For example:

- Lt. Gen. Nathan Twining's letter of September 23, 1947, originally classified "Secret" but declassified since 1969, in response to a Pentagon request for the Air Materiel Command's (AMC) opinion as to what UFOs might be. While Twining said AMC believed that "the phenomenon reported is something real and not visionary or fictitious," he added that "Due consideration must be given the following. . . . *The lack of physical evidence in the shape of crash recovered exhibits which would undeniably prove the existence of these objects*" (emphasis added). The AMC was headquartered at Wright Field, in Dayton, Ohio, then the center of Air Force technical expertise where a recovered crashed UFO would have been sent for scientific analysis. And Twining's letter was written more than two months *after* the Roswell Incident.

- USAF Directorate of Intelligence Analysis of Flying Disc Reports, originally classified "Secret," transmitted on December 22, 1947, by Maj. Gen. George C. McDonald, USAF Director of Intelligence, to USAF's Director of Research and Development. Conclusions of this analysis included the following:

  Flying discs, as reported by widely scattered observers, probably represent something real and tangible, *even though physical*

evidence, such as crash-recovered exhibits, is not available. . . .
On the basis of presently available information, if these discs
actually exist they are foreign in origin, so investigation of the
possible country of development and the place of origin should
continue. . . . (Emphasis added)

• March 17, 1948, members of the recently created Air Force
Scientific Advisory Board (AFSAB), heard a report by Col.
H. M. McCoy, chief of intelligence for the Air Materiel
Command, in Dayton, Ohio. AFSAB's initial and subse-
quent members included eminent scientists such as Dr.
Theodore von Karman, Dr. Edward Teller, Dr. Hans A.
Bethe, Dr. Enrico Fermi, Dr. Irving Langmuir, and Dr.
Vladimir K. Zwarykin. According to the once "Secret" min-
utes of the 1948 meeting, it was late in McCoy's remarks
before he got around to discussing UFOs when he reported:

We have a new project—Project SIGN—which may surprise
you as a development from the so-called mass hysteria of the
past summer [1947] when we had all the unidentified flying
objects or discs. This can't be laughed off. We have over 300
reports which haven't been publicized in the papers from very
competent personnel, in many instances—men as capable as Dr.
K. D. Wood—and practically all Air Force, airline people with
broad experience. We are running down every report. *I can't
even tell you how much we would give to have one of those
[UFOs] crash in an area so that we could recover whatever they
are.* (Emphasis added)

• November 8, 1948, Col. McCoy wrote a letter, classified
"Secret," addressed to the USAF's chief of staff in Washington, which described the results of an AMC analysis of
180 UFO reports. McCoy noted that some had turned out to
be generated by bright planets, meteor-fireballs, and by
weather and scientific balloons. McCoy's letter concluded:
"Although it is obvious that some types of flying objects
have been sighted, the exact nature of those objects *cannot
be established until physical evidence, such as that which*

would result from a crash, has been obtained" (emphasis added).

- December 10, 1948, a report titled "Analysis of Flying Object Incidents in the U.S.," classified "Top Secret," based on Air Intelligence Division Study #203, was submitted to top Pentagon officials and the White House. The report concluded: "The origin of the devices is not ascertainable. There are two reasonable possibilities: (1) The objects are domestic devices. . . . (2) Objects are foreign, and if so, it would seem most logical to consider *that they are from a Soviet source . . ."* (emphasis added). Highlights of this report, which was declassified on March 5, 1985, were published in the July 1985 issue of the *MUFON UFO Journal.*

Additionally, the GAO report could have cited the CIA's once SECRET briefing papers of mid-August 1952 (chapter 6): "The third theory is the man from Mars—space ships—interplanetary travelers. . . . *[T]here is no shred of evidence to support this theory at present"* (emphasis added).

But if such hard evidence had been included in the GAO report, it would surely have antagonized some Roswell residents who are benefiting from the city's newfound fame as the nation's "crashed-saucer capital." While Schiff does not currently need support from voters in Roswell because he represents a different congressional district, that would change if Schiff should some day decide to run for the Senate.

23.

Contaminated Memories

Numerous experiments have demonstrated that the recollections of eyewitnesses can be grossly in error even for recent events. Hence the accuracy of recollections of Roswell "witnesses" is necessarily suspect because they must try to recall an event that occurred forty to fifty years earlier. Many of them are—or were—in their seventies or eighties when interviewed—and advancing years take their toll of one's memory.

A more serious impediment to accurate recollection is "memory contamination" by the news media—and especially TV. During the past decade the public has been bombarded with TV shows that promote the idea that a UFO crashed near Roswell, was recovered by the Air Force, and that the government has tried to keep this startling fact under cover. Still another source of memory contamination can come from interviewers who want to believe in a crashed-saucer coverup and may unwittingly "lead the witness" by the nature of their questions and/or comments.

An excellent example of memory contamination of two persons involved in the Roswell Incident can be found in Randle and

Schmitt's second book, *The Truth About the UFO Crash at Roswell,*
based on interviews with Jason Kellahin and Robin Adair. In July
1947, the two men were employed in the Albuquerque office of the
Associated Press, where Kellahin was a reporter and Adair a photographer. It is known beyond any doubt that Kellahin interviewed
rancher Brazel in the offices of the *Roswell Daily Record* on the
night of Tuesday, July 8. And Adair was present to take pictures of
Brazel and to transmit one of them later to AP clients using then
recently developed portable Wirephoto equipment.

The front page of the July 9 edition of the *Roswell Daily
Record* carried a picture whose caption read:

> Pictured above are Jason Kellahin and R. A. Adair, of the Asso-
> ciated Press bureau in Albuquerque, as they sent out the first AP
> wirephotos ever to be dispatched from Roswell. Dispatch of pic-
> tures of W. W. Brazel, who discovered a reported flying disk on
> the Foster ranch, northwest of Roswell, were made on the
> instruments shown in the picture. The instruments were set up
> in The Record office last night, and the pictures sent out by wire
> at about six o'clock this morning.

It is not known precisely when the AP bureau in Albuquerque
first learned of Lt. Haut's flying disk press release. But it is
known—thanks to Karl Pflock's *Roswell In Perspective*—that
highlights of Haut's release were transmitted by AP's competi-
tor—the United Press—to its clients at 2:41 P.M. (mountain daylight time). Word of the Haut release would certainly have reached
AP's Albuquerque bureau (and AP headquarters in New York) no
later than 3 P.M. AP's headquarters then instructed Kellahin and
Adair to go to Roswell to get photos and more details. Because
Roswell was then roughly four hours away by automobile, Kellahin and Adair could expect to spend the night in Roswell and
would logically have rushed home to pack a few clothes. Thus, it
seems likely that it would be at least 4 P.M. before they would have
left for Roswell, and they would have arrived no earlier than 8
P.M., possibly a bit later if they had stopped for dinner en route.

During interviews in early 1993 with Randle and Schmitt, Kellahin—then in his early eighties—said that he and Adair had interrupted their drive down to Roswell to visit Brazel's ranch. They reportedly had "seen a lot of [military] cars," off Highway 285 and had decided to follow them to the ranch where they reportedly saw a number of military officers. According to Kellahin, Brazel took him and Adair out to the debris site and Adair "took some pictures of the stuff lying on the ground and of the rancher." Kellahin said he interviewed Brazel briefly before military officers came over and said they had finished and were going to take Brazel back to Roswell.

If Kellahin's 1993 recollections were reasonably correct, one should expect that having taken pictures of Brazel, of the debris site, and having had an opportunity to interview the rancher, the two men would then have returned to AP's Albuquerque office to promptly file a story, process the photos taken at the ranch, and transmit them to AP's members. *Instead, it is known that they drove to Roswell to interview Brazel, take his photo, and set up the special equipment to send Brazel's photo taken in Roswell to AP clients.* Kellahin recalled that they had arrived in Roswell before dark. If the two men had diverted to the Brazel ranch and taken time to visit the debris site, they could not possibly have arrived in Roswell "before dark."

Adair's recollections conflicted sharply with Kellahin's. He recalled that he had been in El Paso, Texas, when AP's New York headquarters reached him and told him to go to Roswell. Adair recalled that he was instructed to get to Roswell as fast as possible, so he recalled that he had gone to the expense of chartering a private aircraft to fly him there. This is curious because the distance from El Paso to Roswell is roughly the same as to Albuquerque. Yet Kellahin would drive down while Adair was allowed to charter an airplane to expedite his arrival in Roswell.

According to Adair's recollection, he delayed his arrival in Roswell in order to fly up to the Brazel ranch. From the air he recalled seeing military personnel and said "we could make out a lot of stuff . . . looked like burnt places. . . . You could tell that something had been there. . . . Apparently the way it cut into [the ground], whatever hit the ground wasn't wood or something soft. It looked like it was metal." According to Randle and Schmitt's second book, from the air "Adair could see the gouge and tracks on the ground."

This contradicted Kellahin's recollections of the debris he had seen at the Brazel ranch: "It was a weather balloon. In my opinion that's what we saw. We didn't see anything else to indicate it was anything else." Later, in an affidavit signed on September 23, 1993, following an interview with Karl Pflock, Kellahin provided more details of what he recalled seeing at the Brazel ranch on Tuesday late afternoon, despite the fact that early that morning Marcel, Cavitt, and Brazel had recovered much of the debris. "There was quite a lot of debris on the site—pieces of silver colored fabric, perhaps aluminized cloth. Some of the pieces had sticks attached to them. I thought they might be the remains of a high-altitude balloon package, but I did not see anything, pieces of rubber or the like, that looked like it could have been part of the balloon itself."

In fact, Kellahin's account unwittingly was drawn from the story he wrote forty-six years earlier, based on Brazel's description given in the offices of the *Roswell Daily Record*, and what he had read in the Berlitz/Moore book. Kellahin's article, published the next day in the July 9, 1947 edition of the *Albuquerque Journal*, included the following: "Brazel described his find as consisting of large numbers of pieces of paper covered with a foil-like substance, and pieced together with small sticks much like a kite. . . ."

Clearly, *both* Kellahin's and Adair's recollections were flawed. But Kellahin's description of the debris, and his recollection that the military officers did not object to him and Adair visiting the debris site, challenged the crashed-saucer coverup hypothesis whereas Adair's recollections did not. Not surprisingly, Randle and Schmitt's second book pointed out the flaws in Kellahin's account but did not do the same for Adair's.

Randle and Schmitt noted that Kellahin recalled having learned of Haut's press release in the morning, although it was not released until around noon. They noted that the Brazel ranch is too distant from Highway 285 for Kellahin to have seen military vehicles, and that by Tuesday afternoon, Marcel and Cavitt had already collected most of the debris which was then being flown to Fort Worth. Also, the photos that Kellahin recalled Adair having taken of Brazel at the ranch and of the debris were never published. Randle and Schmitt correctly concluded that Kellahin did not stop at the ranch en route to Roswell.

On the other hand, Randle and Schmitt did not question why Adair would be authorized to charter an airplane to fly from El Paso to Roswell while Kellahin would go by car from Albuquerque which was roughly the same distance from Roswell. Nor did Randle and Schmitt question how Adair would be able to find the Brazel ranch on Tuesday afternoon inasmuch as Haut's press release had not identified where the "flying disc" had been found or mention Brazel's name. However, according to Randle and Schmitt, "Adair having seen some of the military activity on the [Brazel] field, knew that something extraordinary had happened, but didn't know exactly what." Despite the obvious flaws in the recollections of both men, Randle and Schmitt conclude: "The point, however, is that we can take the testimonies of the two men and the documentation, and reconstruct, with a fair amount of accuracy, exactly what happened on July 8 and 9, 1947."

The recollections of Maj. Marcel's son, Dr. Jesse Marcel Jr., provide an interesting example of memory contamination. Dr. Marcel's least-contaminated memories were obtained when William L. Moore interviewed him in March 1979 and sought his thirty-two-year-old recollections. The Berlitz/Moore book quoted Dr. Marcel, who in 1947 was eleven years old, as saying his father

was *gone a couple of days* and returned with a van and part of a car filled with wreckage debris. The material was foil-like stuff, very thin, metallic-like but not metal, and very tough. There was also some structural-like material too—beams and so on. Also a quantity of black plastic material which looked organic in nature. *Dad returned toward evening. He was gone all one night and most of the next day.** He had a 1942 Buick and a Carry-all trailer, and both were loaded with this material which was only a small fraction of the total material. (Emphasis added)

When Dr. Marcel was asked if he had heard anything further after that evening, he replied:

Yes. The story leaked out and we were bombarded with reporters, etc. . . . My main impression was that the metal objects and strips were from some kind of machine, not a weather balloon. I was told that it was some type of aircraft, but it wasn't any type we were familiar with—that's for sure. Dad said that the speed of impact was not in keeping with any type of aircraft we had at the time.

This first interview prompted Dr. Marcel to try to recall more details and several weeks later he wrote Moore the following:

In reference to the UFO incident of 1947 *or 1948*, I omitted one startling description of the wreckage for fear it might have been the fanciful imagination of a 12-year-old. *Imprinted* along the edge of some of the beam remnants there were hieroglyphic-type characters. I recently questioned my father about this, and

---

*This contradicts Dr. Marcel's later recollection that his father had stopped at his house en route back from the Brazel ranch to show the debris to his wife and son. In Maj. Marcel's 1979 interview with Bob Pratt, he said that Capt. Sheridan Cavitt "drove a Jeep carry-all. I drove my staff car. . . . We got to his [Brazel's] place at dusk. It was too late to do anything, so we spent the night there in that little—his—shack, and the following morning we got up and took off. He took us to that place and we started picking up fragments. . . ." Based on Maj. Marcel's 1979 recollections, he and Cavitt returned directly to RAAF, probably arriving around 11 A.M. on Tuesday, July 8. Several hours later Marcel was en route by air to Fort Worth. In my opinion, the debris that Marcel showed his wife and son were fragments that he brought back from Fort Worth Tuesday night to show his family what had kept him away from home since early Monday morning.

he recalled seeing these characters also, and even described them as being a *pink or purplish-pink in color*. Egyptian hieroglyphics would be a close visual description of the characters seen, except I don't think there were any animal figures present as there are in true Egyptian hieroglyphics.

I keep wondering if some remnants of the crash might still be lying on the New Mexico desert floor. According to my father, some of it was left behind when he and his crew investigated the air-crash site. I suspect, however, that after the true nature of the craft became known to the Air Force Intelligence, the whole site was gone over with a vacuum cleaner. As you know, my dad brought a portion of the wreckage into the house and spread it over the kitchen floor, trying to piece some of the larger fragments together. There were quite literally piles of *metallic scrap* along with bits of a black brittle residue that looked like plastic that had either melted or burned. The task was hopeless because there was far too much debris for one kitchen floor to hold. I doubt if all the smaller fragments were picked up from the kitchen, and, indeed, my mother remarked that some of it was probably swept out the back door. . . . (Emphasis added)

In the nearly two decades since Dr. Marcel's first interview, he has been interviewed many times for books and articles and has appeared on many TV shows dealing with Roswell. But so far as is known, he has never mentioned the humiliation that his father, mother, and he experienced when Gen. Ramey identified the debris as being the remnants of a balloon-borne radar target and not from a "flying disc." If Ramey had known about Project Mogul and the New York University experiments, he could have softened the blow to Maj. Marcel's ego. Ramey could have explained that the debris was not from a conventional weather balloon-borne target but from a giant train of twenty-three balloons, several radar targets, and instruments, and this could explain Marcel's inability to identify the debris. But Ramey did not know, and Marcel's reputation suffered as a result.

The July 9, 1947 edition of the *Roswell Dispatch* carried a two-level banner headline on its front page which read: "Army Debunks Roswell Flying Disk As World Simmers With Excitement." The banner headline on that evening's edition of the *Daily Record* read: "Gen. Ramey Empties Roswell Saucer." The next day's edition carried a photo of Maj. Marcel, taken in Gen. Ramey's office, which carried the headline: "NOT a Flying Disc." The caption read: "Maj. Jesse A. Marcel, of Houma, La., intelligence officer of the 509th Bomb Group at Roswell, inspects what was identified by a Fort Worth army air base weather forecaster as a ray wind [*sic*] target used to determine the direction and velocity of the wind at high altitudes. Initial stories originating from Roswell, where the object was found, had labeled it as a 'flying disc' but inspection at Fort Worth revealed its true nature. (AP Wirephoto)." The same photo of Maj. Marcel also was published on the front page of the morning paper, *Roswell Dispatch,* whose caption began: "*NOT A FLYING DISC.*"

It seems safe to assume that young Jesse Jr. must have taken some ribbing from his schoolmates and friends because his father had erroneously identified the debris. One significant indication of the family's embarrassment is that neither Maj. Marcel nor his wife kept a scrapbook of newspaper clippings of the incident. When Maj. Marcel was first interviewed by Stanton Friedman, he was unsure of even the *year* when the incident had occurred, as was Dr. Marcel when he was interviewed by William Moore in 1979. Dr. Marcel has acknowledged that he never discussed the incident with his father until it attracted media interest in the late 1970s.

Thus, if the Moore/Berlitz book *The Roswell Incident,* and those that followed a decade later were correct and the Brazel ranch debris was from a crashed saucer, *then Dr. Marcel's father was vindicated.* This provided an incentive for Dr. Marcel to embellish his recollections to strengthen the case for a crashed saucer, but he resisted such temptation with one exception. At some point between his Moore interview in the spring of 1979 and mid-1980 when Dr. Marcel was interviewed for a UFO series produced by Johnny Mann of New Orleans TV station WWL, he recalled that one of the objects his father brought home was a thin beam shaped like an *I*. The I-beam, as Dr. Marcel recalled, was about ⅜-inch thick and perhaps 12 to 18 inches long.

In mid-October 1988, Dr. Marcel became a nationally famous Roswell TV celebrity when he was flown from his home in Helena, Montana, to Washington, D.C., to appear on a widely publicized two-hour UFO special, "UFO Coverup? Live." Shortly after William Moore and Stanton Friedman were interviewed, Marcel joined them to briefly describe the debris his father had shown him. Marcel described it as a "foil-like sheathing alloy. It was metallic and looked like the skin of an aircraft, but it was unlike anything I had ever seen before. Also there was an *I-beam*, about a foot or foot and a half in length, about one-half inch across . . ." (emphasis added).

In the closing moments of the interview, the program host said: "Dr. Marcel, you've examined the material firsthand, you've had a long time to think about it. What is your assessment of the Roswell incident?" Dr. Marcel responded: "I held this material in my hand. It was not from this earth or this universe. That's what I think. We're not alone."

When Dr. Marcel was interviewed the following August (1989) by Randle and Schmitt, he again mentioned the I-beam, which was reported in the first Randle/Schmitt book, *UFO Crash at Roswell.* So far as is known, Maj. Marcel—who died in June 1986—was never questioned by Roswell researchers about the I-beam shape. However, when he was interviewed in late 1979 by Bob Pratt, Marcel made no mention of an I-beam. Instead, he described *"rectangular members, just like a square stick,"* and drew a sketch for Pratt which was *not* shaped like an I-beam. Marcel told Pratt that these "members . . . didn't look like metal. It looked more like wood." It would be extremely difficult to fabricate a small I-beam-shaped stick out of wood.

Except for the I-beam, Dr. Marcel's recollections of the debris correlate very closely with the forty-plus-year-old recollections of his father, of Bessie Brazel Schrieber, of meteorology officer Irvin

Newton and Prof. Charlie Moore, and with the photos taken in Gen. Ramey's office. But so long as Dr. Marcel sticks with his I-beam claim, it seems to rule out a Project Mogul explanation and thereby seems to vindicate his late father.

Maj. Marcel died before publication of the two books by Randle and Schmitt and the one by Friedman and Berliner, *Crash at Corona,* which claim that the Air Force recovered ET bodies as well as a crashed saucer—something that was never mentioned by Marcel, even to members of his family. We can only speculate as to what Marcel's reaction would have been to such claims. But a possible clue to his reaction was contained in a letter written on September 11, 1982, by Roswell researcher Lee Graham to Dr. Marcel, who had earlier provided Graham with his father's address and phone number. Graham wrote that he had talked by telephone with Maj. Marcel and quoted him as saying: "I do not know what it was I picked up." But Graham said that Marcel added: "I do not believe in flying saucers and little green men. . . ."

24.

The Nurse Who Never Was

When I interviewed mortician Glenn Dennis in Roswell in early December 1991 and heard him describe the "sacred oath" he claimed he had given to the nurse to keep secret her ET-autopsy story and sketches (chapter 8), I expected Dennis would offer some moral justification for violating his "sacred oath." But there was none. Dennis said that his wife had "talked me into it. . . . She thought this was a very important story." Dennis added: "I think the public has the right to know."

Later, when I studied the transcript of our tape-recorded interview, my doubts increased about the veracity of Dennis's story. For example, Dennis claimed the RAAF's mortuary officer had called to ask whether fluids used for embalming might affect "blood content. Would it change tissue, would it change stomach contents." If ET bodies had really been recovered, an autopsy would be conducted *before* the bodies were embalmed for burial. Dennis said he had recommended that the mortuary officer call the Army's own Walter Reed Hospital in Washington for more authoritative answers to such questions.

187

In early 1995, Dennis was interviewed by Tim Korte, a reporter from the Associated Press bureau in Albuquerque, and the resulting story was published in mid-January. Korte's article included a new detail provided by Dennis whose significance was not apparent to the AP reporter. It quoted Dennis as saying that his nurse friend had told him that *"the two pathologists were from Walter Reed Hospital"* (emphasis added). If true, why had the base mortuary officer called Dennis to ask about the effects of embalming fluid when top Army pathologists had been flown in from Washington?

This new detail revealed more serious flaws in Dennis's account. In Pflock's *Roswell In Perspective* (chapter 17) he had reported a recent "blinding flash recall" by Dennis. Dennis now "remembered" that shortly after he had returned from having lunch with his nurse friend, the July 8 edition of the *Roswell Daily Record* had arrived with its giant headline about RAAF having recovered a flying disc. This meant that the (alleged) ET autopsy had taken place *Monday afternoon, July 7.* This would require the Army pathologists to have departed Washington by *9 A.M., Monday, July 7—several hours* before *rancher Brazel had arrived in Roswell and contacted RAAF to report finding the unusual debris.*

If Dennis's latest recollection about the pathologists from Washington was true, then the ET bodies must necessarily have been discovered sometime *before* Monday morning, July 7, so they could be recovered and brought to RAAF by that afternoon. But if RAAF had discovered the ET bodies sometime prior to Monday morning, Marcel and Cavitt would have been dispatched to *that* site by early Monday morning. They would not have been available to journey to the Brazel ranch Monday afternoon.

These serious discrepancies were reported in the March 1995 issue of my *Skeptics UFO Newsletter* (*SUN*), to which Karl Pflock subscribes. When Pflock called me on March 27 to discuss other matters, I learned that *SUN*'s article had prompted him to talk with Dennis about Korte's article. Pflock told me that Dennis claimed that Korte had misunderstood when Dennis said he had suggested the RAAF mortuary office should *consult* with Walter Reed Hospital. My response was to read to Pflock portions of a report titled "The Glenn Dennis Story," which I had recently purchased from the Roswell International UFO Museum. The report, written by mortician John Sime and based on an interview with Dennis, *also said the two pathologists were from Walter Reed Hospital in Washington.*

I discovered further confirmation in a videotape of a UFO show, given to me by friends, Mr. and Mrs. Bernard Levine, in Dayton, Ohio, which had been produced by Carl Day of TV station WDTN and which had aired on March 20, 1994. Because Dennis had been interviewed in Roswell for the show I wrote to Day on March 25, 1995, to ask if he would review all the footage of the Dennis interview to see "if he discussed or mentioned the two [alleged] pathologists/doctors involved in the autopsy—and if Dennis mentioned where they [allegedly] were from." On April 10, Day called me and read the following statement that Dennis had made on camera: "The guys—they were in with the nurse— *they were flown in from Walter Reed Hospital in Washington* and they were doing a partial autopsy. They have their names *and we know who they were*" (emphasis added).

When these contradictions were reported in the May issue of *SUN,* Pflock wrote me to say that Dennis no longer denied having told Korte that the two pathologists were from Walter Reed Hospital. Now, according to Pflock, Dennis claimed that he "didn't recall" making such a statement to Korte. As for Dennis's on-camera statement to Carl Day/WDTN that "They have their names and we know who they were," Pflock explained that Dennis was simply repeating information he had recently heard from "two separate sources, one of whom has proven to be, shall we say, less than reliable."

During our 1991 interview, when Dennis described how the nurse (allegedly) had violated her security oath by providing him with ET-autopsy details and sketches, I wondered if perhaps he had had a romantic relationship with the nurse and asked if he had dated her. Dennis replied: "No, no, no. She had no interest in men whatsoever. Her whole life was planned. She was gonna be a [Catholic] nun" after she finished her military service.

But in early 1993, when I viewed a new video titled *UFO SECRET: The Roswell Crash,* in which Dennis was interviewed, the narrator said: "We should note here that Glenn's concern for Judy [pseudonym for the nurse] was serious. *Marriage had been discussed"* (emphasis added). I wrote to Mark Wolf, who had produced the video, to ask him "how certain are you of the accuracy" of this narrator's statement. Wolf replied on March 29, 1993, explaining that he "spoke to Dennis almost daily over a period of two weeks, in sessions sometimes spanning as much as ten hours. That is what he disclosed to me during one of several lengthy background discussions prior to taping [the interview]. He added that her family did not approve of him, since they were Catholic and he was Protestant." At the time of the videotaping sessions, Wolf did not know that in mid-1947, Dennis already had a wife.

The fall 1995 issue of *Omni* magazine carried three feature articles on the Roswell Incident. One, authored by Pflock, was titled: "Star Witness: The Mortician of Roswell Breaks His Code of Silence." The nearly seven-page article, which included a full-page photo of Dennis, consisted of Dennis's response to Pflock's questions. When Pflock asked why the nurse had made the ET sketches for Dennis, he replied: "She made the drawings for me—but only after I'd made a solemn oath I'd never reveal her connection to them. She wanted to know if I saw the same things she saw. She asked me if they brought—I think she called them 'creatures'—to the funeral home. I told her I hadn't seen the bodies, that they hadn't been taken to Ballard's." *This was the first time Dennis had offered this curious explanation for why the nurse had provided him with sketches of the ETs.*

Pflock asked: "Why do you think the nurse and everything about her seem to have vanished?" Dennis replied: "This is just my surmise, but I think that when she was transferred [out of RAAF], they discharged her and arranged for her to join an order, enter a convent. Everything was covered up with the [Catholic] church's help." When Pflock asked Dennis why he had provided some Roswell researchers with the name of the nurse, Dennis replied: "I would like to know what happened to her and have someone verify my story."

The very next article in the same issue of *Omni*, titled "The Case of the Vanishing Nurses," by Paul McCarthy, reported on the results of his efforts to locate Dennis's nurse. (See chapter 20.) McCarthy discovered that four of the five military nurses at the RAAF base hospital were no longer alive. But he did locate and interview the former chief nurse, Lt. Col. Rosemary McManus (Brown). She told McCarthy that she recalled the other four Army nurses who had been stationed at RAAF in July 1947, *but not Nurse X*. Nor did she remember Dennis.

When Stanton Friedman first interviewed Dennis in 1989, he had asked for the name of the nurse so he could try to locate her and Dennis had supplied it. He also provided the nurse's name to Randle and Schmitt, and later to Pflock. The name—*Naomi Maria Selff*—was first made public in the January 1995 issue of *SUN*. (I had obtained the name from a third party, who had learned of it from one of the researchers.)

By the spring of 1995, McCarthy and Don Schmitt were not the only persons trying to locate Naomi Maria Selff. Capt. Jim McAndrew,* a USAF historian-researcher, who had played a key role in the USAF/Weaver Roswell report released in the fall of 1994 and the USAF's Project Mogul report released in 1995, was searching military records for Dennis's nurse. UFO researcher Victor Golubic was also searching, based on Dennis's claim that the nurse had been raised in the Minneapolis/St. Paul area and had a brother named Billy. When that effort was unsuccessful, Golubic turned to military archives, including records of the training center for military nurses.

Both McAndrew and Golubic talked to chief nurse McManus before her death. More importantly, both were able to locate

---

*Earlier referred to as Lt. McAndrew. By this time he had become a captain.

archival records for all military nurses who had been in the Army in 1947. None of the researchers could find a nurse whose name matched or even resembled Dennis's alleged nurse. And none of the Army nurses based at RAAF, whose pictures were published in the annual RAAF yearbook, resembled Dennis's description of his nurse friend. When Golubic informed Dennis in late 1995 of his negative findings, Dennis responded that the name he had provided to Friedman, Randle, Schmitt, and Pflock was *not the nurse's real name*. He declined to give Golubic the correct name but did provide what Dennis claimed was the first letter of her last name.

By late 1996, Pflock had learned of the results of the search for Dennis's nurse by Golubic and McAndrew, as well as the earlier effort by McCarthy, and faced a difficult decision. Pflock had formed a close friendship with Dennis—so close that when a journalist requested an interview with Dennis he would often decline and suggest they interview Pflock instead. On January 6, 1997, Pflock wrote Dennis as follows:

> I think you need to know my current views on the Roswell case in general and your story in particular. The first is easy. Based on my research and that of others, I'm as certain as it's possible to be without absolute proof *that no flying saucer or saucers crashed in the general vicinity of Roswell or on the Plains of San Agustin in 1947. The debris found by Mac Brazel and brought to the Roswell air base by Brazel, Major Marcel and others was the remains of something very earthly, all but certainly something from the Top Secret Project Mogul.*
>
> The recollections of the real Roswell witnesses and those involved with Mogul and the 1947 press accounts, official records having to do with Mogul, and weather data from the time, support the conclusion that what Brazel found was from Mogul and that he found it in mid-June, not early July. The formerly highly classified record of correspondence and discussions among top Air Force officials who were responsible for cracking the flying saucer mystery from the mid-1940s through the early 1950s makes it crystal clear not only that *they didn't*

(fig. 1a)

Fig. 1a: The headline and story that helped trigger the "Roswell Incident," in the July 8, 1947 edition of Roswell's evening newspaper-based on a press release by Lieutenant Walter Haut. (*Roswell Daily Record*)

(fig. 1b)

(fig. 1c)

(fig. 1d)

Figs. 1b, 1c, 1d: When the Brazel ranch debris was flown to Eighth Air Force Headquarters in Fort Worth for examination, it was identified by Gen. Ramey as the remnants from a weather balloon and its kitelike radar target, as reported in Roswell's July 9 newspapers. (*Roswell Daily Record; Roswell Dispatch*)

(fig. 2)

Fig. 2: Maj. Jesse A. Marcel, intelligence officer for the 509th Bomb Group based at Roswell Army Air Field, is shown holding some of the Brazel ranch debris in the office of Gen. Ramey. The kitelike radar target was fabricated from balsa-wood sticks and metal foil (to reflect radar signals) which were attached to parchmentlike paper for structural rigidity. When this photo was published on the front pages of both Roswell newspapers on July 10, 1947, indicating that Maj. Marcel had "goofed," it was embarrassing for Marcel and members of his family. (Fort Worth Star-Telegram Photograph Collection, The University of Texas at Arlington Libraries)

(fig. 3)

Fig. 3: Gen. Roger Ramey, commander of the Eighth Air Force, is shown alongside some of the debris that Maj. Marcel recovered. It would be more than forty years later before Roswell researchers would discover that the debris was from a 600-foot-long string of twenty-three weather balloons and three radar targets that had been launched from Alamogordo Army Air Field as part of a "Top Secret" Project Mogul (see **fig. 4**). (Fort Worth Star-Telegram Photograph Collection, The University of Texas at Arlington Libraries)

(fig. 4)

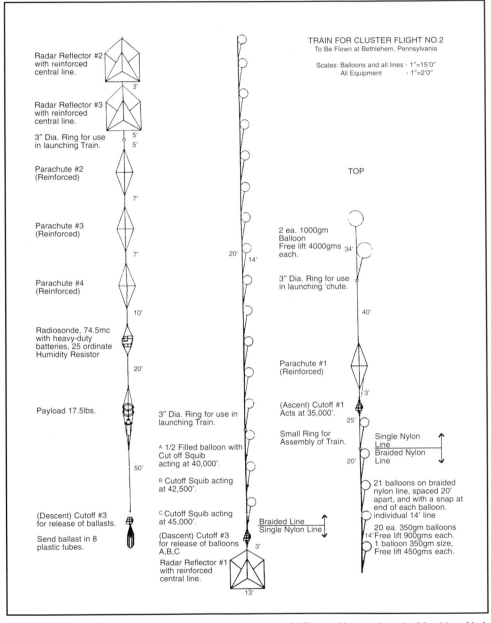

Fig. 4: A train of balloons, radar targets, and instruments similar to this was launched by New York University scientists on June 4, 1947, and tracked by radar to within 20 miles of the ranch where its unfamiliar debris was discovered by Brazel on June 14. ("The Roswell Report: Fact vs. Fiction in the New Mexico Desert," USAF /1995)

(fig. 5)

Fig. 5: Prof. Charles B. Moore, who headed the New York University team based in Alamogordo which launched balloons for Project Mogul, is shown with a radar target similar to the one that crashed on the Brazel ranch and which Moore recently constructed. (David Thomas)

(fig. 6)

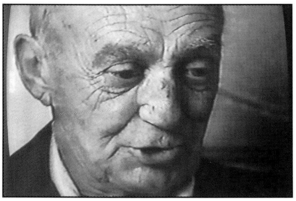

Fig. 6: In the late 1970s, Maj. Marcel emerged from obscurity and retirement as a TV repairman to become a TV celebrity with his claim that the Brazel ranch debris was really from a crashed flying saucer. He was featured in a UFO special produced by New Orleans TV station WWL and later in a Hollywood-made video. (WWL-TV "Eyewitness News")

(fig. 7)

Fig. 7: Dr. Jesse Marcel Jr., who was eleven years old at the time of the incident, also became a TV celebrity by recounting his recollections of the debris his father had brought home more than forty years earlier to show his family. (KTVU-TV "Segment Two")

(fig. 8)

Fig. 8: Dr. Marcel sketched this recollection of unusual pink-and-lavender-colored symbols on an I-beam-shaped "stick" his father brought home more than forty years earlier. (WWL-TV "Eyewitness News")

(fig. 9)

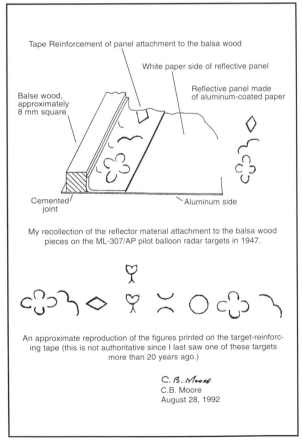

Tape Reinforcement of panel attachment to the balsa wood

White paper side of reflective panel

Reflective panel made of aluminum-coated paper

Balsa wood, approximately 8 mm square

Cemented joint

Aluminum side

My recollection of the reflector material attachment to the balsa wood pieces on the ML-307/AP pilot balloon radar targets in 1947.

An approximate reproduction of the figures printed on the target-reinforcing tape (this is not authoritative since I last saw one of these targets more than 20 years ago.)

C.B. Moore
August 28, 1992

Fig. 9: Prof. Moore recalled that his radar targets had similar colored symbols on the tape used to strengthen the kitelike structure, as shown in his sketch. The radar targets were produced by a New York toy manufacturer who used the tape with colored symbols for toys it also produced. ("The Roswell Report: Fact vs. Fiction in the New Mexico Desert," USAF/1995)

(fig. 10)

(fig. 11)

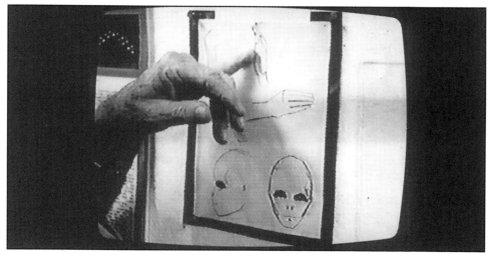

Fig. 10: Former mortician Glenn Dennis claims that a nurse at the Roswell Army Air Field revealed to him that she had participated in an autopsy of three strange-looking ET creatures and drew sketches of their appearance, which she gave to him **(fig. 11)**. Rigorous investigation has failed to substantiate that an Army nurse with her name, appearance, or background ever existed. (Both photos KTVU-TV "Segment Two")

(fig. 12)

(fig. 13)

Fig. 12: Roswell researchers and book authors Kevin Randle (*left*) and Don Schmitt (*right*) with their star witness Frank Kaufmann (*center*). This photo was taken by the author in March 1994, when the new Randle/Schmitt book revealed the location of the "new impact site," which Kaufmann claimed was really 35 miles north of Roswell. (Philip J. Klass)

Fig. 13: The new Kaufmann "impact site" located on the ranch owned in 1947 by the McKnight family. However, a member of the McKnight family recently has flatly denied that any UFO crashed on their ranch. (Philip J. Klass)

(fig. 14)

(fig. 15)

Fig. 14: Some "witnesses" claim that they saw military guards at this point near Highway 285, whose mission was to keep civilians from going to the Kaufmann "impact site." In reality, the site is located 6 miles to the west and is not visible to persons on the highway, so it would be foolish to station military guards here to attract the attention of passing motorists. (Philip J. Klass)

Fig. 15: The McKnight family ranch house, located approximately 4 miles west of Highway 85 and about 2 miles east of the Kaufmann "impact site." If a UFO had crashed there, the military convoy allegedly sent to recover the saucer would have passed directly in front of this house. (Philip J. Klass)

(fig. 16)

(fig. 17)

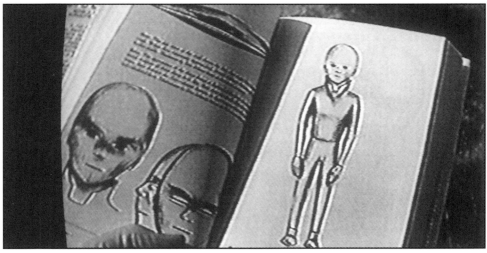

Fig. 16: During Frank Kaufmann's first appearances on TV, he declined to give his real name and required that his face be electronically disguised. But in later TV appearances, he allowed his name to be used and his face to be shown. (CBS News "48 Hours")

Fig. 17: Kaufmann's sketches of the ETs he claims he saw at the crashed UFO site. They differ significantly from those which Glenn Dennis claims his nurse friend sketched and described. (CBS News "48 Hours")

(fig. 18)

(fig. 19)

Fig. 18: Congressman Steven Schiff of Albuquerque, N.M., who asked the General Accounting Office to investigate the Roswell Incident, achieved considerable publicity as a result. The GAO investigation turned up no evidence of a crashed saucer or a government coverup. (CBS News "48 Hours")

Fig. 19: Jackie Rowe, who has become a TV celebrity because of her claim that her fireman father was called to the UFO crash site and later let her handle some of the debris, which she said flowed like mercury. Her description differs dramatically from those given by persons who are known to have seen and handled the debris. (CBS News "48 Hours")

(fig. 20)

(fig. 21)

Fig. 20: Walter Haut, who as a young lieutenant at Roswell Army Air Field put out the press release saying a flying disk had been recovered. Haut, who has lived in Roswell since that time, admits that for more than thirty years he accepted the weather balloon-borne radar target explanation and that he never heard any rumors of a crashed saucer or ET bodies until after the first Roswell book was published in 1980 which promoted such claims. (CBS News "48 Hours")

Fig. 21: Roswell researcher Karl T. Pflock, who began his several-year investigation hoping to find evidence of a crashed saucer and government coverup, had concluded by early 1997 that no UFO crashed in New Mexico in 1947. (Gildas Bourdais and Karl Pflock)

(fig. 22)

Fig. 22: Airline pilot Kent Jeffrey, who originally suspected a crashed saucer and government coverup, has recently changed his views based on results of his own investigation. (Photo: Joanne Pianka)

Fig. 23: Stanton Friedman, a leading promoter of the Roswell crashed-saucer tale, earns his living from UFO lectures, videos, and books. Friedman, who accuses the government of a coverup, withholds from his readers and his audience the once-"Secret" and "Top Secret" documents which would show his claims to be false. (Philip J. Klass)

(fig. 23)

(fig. 24)

(fig. 25)

Fig. 24: The UFO Enigma Museum, near the former Roswell Army Air Field, offers visitors a seemingly realistic view of the UFO crash site and its ET occupants **(fig. 25)**. (Both photos by Philip J. Klass)

(fig. 26)

(fig. 27)

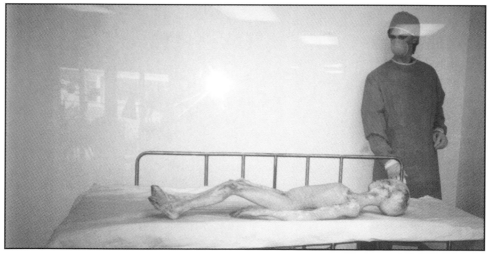

Fig. 26: Roswell's International UFO Museum recently moved to larger quarters–a former movie theater–to accommodate its many visitors. Since the museum opened in early 1992, it has had visitors from sixty-one foreign countries. Its exhibits include a model of an ET **(fig. 27)**. Former mortician Glenn Dennis is the current head of the museum. (Both photos Roswell International UFO Museum & Research Center)

(fig. 28)

(fig. 29)

Fig. 28: Many persons are exploiting the Roswell Incident as a tourist attraction for financial gain. For example, "Hub" Corn, who now owns the Kaufmann "impact site" property, offers tours of the site for $15 per person. (Ken Hanslik)

Fig. 29: Author Philip J. Klass, photographed with a "friend" in the Roswell International UFO Museum during his 1994 trip. (Philip J. Klass)

have any crashed-saucer wreckage or bodies of saucer crews,
but that they were desperate to have such evidence and [were]
tearing their hair out because they didn't.

The other part—your story—is, well, another story. . . .
Here's what I think and why. I believe you were called by the
base mortuary officer as you say you were, but I think the calls
had nothing to do with the bodies that were at the base hospital
when you showed up there. Moreover, they probably didn't
come in on the day you got into a fix* at the hospital. As for the
strange bodies, I believe there were bodies, but they had nothing to do with what Brazel found or anything from another
planet, regardless of who found it and where. In fact, I now
think it very likely what happened to you did not happen *when*
you now recall it did—more likely, it was a year or two later.
Finally, while I still believe there was an army nurse who was
your friend, who got mixed up in the examination of the bodies,
and who later told you about it, I no longer believe she mysteriously disappeared or had a name anything like Naomi Selff—
and I don't think you do either. (Emphasis added)

Pflock's letter, which he told Dennis was being sent to other
Roswell researchers, suggested that perhaps the "bodies" were the
result of a B-29 crash (one had occurred on May 22, 1947),

which the army was concerned to keep quiet or at least under
military control until an investigation could be completed. . . . It
is also possible the accident involved a highly classified program of some type, perhaps some activity which went beyond
authorized limits. . . . Many researchers, including Yours Truly,
have done a lot of digging to find some trace of "Naomi" and
the plane crash in which she is alleged to have died. One private
researcher [Golubic] has established that David Wagnon a former base hospital technician who said he remembered your
nurse is actually remembering one of the five [nurses] who
appear in the [RAAF] yearbook. . . . There is no record or reliable recollection of any abrupt transfer of any member of the

alleged AAF threats to Dennis if he talked

base-hospital nursing staff or of any mysterious activity at the hospital—including an order for the regular staff not to report for duty—in early July 1947. This includes the recollections of the man who commanded the hospital at the time.

The simple truth is, no matter how efficient and far-reaching a group of coverup conspirators might be, there is absolutely no way they could possibly have eliminated all record *and recollections* of "Naomi." She simply did not exist, Glenn. (Emphasis added)

Pflock's January 6 letter then offered Dennis a possible alternative explanation than that he had knowingly concocted a tall tale:

So what do I think is the truth? When you were approached by Stan Friedman in 1989, in his usual fashion with leading questions . . . and his advance packet of information about himself and what supposedly happened near Roswell (which we know from your interview with Friedman [that] you had read before the interview), I believe you got to thinking: "You know, there was that time I got into trouble at the base hospital, that time my friend who was the nurse there got so shook up. I wonder if it had anything to do with that?" Then you quite honestly told this to Friedman and, realizing you had nothing to back up the story, you decided to mention both the pediatrician and the nurse, giving a false name for the latter (Naomi Self—one "f" at the time of the interview with Friedman) because you and she had been a bit more than friends and you were married at the time. Why? Because if she were still alive you wanted to protect her from scandal.

Since then, naturally, you spent a fair amount of time trying to recall more details and fill in the blanks. Through the fog of many years, unrelated events became part of the story and you recalled or thought you recalled many more "interesting" details and made "adjustments" to your story (like seeing the newspaper headline about the crashed saucer just hours after meeting with the nurse). . . .

Glenn, I think you got into this whole business quite honestly, sincerely trying to help Friedman and others with their investigations. At some point, you probably began to realize [that] what you recalled probably had nothing to do with a flying saucer crash, but you thought you were in too deep to say so. So you've stuck with your story. . . . What started out as an honest attempt to recall events you thought might be connected with a crashed flying saucer story got out of hand, grew into a tall tale, and became part of the Roswell myth which now is more "real" to thousands than the facts of the case.

If Pflock's hypothesis were reasonably correct and Dennis had not intentionally and knowingly concocted his nurse/ET autopsy tale, he could promptly have responded by endorsing Pflock's theory. But Dennis did not do so. As of late March—nearly three months later—Pflock told me he had not received any written response from Dennis.

Another Roswell researcher, who spoke with Dennis shortly after he received Pflock's letter, reportedly was told by Dennis that he had never trusted Pflock because he had earlier been employed by the CIA and later had held a high Pentagon post. Yet less than two years earlier, when freelance writer Dava Sobel had requested an interview with Dennis for an article she was writing for the Fall 1995 issue of *Omni* magazine, he had declined and urged her to interview Pflock.

By the time Dennis received Pflock's letter, he had been named president of the Roswell International UFO Museum, following the decision of Walter Haut to retire in mid-1996. Dennis's museum had moved to larger quarters and was deeply involved in preparing for a weeklong fiftieth anniversary crashed-saucer celebration to be held in Roswell on July 1–6. If Dennis had admitted in writing that his nurse/ET autopsy tale was in error, and had this admission received the national media coverage it deserved, this could have spoiled the upcoming celebration.

As of early 1997, practically all of Roswell's available hotel/ motel rooms were already booked for the affair. *Invited speakers included Stanton Friedman and Don Schmitt—who continued to endorse Dennis's story. Not surprisingly, Karl Pflock was not invited. Nor was Kevin Randle, whose new book,* The Randle Report, *expresses serious doubts about the veracity of Dennis's nurse/ET autopsy tale.*

25.

Randle Ignores His Own Advice

Because Kevin Randle has achieved international fame as the coauthor of two books that promote the reality of the Roswell crashed saucer, it might seem surprising that in his new book one chapter is titled: "The Decline and Fall of Roswell—1996." Randle admits that two key witnesses—Jim Ragsdale and Glenn Dennis—have forfeited their credibility. Randle cautions Roswell researchers: "We must not accept stories told by seemingly credible sources because it is what we want to hear."

But Randle adds: "There is no doubt in my mind, based on the evidence I have seen, that there was an alien spacecraft that crashed outside of Roswell." Randle says his belief is based on "military sources to whom I have spoken" and several civilian witnesses—who were only briefly mentioned in his two previous books. *Curiously, Randle does not cite Frank J. Kaufmann (a.k.a. Steve MacKenzie) who emerged in his second Roswell book* (The Truth About the UFO Crash at Roswell) *as a key witness*. It was Kaufmann who first informed Randle and Schmitt of the location of the "impact site," 35 miles north of Roswell, and prompted them to come up with their revised scenario in their second book. In their first book, *UFO Crash at Roswell,* based on their first interview with Kaufmann on January 27, 1990, he claimed only hearsay knowledge of a crashed saucer. But after being relegated to a minor role in their first book, and not being invited to appear on TV programs like Dr. Marcel, Dennis, and Haut, Kaufmann greatly embellished his account in subsequent Randle and Schmitt interviews and became a Roswell TV celebrity.

For example, Kaufmann claimed he had been selected as a member of an elite nine-man team to visit the "impact site" and to direct recovery operations. As reported in the second book, the nine-man team "was restricted to those with the highest [security] clearance and a real need to know." Yet in July 1947, Kaufmann was a civilian employee at RAAF, working in its personnel department. Kaufmann told Randle and Schmitt that he had been a member of a military team which had discovered the crashed saucer on Friday night, July 4, and that recovery operations began early Saturday morning, July 5. He went so far as to claim that one ET survived and that he saw it walk into the base hospital!

These Kaufmann claims should have prompted Randle and Schmitt suspicions. If Kaufmann's tale were true, then certainly Maj. Marcel, as RAAF's top intelligence officer, and Capt. Cavitt, who headed the counterintelligence operation, should have been named to the (alleged) nine-man recovery team. They had top security clearances and a definite need-to-know. But then Marcel and Cavitt would have been much too busy at the "impact site" to have driven up to the Brazel ranch to acquire any debris. Marcel *never* mentioned any such flying saucer/ET body recovery operation, and Cavitt disavows any such assignment.

If an ET craft had really visited New Mexico, it might be the precursor to an ET attack. Certainly top Pentagon and White House officials would have been informed by early Saturday morning, July 5. And there would have been a national military alert, with AAF fighter pilots around the nation being recalled from their three-day holiday. Yet no such military alert occurred.

Certainly Col. Blanchard would have been warned to keep word of the crashed saucer under wraps, and Lt. Haut would never have issued his famous press release on Tuesday, July 8. If a crashed saucer and ET bodies had been discovered on the night of July 4, Gen. Ramey would not have told Col. Blanchard to fly the Brazel ranch debris to Fort Worth. Instead, Gen. Ramey and other top AAF officials would have flown to Roswell to inspect the crashed saucer and ET bodies. During Ramey's visit to Roswell, he could also have examined the Brazel ranch debris. Yet it is known with certainty that Marcel flew the Brazel ranch debris to Fort Worth for Ramey's examination.

Shortly before *The Truth About the UFO Crash at Roswell* was published, Randle and Schmitt provided a preview of their new Roswell scenario in the January/February 1994 issue of *International UFO Reporter* (*IUR*). In support of their new "impact site," 35 miles north of Roswell, they cited the testimony of Jim Ragsdale and "a former military and intelligence officer who was at Roswell in 1947. *He was involved with the recovery of the object and bodies, and he kept a diary of the events. . . . [H]is log does note military activity related to the recovery taking place early on the morning of July 5*" (emphasis added). This alleged "former military and intelligence officer" was Frank J. Kaufmann, although he was not identified by name in the *IUR* article.

But when the second book was published several months later, although Kaufmann and "Steve MacKenzie" were prominently featured, there was *no mention of Kaufmann's alleged diary*. However, Randle and Schmitt did include sketches of the bat-shaped crashed UFO and an ET crew member. These had been drawn by Schmitt based on sketches which Kaufmann showed the authors, which allegedly came from his diary. Kaufmann had also shown his sketches to Karl Pflock during an interview and allowed him to make crude copies.

Randle was quite familiar with the forensic tests that had been conducted on the ink used in what Gerald F. Anderson claimed was a diary written by his uncle Ted in 1947. These tests revealed that the diary was bogus because the ink used had not been available until the 1970s, as reported in chapter 9. This prompted me to call Randle on November 4, 1996, to ask if similar forensic tests had been conducted on Kaufmann's alleged diary. Although Kaufmann had "gone public" under his true name on British TV with his Roswell account more than a year earlier, Randle felt obligated to simply refer to him as his "witness."

Randle admitted that he had not yet been able to obtain any of the *original* pages of Kaufmann's diary but only photocopies of a few pages. Randle indicated that he had been "promised" he could obtain an original for forensic testing but that his "witness" insisted that he come to "a certain city" (Roswell). Randle explained he had been too busy working on two new books to make the trip but hoped to do so shortly. He added: "There is one document, if we can get our hands on it and have it tested properly, *it could be a very devastating document if it proves to be authentic. And I'm hoping to get my hot little fists on it.*" (I offered to contribute $100 or maybe $200 to help underwrite the cost of forensic testing.)

More than four months later, on March 18, 1997, I called Randle to find out if he had visited Roswell and been able to obtain a single page from Kaufmann's diary to verify that it had indeed been written in 1947. Randle said he had "visited city X," and had met with his "witness," but had not been able to obtain a single page of the original diary for forensic tests. However, Randle was allowed to examine a *photocopy* of one page from what the "witness" claimed was his formal report on the crashed-saucer recovery operations. This page was on paper which bore a Roswell Army Air Field letterhead that appeared to be of 1947 vintage. The identity of the intended recipient of the report had been blacked out by the "witness." Curiously, the report was *dated July 26, 1947. Seemingly, it had taken Kaufmann three weeks to get around to writing his report on the crashed saucer and its ET occupants.*

Another anomaly was that the first page of this report contained Kaufmann's sketches of the craft and its ET occupants. Yet according to "MacKenzie" (Kaufmann), "two photographers on the [crash] site had come from Washington," as reported in Randle and Schmitt's second book (p. 10). If two photographers had been flown in from Washington to take pictures of the craft and its ET occupants, there would be no need for Kaufmann to make and submit his own sketches. (During Randle and Schmitt's January 27, 1990 interview with Kaufmann, he told them that pictures had been taken by *one* photographer from RAAF, not two flown in from Washington.)

Still another curious anomaly in this one page from Kaufmann's (alleged) report is that the original—with the RAAF letterhead—should have been sent off to its intended recipient. Because the photocopy machine had not yet been introduced, Kaufmann would have retained a carbon copy *without* the RAAF letterhead. Yet the copy Kaufmann showed Randle did have an RAAF letterhead. When I raised this objection, Randle suggested that perhaps the "witness" had made *two* originals and kept the first draft. If so, the first-draft original in the possession of the "witness" could be used for authentication tests if he would release it to Randle. But later Randle admitted: "Getting my hands on originals for authentication probably will not happen."

Kaufmann was interviewed for the British TV show "The Roswell Incident," broadcast on August 28, 1995. The narrator introduced Kaufmann, noting that he claimed "he was also a covert member of a highly secret counterintelligence group, code-named Lion. Tonight, Kaufmann reveals for the first time what he says is the true story of the Roswell incident." Later the narrator said: "Frank Kaufmann provided us with what he claims is a copy of his official report on the Roswell incident—a Top Secret document containing observations and sketches of what he saw at the time."

Near the end of the Kaufmann interview segment, the narrator said: "The fact is that there is no proof, documentation, physical evidence of any sort to prove that your story is true." Kaufmann responded: "That's right. You have to accept it. I mean, you either believe it or you don't." *In reality, if Kaufmann would release only one page of the many "original" documents he claims to have for forensic testing, this could authenticate the documents and support his tale—if it is true. But Kaufmann refuses to release any of his "original" documents to permit forensic testing.*

Important new evidence to further challenge Kaufmann's story emerged in early 1997 in the form of a sworn statement by Jim McKnight whose Aunt Florence owned the ranch on which the flying saucer allegedly had crashed. McKnight's father owned adjacent land. (McKnight's affidavit, dated February 3, 1997, was obtained by officials of the Roswell International UFO Museum, in response to Randle's challenge to the "new Ragsdale impact site" west of Roswell.) In McKnight's affidavit he said: *"No one in my family had any knowledge of such a [UFO] crash or military retrieval. . . . I cannot believe that a convoy of Army trucks and cars could have come and gone without them noticing. If they had seen it, they would have told us about it"* (emphasis added).

If there had been a military convoy, including a large crane to recover the crashed saucer, as Kaufmann claimed, it would have passed within a hundred yards of his Aunt Florence's ranch house, McKnight told me during a telephone interview on March 21, 1997. According to McKnight, although his aunt then resided in Roswell, where she taught school, during the summer months she usually lived on the ranch. His aunt employed a hired hand to look after the ranch. He lived there permanently. Furthermore, there was no roadway west of the McKnight ranch that a military convoy could have used to reach the "impact site," because of a macho—a large creek bed that often flooded. It was not until *1960*, according to McKnight's affidavit, that his aunt "hired a bulldozer to build a crossing" over the macho that would enable cars to reach the Kaufmann "impact site."

McKnight's affidavit noted that the RAAF "had a practice bombing range on the ranch about 10 miles west of the alleged UFO impact site and one airplane had crashed on the ranch." This aircraft crash naturally was much-discussed among nearby ranchers. But his affidavit added: "Never, never did the subject of such an event as the Roswell Incident come up for discussion. I know the people who settled in that harsh environment. . . . No amount of military threats would have silenced them, especially when they talked among themselves."

Several of Randle's still-credible witnesses had recalled seeing a military patrol near Highway 285, seemingly positioned to keep any unauthorized visitors from turning off and driving to the "impact site" on the McKnight ranch. But if there had not been a UFO crash on the McKnight ranch, then the recollections of these witnesses were seriously flawed. And, none of the residents living near the Ragsdale "impact site" recalled any UFO crash in 1947, according to William Barrett's investigation, as reported in chapter 19. The only substantiated element of the entire Roswell Incident is that Mac Brazel found some unfamiliar debris on his ranch on June 14, 1947.

26.

The REAL Roswell Crashed-Saucer Coverup

In contrast to the flawed recollections of some Roswell witnesses, and the tall tales told by others, there is hard, credible evidence that shows that no ET craft crashed in New Mexico in 1947. This hard evidence shows that the *only coverup is by those who accuse the Air Force and U.S. government of a crashed-saucer coverup.* This evidence is found in once-classified "Secret" or "Top Secret" documents—some of which had been declassified and made public years *before* the first Roswell crashed-saucer book was published. Still more of these documents had been declassified before the next three Roswell books were written in the early 1990s. But the existence of these documents and/or their revealing contents were withheld by the authors of those books.

For example, consider the letter of September 23, 1947, from Lt. Gen. Nathan Twining to Brig. Gen. George Schulgen, a top Air Force intelligence official in the Pentagon, offering the opinion of the Air Force's top scientists at Wright Field as to what UFOs might be. The Twining letter, originally classified "Secret," was written more than two months *after* the Roswell Incident. It had been declassified for publication in the University of Colorado UFO study report published in 1969.

The Roswell Incident by Berlitz and Moore, published in 1980, quoted portions of the Twining letter, including the opinion that "The phenomenon reported is something real and not visionary or fictitious." *But the Berlitz/Moore book omitted Twining's important comment about "the lack of physical evidence in the shape of crash recovered exhibits which would undeniably prove the existence of these objects."* The first Randle/Schmitt book, *UFO Crash at Roswell,* published in 1991, made only brief reference to this Twining letter, noting that it had characterized UFOs as "something real and not visionary or fictitious." Twining's comment about "the lack of physical evidence in the shape of crash recovered exhibits which would undeniably prove the existence of these objects" was *not* mentioned. The Friedman/Berliner book *Crash at Corona,* published in 1992, also made a brief reference to the Twining letter, quoting only "The phenomenon is something real and not visionary or fictitious." There was no mention of "the lack of physical evidence. . . ."

Not one of these three books mentioned the once-"Secret" CIA briefing documents of mid-August 1952, prepared for the Director of Central Intelligence, which had been declassified and made public in 1978. (See chapter 6.) Not one of the three books quoted the August 14, 1952 briefing-document reference to possible explanations for UFO reports: "The third theory is the man from Mars—space ships—interplanetary travelers . . . *there is not a shred of evidence to support this theory at present"* (emphasis added). Nor was there any mention of the August 15, 1952 briefing-document comment: *"Finally, no debris or material evidence has ever been recovered following an unexplained sighting"* (emphasis added). Recall that this CIA document was written five years *after* the Roswell Incident.

Not until 1994, with publication of the second Randle/Schmitt book, was the full content of the Twining letter published. After quoting the letter, Randle and Schmitt made the following admission:

The problem for researchers today is that one paragraph about
the "lack of physical evidence in the shape of crash recovered
exhibits." Clearly Twining and the highest ranking members of
his staff would have been notified if a flying disk had crashed.
The laboratories and facilities to examine and exploit such a
find were at the Wright-Patterson Field complex in Dayton.

Randle and Schmitt were hard-pressed to try to explain why
Twining's letter makes *no* mention of a crashed saucer recovered
at Roswell and refers to the "lack of . . . crash recovered exhibits."
To try to invent an explanation they assume that the Roswell Incident would have been classified "Top Secret." They are not foolish enough to claim that Twining, who commanded the Air Force's
Air Materiel Command and its Foreign Technology [intelligence]
Division, was not cleared for "Top Secret." Nor that Schulgen, one
of the Air Force's top intelligence officials, was not cleared for
"Top Secret." Instead, Randle and Schmitt point out that the pro-
cedure for handling "Top Secret" material is more complicated
than for "Secret" material. So they imply that perhaps Lt. Gen.
Twining intentionally lied to Brig. Gen. Schulgen about the lack
of any recovered crash debris so his letter could be classified
"Secret" to spare Schulgen the inconvenience of handling a "Top
Secret" document. (If Twining had knowingly lied to Schulgen, he
could be dismissed from the USAF. In fact, Twining rose to later
become the first USAF officer to be named Chairman of the Joint
Chiefs of Staff.)

Such nonsensical explanations for the failure of Twining's letter to mention Roswell or recovered crash debris should have been
laid to rest in early 1985 when a once-"*Top Secret*" report on
UFOs, which made *no mention of recovery of an ET craft*, was
declassified. This was Air Intelligence Division Study Report
#203, titled: "Analysis of Flying Object Incidents in the U.S." The
"Top Secret" report was dated December 10, 1948—more than a
year *after* the Roswell Incident. The report began with a statement
of the problem it addressed: "To examine pattern of tactics of 'Fly-

ing Saucers' (hereinafter referred to as flying objects) and to develop conclusions *as to the possibility of [their] existence*" (emphasis added).

The second page of the report states:

> The origin of the devices is not ascertainable. There are two reasonable possibilities: (1) The objects are domestic [U.S.] devices.... (2) Objects are foreign, and if so, *it would seem most logical to consider that they are from a Soviet source.* The Soviets possess information on a number of German flyingwing type aircraft.... (Emphasis added)

This report was declassified on March 5, 1985, largely through the efforts of researcher Robert G. Todd. And the highlights of the report were published in the July 1985 issue of the *MUFON UFO Journal*. Thus, this report's existence and contents must certainly have been known to Randle, Schmitt, Friedman, and Berliner at least several years prior to writing their Roswell books. *Yet not one of their books even mentions Air Intelligence Report #203, let alone revealing that as of late 1948, top Pentagon officials suspected that UFOs were covert Soviet craft, based on German designs.*

It is not surprising that these authors and others who promote the crashed-saucer myth have resorted to this coverup. They have spent many years searching for a "smoking gun" in USAF, CIA, National Security Agency, and FBI files, using Freedom of Information Act requests. This effort has turned up hundreds of once-"Secret" documents—*not one of which indicates the Air Force ever recovered a crashed saucer, and others which show there was not any crashed saucer.* For example, there is a once-"Secret" letter, dated November 8, 1948, to the Air Force Office of Intelligence Requirements in the Pentagon, signed by Col. H. M. McCoy, chief of the Intelligence Department at Wright-Patterson AFB, in Dayton, Ohio. In McCoy's letter, he reports on his department's conclusions "as to the nature of unidentified flying object incidents" based on a study of 180 such incidents. McCoy offers the following assessment:

There is as yet no conclusive proof that unidentified flying objects, other than those which are known to be balloons, are real aircraft. Although it is obvious that some types of flying objects have been sighted, *the exact nature of those objects cannot be established until physical evidence, such as that which would result from a crash, has been obtained.* (Emphasis added)

In the spring of 1996, UFO researcher William P. LaParl obtained declassification of once-"Secret" minutes of the March 17, 1948 meeting of the Air Force Scientific Advisory Board. The AFSAB had been created in mid-1946 to enable the Air Force to utilize the expertise of thirty-one of the nation's top scientists. Initial and subsequent members would include such eminent scientists as Dr. Theodore von Karman, Dr. Edward Teller, Dr. Hans Bethe, Dr. Enrico Fermi, and Dr. Irving Langmuir.

The March 17, 1948 meeting included a briefing by Col. McCoy on some of the technical advances achieved by the Soviet Union and other potential enemies. Near the end of Col. McCoy's briefing, he disclosed that as of early 1948, the USAF had launched a new effort to determine what UFOs might be.

We have a new project—Project Sign—which may surprise you as a development from the so-called mass hysteria of the past summer [1947] when we had all the unidentified flying objects or discs. This can't be laughed off. We have over 300 reports which haven't been publicized in the papers from very competent personnel, in many instances—men as capable as Dr. K. D. Wood—and practically all Air Force, airline people with broad experience. We are running down every report. *I can't even tell you how much we would give to have one of those crash in an area so that we could recover whatever they are.* (Emphasis added)

McCoy's statement was made less than a year after it is claimed that a crashed saucer was recovered near Roswell and shipped to Wright-Patterson AFB. If true, it would have been turned over to McCoy's technical specialists for analysis. During the same AFSAB meeting, McCoy revealed that a Soviet IL-7 aircraft which had crashed in South Korea had been recovered and sent to his group for analysis.

Five years later, in early 1953, Capt. Edward Ruppelt, who then headed the USAF's Project Blue Book office which had been created to investigate UFO reports, briefed the Air Defense Command (ADC). If any UFOs were ET craft and if they turned hostile, ADC pilots would be responsible for defending our nation. Thus it was essential that ADC be accurately informed as to what was known about UFOs. Ruppelt said:

> the majority of the [UFO] information is currently being carried as "Restricted" [then the lowest security classification level which later was dropped]. This is merely to protect the names of the people who have given us reports; it is not any attempt to cover up any information that we have.
>
> The required security classification for admittance to this briefing is "Secret," however. The reason for this is that in some instances we may get into a discussion of classified equipment, classified locations, or classified projects during the question and answer period that follows this briefing. *When the project was first started, it was classified as "Top Secret."* This is probably the reason for the rumors that the Air Force has Top Secret information on this subject; *it does not. The only reason for the original classification was that when the project first started, the people on the project did not know what they were dealing with and, therefore, unknowingly put on this high classification.* (Emphasis added)

Later, Ruppelt said that most scientists acknowledge the possibility that other planets could have intelligent life and that they might "send beings down to earth. However, there is no, and I want to emphasize and repeat the word *no* evidence of this in any report the Air Force has received . . . we have never picked up any hardware. By that we mean any pieces, parts, whole articles, or anything that would indicate an unknown material or object." Ruppelt's declassified report to ADC was published in the mid-1970s in the book *Project Blue Book,* edited by Brad Steiger. But Ruppelt's once-"Secret" briefing is never mentioned in *any* of the Roswell crashed-saucer books.

The Friedman/Berliner book does mention Blue Book Special Report #14, consisting of a statistical analysis of 2,199 UFO reports received by the USAF from 1947 through 1952. The analysis was performed by scientists at the Battelle Memorial Institute, Columbus, Ohio. The Friedman/Berliner book says that "perhaps the most telling revelation of the Battelle independent analysis can be found in a set of pie charts illustrating the relationship between the technical qualifications and reliability of the witnesses, and the percentage of unexplained cases." The Friedman/Berliner book withheld from its readers a far more significant comment in the Battelle report's conclusions:

> *It is emphasized that there was a complete lack of any valid evidence consisting of physical matter in any case of a reported unidentified aerial object....* Therefore, on the basis of this evaluation of the information, it is considered to be *highly improbable* that any of the reports of unidentified aerial objects examined in this study represents observations of technological developments outside the range of present-day scientific knowledge. (Emphasis added)

It is hardly surprising that Friedman/Berliner withheld the Battelle report statement about the "complete lack of any valid evidence of physical matter. . . ." The reason is that in the 1940s and 1950s, Battelle was acknowledged to be one of the nation's top facilities for metallurgical expertise and had conducted "Top Secret" research for the atomic bomb Manhattan Project. If metallic material with unusual characteristics had been recovered in New Mexico and sent to Wright Field for analysis, the Air Force would certainly have sent samples to the nearby Battelle facility for analysis by its metallurgical experts.

Ms. Jennie Zeidman, a longtime UFO researcher and associate of Dr. J. Allen Hynek, had been employed at the Battelle facility in the early 1950s when it had conducted its statistical analysis of UFO reports for Project Blue Book Report #14. As a result, she knew some of the metallurgical experts who had then worked there. In the early 1990s, Zeidman decided to interview some of these metallurgists to see if they were involved or had ever heard rumors of Battelle's analysis of crashed-saucer debris. The results of Zeidman's investigation were published in the May/June 1993 issue of *International UFO Reporter* (*IUR*).

The article reported that *"none of our interviews and none of our other research has yet provided any evidence that Battelle has ever been in possession of UFO artifacts, for Roswell or any other UFO case"* (emphasis added). For those who might suspect that perhaps these metallurgists were resorting to coverup, the article noted: "As for the elderly gentlemen whom we interviewed . . . their choice of words, their directness, their body language all indicate that *to their knowledge, no UFO artifacts were ever analyzed at Battelle"* (emphasis added).

The results of Zeidman's investigation were published a year *after* the Friedman/Berliner book. But the paperback edition of the book was published in 1995, two years *after* the Zeidman article appeared. However, there is no mention of Zeidman's findings in the 1995 paperback version. Nor does this recent edition inform its readers that Friedman/Berliner's key crashed-saucer "witness," Gerald F. Anderson, has been exposed as a spinner of tall tales.

Yet in Friedman's frequent lecture and TV appearances, he repeatedly accuses the U.S. government of Roswell crashed-saucer coverup. These false accusations against the U.S. government of coverup, which Friedman so frequently makes, recall the sage observation of President Thomas Jefferson: "He who permits himself to tell a lie once, finds it much easier to do it a second time and third time, 'till at length it becomes habitual."

27.

Kent Jeffrey Shouts the Truth

Kent Jeffrey, an airline pilot for twenty-six years and now employed by a major U.S. airline, has had a long-standing interest in UFOs although he has never seen one in his many thousands of flight hours. Like many others, he became interested in the Roswell Incident in the early 1990s as a result of numerous books and TV shows on the case. Additionally, his father—a retired colonel in the USAF—had worked under Blanchard who was the Roswell Army Air Field base commander in 1947.

I first met the tall, handsome Jeffrey—then in his late forties—during my second visit to Roswell in late March 1994, shortly after he had launched what he called "International Roswell Initiative." Its objective was to get the President to issue "an Executive Order declassifying any information regarding the existence of UFOs or extraterrestrial intelligence." Jeffrey hoped to accomplish this by getting many persons to sign a one-page "Roswell Declaration" requesting such Presidential action. Jeffrey's then-current views were summarized in a five-page position paper titled "Time for the Truth About Roswell." By late

1995, more than twenty thousand persons had signed Jeffrey's Roswell Declaration.

Like many others, while Jeffrey did not then accept all the claims made by some of the alleged witnesses, he believed there was a "significant possibility" that the crashed-saucer coverup claim was true, but he was not "absolutely certain." However, as Jeffrey more recently explained: "Even if I had only felt that there was a *slight* chance that Roswell involved the crash of an alien spaceship, I still would have pursued the matter vigorously because if true, it would have been the story of the millennium."

In late March 1993, Jeffrey received a letter from Roswell researcher Don Schmitt which claimed that he had recently located a new "first-hand witness to the [ET] bodies. This brings our total to *EIGHT* with yet additional prospects." These "first-hand witnesses" allegedly were reluctant to speak out for fear of the consequences of violating military security oaths. So Jeffrey hired a Washington law firm and paid the cost of sending two lawyers to New Mexico to counsel the witnesses. But when they arrived in Roswell, they were able to meet with only one of the eight (alleged) witnesses claimed by Schmitt—and they considered his tale "outlandish," according to Jeffrey.

In the spring of 1996, Jeffrey's views on Roswell were jolted when he received portions of a 289-page "Secret" document which had just been declassified under a Freedom of Information Act (FOIA) request by UFO researcher William P. LaParl. The document contained the minutes of the March 17–18, 1948 meeting of the Air Force's Scientific Advisory Board, at which Col. McCoy, the Air Materiel Command's chief of intelligence, reported on then current efforts to investigate UFO reports (see chapters 22 and 26). Jeffrey was taken aback by McCoy's statement: "I can't even tell you how much we would give to have one of those [UFOs] crash in an area so that we could recover whatever they are."

Any doubts Jeffrey had about the veracity of McCoy's report to the AF Scientific Advisory Board would vanish later when

Jeffrey acquired other once highly classified documents in which McCoy made similar statements to top USAF officials. For example, McCoy's November 8, 1948 letter to Maj. Gen. C. P. Cabell, USAF's Director of Intelligence, originally classified "Secret." (See chapter 26.) Gen. Cabell's memorandum of November 30, 1948, to Defense Secretary James Forrestal was based on McCoy's information.

In September 1996, Jeffrey was invited to attend a reunion of alumni of the 509th Bomb Group, held in Tucson, Arizona. Prior to the reunion, he had sent out more than seven hundred letters to members, hoping to locate persons who were based at RAAF in mid-1947 who might have information on the Roswell Incident. But he received only two responses: one telling of a UFO sighting from another air base. The other respondent said he recalled seeing a lot of extra activity near one of the hangers around the time of the incident but could offer no more useful information.

During the Tucson reunion, Jeffrey met several pilots who had been based at Roswell in 1947. They informed Jeffrey that so far as they were aware, there had been no crashed saucer. One pilot, Jack Ingham, who was assigned to the 509th from February 1946 until July 1962, assured Jeffrey that if something as spectacular as the recovery of an alien spaceship had occurred, word of it would certainly have spread within the close-knit 509th. Since the Tucson reunion, Jeffrey has communicated with a total of fifteen B-29 pilots and two navigators who were based at Roswell in mid-1947. Most of them had never heard claims of a crashed saucer until many years later. A few who did recall the incident did not challenge the explanation that the debris was from a balloon-borne radar target. Not one of these men of the 509th had ever encountered any other person who had firsthand knowledge of a crashed saucer near Roswell, according to Jeffrey—the first Roswell researcher to rigorously explore this potential source of information.

As a result of Jeffrey's investigation, he met a former 509th navigator who had been based at RAAF in mid-1947, who would certainly have known if a crashed saucer had been recovered near

Roswell—retired Col. Walter Klinikowski. From 1960 until 1964, Klinikowski had served as Deputy Director of Intelligence Collections at the USAF's Foreign Technology Division, at WPAFB in Dayton, Ohio. If a crashed saucer had been recovered near Roswell in 1947, it would certainly have been sent to WPAFB for analysis, and discovering its advanced aerodynamic and propulsion technology secrets would have been the FTD's top priority.

If these crashed-saucer secrets had been "uncovered" prior to Klinikowski's arrival in 1960, these advanced technologies would have begun to appear in new USAF saucer-shaped craft with novel propulsion systems by the early 1970s—which they did not. And if the USAF had not been able to crack the secrets of UFO technology by 1960, it would have been Klinikowski's highest priority program, lest the USSR recover a crashed saucer and unlock its secrets before the United States did. Klinikowski assured Jeffrey that there was no crashed saucer at WPAFB—from Roswell or elsewhere. Klinikowski arranged for Jeffrey to talk with other former FTD officials who provided the same assurance.

By early 1997, all of the foregoing had prompted serious doubts in Jeffrey's mind about a crashed-saucer coverup and many of the alleged witness tales. But he viewed Dr. Jesse Marcel as a key witness who was honestly trying to describe his forty-plus-year-old recollections of the debris that his father had brought back from the Brazel ranch. To try to enhance the accuracy of Dr. Marcel's recollections, Jeffrey arranged for Marcel to fly to Washington and to undergo regressive hypnosis. It would be administered by Dr. Neil Hibler, a clinical psychologist with extensive experience in the use of hypnotic recall for forensic purposes for the FBI and U.S. intelligence agencies.

During the January 10–12 weekend, Marcel spent more than six hours, under Dr. Hibler's guidance, trying to enhance his recollection of the debris his father had brought into the kitchen of their Roswell home nearly fifty years earlier. Initially Marcel's recollections were without hypnosis, and the entire proceeding was videotaped to assure that Dr. Hibler's questions did not unwittingly influence Marcel's comments. Although Marcel was able to recall a few additional details, *there was no significant new information. The Brazel ranch debris he recalled consisted of torn pieces of thin metal-foil, a few pieces of dark plasticlike material, and a thin I-beam-shaped stick with unusual colored symbols. Except for the I-beam shape, Dr. Marcel's recollections closely matched those recalled by his late father in his 1979 interview with Bob Pratt and with the description given by rancher Brazel during his interview on July 8, 1947.* (See chapters 1 and 23.)

For Jeffrey the most significant information to emerge from the more than six hours of recollection-sessions was "what *didn't* come out of them. There were no descriptions or memories of *any kind of exotic debris or wreckage.*" The reason, Jeffrey concluded, was because "there simply was no such exotic debris or wreckage for Jesse to remember. If there had been, in all probability he would have remembered it consciously." Jeffrey acknowledges that "hypnosis can elicit [false] memories of things that didn't happen, but it can't take away memories of things that *did* happen."

As Jeffrey weighed the total evidence, he could no longer believe there was *any* possibility of a Roswell crashed saucer despite his earlier hopes. Jeffrey might have opted to suppress his new skepticism to avoid embarrassment and the criticism of UFOlogists who believed in the Roswell crashed saucer. But Jeffrey was too intellectually honest to do so. Instead, he candidly informed a few other Roswell researchers, including officials of CUFOS, whom he assumed would find the new information of sufficient interest to be published in *International UFO Reporter.* But they sought to convince him that his new views were wrong. When Jeffrey then offered to report his new findings in the *MUFON UFO Journal,* its editor, Dennis Stacy, agreed to publish the article. Jeffrey's lengthy article was published in the June 1997 issue, an ironic commemoration of the fiftieth anniversary of the Roswell Incident.

In the *MUFON UFO Journal* article Jeffrey wrote:

There are apparently those who feel that by reversing my position on Roswell I am letting down the 20,000 plus individuals who have signed the Roswell Declaration. . . . First, with regard to reversing my stance, it is important to remember that the objective of the Roswell Initiative has been *to find the truth,* not define it. Unfortunately, the truth turned out to be different from what I thought it might be, or hoped it would be. However, now that it is absolutely certain that the debris recovered from Roswell *was not that from an extraterrestrial craft, I feel an obligation to get that information out as well. Not to do so would be less than forthright and less than honest.* (Emphasis added)

The article detailed what prompted his change of views on Roswell.

Jeffrey said he still planned to deliver the twenty-thousand-plus signed petitions to the White House during the fiftieth anniversary of the Roswell Incident in early July.

As is stated in the Declaration, if no information is being withheld, such action would, nonetheless, have the positive effect of setting the record straight and clearing up years of suspicion and controversy. On the other hand, if information is actually being withheld, it would represent knowledge of profound importance to which we are all entitled, and its release would unquestionably be acknowledged as a historic act of honesty and goodwill.

While I greatly admire Jeffrey's actions in publicly revealing his new views, I disagree with his hope that if the President were to issue an Executive Order declassifying all UFO information that this would "clear up years of suspicion and controversy." That was the expectation when the USAF declassified all of its voluminous Project Blue Book UFO files in the mid-1970s and made them available to the public in the National Archives. When UFOlogists were unable to find a single "smoking gun," they then sought UFO records from the CIA, which were made public in 1978.

When UFOlogists were unable to find a single iota of evidence that the government knew any UFOs were ET craft, then UFOlogists sought UFO files from the National Security Agency (NSA). (One of the NSA's missions is to covertly intercept and decode radio/telephone communications of potential enemies.) Because most of the fewer than 200 documents in the NSA's vast files which referred to UFOs would reveal that the NSA was covertly eavesdropping on Soviet air defense radar sites, the NSA initially refused to release about 150 Top Secret documents. In early 1997, following the collapse of the Soviet military threat and in response to my request, the NSA released these documents. Analysis revealed that most of the "UFOs" reported by the Soviet air defense radar sites were only balloon-borne radar targets which were used to periodically test the capabilities of Soviet radars and the alertness of their operators. It was the NSA translator-analyst, not the Soviets, who referred to the objects as "UFOs." (Highlights of these once-Top Secret NSA reports were first disclosed in the January 1997 issue of my *Skeptics UFO Newsletter.*) Most important, the NSA papers failed to reveal any "smoking gun."

In my opinion, a Presidential Executive Order is not likely to trigger the release of more than a handful of documents—compared to the many thousands already made public. If and when researchers browse through ancient documents, such as the 289-page minutes of the 1948 meeting of the Air Force's Scientific Advisory Board, they may find brief references to UFOs, such as Col. McCoy's illuminating comment about his hope that a UFO would crash.

There is nothing that the President or the Congress can possibly do to eliminate suspicions of a government UFO coverup in the minds of paranoid UFOlogists. This is demonstrated by the refusal of many UFOlogists to believe what they see in the once-"Secret" and "Top Secret" USAF documents of the late 1940s and CIA documents of the early 1950s, such as those cited in chapter 26.

If any President were to issue such an Executive Order, when no one came forward with credible evidence that any UFOs are ET craft, paranoid UFOlogists would claim that the President covertly issued a "Top Secret" Executive Order warning military personnel *not* to come forward and speak out. If every former President, Defense Secretary, CIA Director, and USAF chief of staff now alive were to sign affidavits swearing there was no government UFO coverup, paranoid UFOlogists would find it easier to believe that all of these former top officials were liars rather than admit that they themselves were wrong about the alleged government coverup.

If a genuine extraterrestrial spacecraft were to land on the White House lawn, and its occupants were to say that they have had planet Earth under surveillance for hundreds of years and that theirs was the very first extraterrestrial visit, stubborn UFOlogists would not believe them. The ETs would be accused of being a part of the government's UFO coverup. It is a no-win situation when dealing with the paranoid, the gullible, and those who exploit the situation for their own financial gain.

28.

TV's Role in the REAL Roswell Coverup

If you watch the evening news on the CBS-TV network with Dan Rather as its host ("anchor"), you expect—and usually get—a fair, balanced treatment of controversial issues. So you naturally expect the same when you see him several hours later as the host of the CBS News TV program "48 Hours." But that did not occur on April 20, 1994, for the Roswell segment on the "48 Hours" program titled "Are We Alone?" Those interviewed included mortician Glenn Dennis, Frank Kaufmann, Frankie Rowe, Kevin Randle, Don Schmitt, and Congressman Schiff. *Not a single skeptic appeared in the Roswell segment to challenge claims of government coverup.*

Several months earlier, CBS News had called me to arrange an interview. When the CBS News caller learned that we both would be in Roswell in late March for the unveiling of the new "impact site" and the debut of the new Randle/Schmitt book, it was agreed that our interview would take place there. During the interview in Roswell, I whipped out a copy of the once-"Top Secret" Air Intelligence Report #203, held it up before the TV camera, and briefly summarized its conclusions. At long last, I expected, the public would learn about this important document which had been declassified nearly a decade earlier.

I was wrong. My entire interview, including the Air Intelligence report which denied the Roswell crashed-saucer tale, ended up "on the cutting room floor." CBS could have been the first TV network to inform its viewers of this hard evidence to challenge the Roswell crashed-saucer myth, but they knowingly withheld it from their viewers.

Shortly afterward I was interviewed for an NBC-TV "Unsolved Mysteries" program on the Roswell Incident. Before I sat down for the tape-recorded interview, I handed the producer a photocopy of the Air Intelligence Report #203 as well as copies of some of the other once-"Secret" documents cited in chapter 26. I explained that these had never before been shown on TV. But when the program later aired on the NBC-TV network, *not one of these documents was shown or even mentioned.*

A few weeks later, I was interviewed for a special program on UFOs, produced by Cable News Network (CNN), with famed talk-show host Larry King as the moderator. The program, titled "UFO Coverup? Live From Area 51," aired on October 1, 1994. Approximately one hour of the two-hour program was devoted to live interviews with three strongly pro-UFO guests, including Stanton Friedman, Kevin Randle, and Dr. Steven M. Greer, who heads a small UFO group that offers training seminars in how to communicate with UFOs and to prepare its members for "off-planet" experiences. The fourth live guest, Glenn Campbell, was only slightly pro-UFO. But there was not a single *live skeptic.* Dr. Carl Sagan and I appeared in a few brief pre-taped segments— each typically less than fifteen seconds long—*for a total combined time of about three minutes.* Because our comments had been taped some weeks earlier, we could not respond to spurious claims made by the live pro-UFO guests.

When I had gone to the CNN studios in Washington to tape the interview, I brought along photocopies of the Air Intelligence

Report #203 and other once-"Secret" documents. When I handed them to the producer, I informed him that these documents had never been shown on TV and he could be the first. But during the two-hour program, not one of these documents was shown or even mentioned. However, during the closing segment of the show, Larry King commented: "Crashed saucers? Who knows? *But clearly the government is withholding something. . . .*" In reality, it was those who produced this TV show who were withholding significant evidence from the public. Larry King's closing words were: "We hope that you learned a lot tonight and that you found it both entertaining and informative at the same time."

Television has become the most pervasive influence in shaping what people believe. This explains why companies spend billions of dollars every year to convince the public that their brand of automobiles are superior to their competitors or that their pills are the best cure for a headache or indigestion. While the U.S. government imposes some truthfulness constraints on claims that advertisers can make for their products, *there are no such constraints on the content of the TV programs that accompany these advertisements.*

The influence of TV is illustrated by the problem encountered by the Audi 5000 automobile, following its introduction in 1978. During the next four years only *thirteen* owners complained that their cars seemed to have mysteriously accelerated and crashed into the front of their garage. But in November 1986, CBS featured this alleged problem in one segment of its popular "60 Minutes" program. During the following month, approximately *fourteen hundred* owners complained that their Audi 5000 had also experienced this same problem. Subsequent investigation and tests by the National Transportation Safety Board revealed that the problem was the result of driver error—stepping on the car's gas pedal when intending to step on the brake pedal.

In mid-1986, I received a call from a CBS News producer who was producing a documentary titled "Search for ETs" for the Arts & Entertainment (A&E) cable television channel, and who wanted to interview me on the Roswell Incident and UFOs. Several weeks later, when she came to Washington to tape the interview, I told her about how CBS News had opted to not use any of my 1994 Roswell taped interview in which I showed the once-"Top Secret" Air Intelligence Report #203. She asked me for a copy of this report and several other "Secret" documents for use in her program. But when "Search for ETs" aired in late 1996, *not one of these documents was used or mentioned.*

One should expect to see a balanced—or even a skeptical—treatment on Roswell and UFOs on the "Science Frontiers" TV program carried on The Learning Channel. But that was not the case in the spring of 1996 when "Science Frontiers" aired a one-hour program titled "UFO." *Not one of the many "UFO experts" interviewed on the program was a skeptic.* The British producer had sent a film crew to Washington, D.C., to interview pro-UFOl-ogist Fred Whiting. He was given nearly three minutes of airtime during which he assured viewers that "there is indeed a coverup." Although I live in Washington, the TV producer apparently feared that the appearance of even one skeptic on the program might poison the minds of the viewers.

The problem is exacerbated by the fact that typically these TV shows are seen by *tens of millions* of viewers—far more than ever read a magazine or newspaper article about UFOs. The NBC "Unsolved Mysteries" show on Roswell reportedly was seen by a total of more than *thirty million* persons in its original 1989 airdate and repeat broadcast in early 1990. Visual recreations of flying saucers, which are used to dramatize "witness" accounts, seem to viewers to substantiate the UFO tales.

There is no simple solution to this problem. The primary objective of those who produce such TV shows is to attract a large audience for the benefit of advertisers. This provides increased profits for TV broadcast and cable networks, and in turn for those who produce such shows. Most human beings—myself included—are attracted by the challenge of the mysterious and the unexplained, so it is not surprising that TV show producers exploit that attraction. The problem is that TV news programs normally provide a reasonably balanced report on controversial issues, so we expect a similar balanced treatment when we see a "documentary" on Roswell with its claims of government coverup.

Perhaps a partial solution to this problem would be to require the narrator of such shows to announce at the beginning of each segment: "This program deals with a controversial issue and we do not claim that you will get a balanced treatment. Our objective is to entertain, not to educate you."

One indication of the impact of such TV "pseudodocumentaries" on public opinion was revealed in a telephone survey of 1,006 adult persons living in all fifty states, conducted by Ohio University and the Scripps Howard News Service in early 1995. The survey showed that *50 percent of U.S. citizens believe that the federal government "is hiding the truth" about UFOs,* which was widely reported in the news media. But the way the question was phrased and the answer-options offered revealed a bias by those responsible for preparing the survey. Persons polled were told: *"Some Americans feel* that flying saucers are real and that the federal government is hiding the truth about them from us." Then they were asked: "Do you think this is *very likely, somewhat likely,* or *unlikely?"* (emphasis added). Half of the persons surveyed responded: "very likely" or "somewhat likely."

This prompted me to write the president of Ohio University. My letter began: "Suppose you received a telephone call from a pollster who said: 'Some Americans think Ohio University is a second-rate institution. Do you think this is: Very likely? Somewhat likely? or Unlikely?' Would you consider the question posed and choice of answers offered to be biased?" I received a reply from Professor Guido H. Stempel III, of the Scripps School of Journalism, who was co-director of the survey. He disagreed that the survey question and its answer-options were biased.

Stempel added: "If indeed the government has been totally candid with the public on this issue, it is still significant that half the American people do not think so." He did not venture an opinion as to why half the American people could be so grossly in error. But his survey results showed that 56 percent of the adults polled who believed in a government coverup were *under thirty-five years of age* and thus had grown up in the TV era. For older persons in the fifty-five to sixty-four age bracket, the number who believed in government coverup fell to 37 percent, and it dropped to 34 percent for those over age sixty-five.

If a friend—a well-educated, intelligent person—or a member of your family believes that a flying saucer crashed in New Mexico in 1947 and for half a century the U.S. government has tried to keep it secret, don't be surprised. Their view simply demonstrates the power of TV to influence what people believe. TV advertisers discovered this fact of life years ago.

29.

From My Own Perspective

If the U.S. government had recovered a crashed saucer in 1947, almost certainly it would have turned to scientists in the world-famous General Electric (GE) Research Laboratory to help analyze the craft's foil-like material and its propulsion and control systems. GE scientists had been deeply involved in the ultrasecret Manhattan Project for the atomic bomb during World War II. In late 1944, GE was selected to analyze portions of German V-2 ballistic missiles which been captured when Allied Forces invaded Germany. This led to GE being selected by the Army to develop the first U.S. ballistic missiles under a highly classified program called Project Hermes.

If the Air Force had recovered an extraterrestrial craft in mid-1947, with the many UFO sightings being reported that summer, Pentagon officials would certainly have been gravely concerned about the possibility of an ET attack. The Pentagon would have sought GE's help in trying to develop a defense against this potential threat as it did in 1948, to protect against Soviet bombers armed with nuclear weapons. As a young GE engineer I was a junior member of the large team GE assembled to deal with the Soviet nuclear attack threat. Thus, had the Pentagon recovered an ET craft in 1947, I would probably have been similarly involved in GE's efforts to analyze the ET threat and to devise a possible defense. At the very least I would have heard veiled references to such an effort from my associates in GE's Aircraft, Federal & Marine Division, which coordinated such major projects.

In mid-1947—at the time of the alleged Roswell Incident— the USAF had contracts with GE and Ryan Aeronautical Corp. to develop supersonic air-to-air missiles. If the Pentagon knew that high-speed ET craft were visiting Earth and might suddenly turn hostile, these supersonic air-to-air missiles might be able to destroy such craft. *But by mid-1948, both these contracts to develop supersonic air-to-air missiles had been terminated.*

Shortly after the USSR startled the world by orbiting its small *Sputnik* I satellite in October 1957, and a relatively huge *Sputnik* II two months later, Pentagon planners became concerned that the Soviets might secretly launch satellites containing atomic bombs, and that when the USSR had a dozen or two dozen such weapons in low-altitude orbit, they could threaten to de-orbit these satellites and rapidly destroy our major cities—unless the United States withdrew all its forces from Western Europe. Thus there was a pressing need for the Pentagon to know how many satellites the USSR was launching, and how many were in low orbit where they posed a potential threat.

Scientists at the Naval Research Laboratory, in Washington, D.C., came up with a novel idea for constructing an "electronic fence" that could detect every object in space which passed over the United States. To enable this "electronic fence" to be quickly deployed, it would use off-the-shelf radio/TV station transmitters and giant arrays of low-cost antennas similar to those then used for home TV receivers. By late 1960, this Navy Space Surveillance System was operational and could detect objects as small as six inches in length.

If the Pentagon knew in 1947 that ET craft were penetrating our airspace, it would want to know how many were in our skies, in case they proved hostile. The Navy's "electronic fence" could provide the answer, and it could have been constructed with technology then available. *Yet it wasn't.* If the system had been deployed in the late 1940s to cope with a potential "UFO threat," it would already have been operational in 1957 when the potential Soviet bombs-in-orbit threat emerged.

In early 1952, I joined the editorial staff of *Aviation Week* magazine which had been created in mid-1947 by McGraw-Hill via the merger of three existing aviation publications. By late 1947, the magazine had acquired the nickname *"Aviation Leak"* when its December 22 issue revealed that the Bell Aircraft XS-1 aircraft had become the first in the world to fly at supersonic speeds, i.e., "break the sonic barrier." Because many aeronautical engineers then believed that swept-back wings would be needed to achieve supersonic speed and the XS-1 had straight wings, *Aviation Week* was widely considered to have revealed "Top Secret" information. The FBI was asked to investigate the leak but no legal action was taken against the magazine.

There would be many more such articles published by *"Aviation Leak,"* revealing information that the Pentagon or CIA considered to be classified. For example, in the early 1950s, *Aviation Week* carried a feature story which revealed the projected performance capability of the B-58—the world's first supersonic bomber which was still under development. In the mid-1950s, *Aviation Week* disclosed that the United States had installed two giant radars in Turkey which were monitoring experimental long-range Soviet ballistic missiles launched from Kapustin Yar. These radars revealed that the USSR was then ahead of the United States in developing long-range ballistic missiles whose thermonuclear warheads could devastate the nation.

In 1954, the United States had launched a crash-program to develop our own Atlas and Titan intercontinental ballistic missiles (ICBMs), but a key challenge was to reduce the weight of the giant rockets without adversely affecting their strength. If an ET craft recovered in New Mexico had been constructed from thin metal foil with the remarkable properties now claimed by some Roswell "witnesses," it would be ideal for use in our ICBMs and would enable the United States to overcome the USSR's lead. By the late 1940s, the nation's top metallurgists would have been brought in to analyze and to replicate the remarkable Roswell debris. But when the Atlas and Titan ICBMs went into production, their giant rockets did not use "Roswell thin-foil" material. If the mystery of the "Roswell thin-foil" material could not be mastered in time for use in our first ICBMs, surely it would have been during the intervening fifty years for use in newer-generation missiles and aircraft. But not one of these uses "Roswell thin-foil technology."

In the early 1960s, *Aviation Week* periodically reported on the "spy satellites" which were then being used to take photographs of key Soviet military facilities after the USSR shot down Gary Powers in a high-flying U-2 aircraft. At the time the existence of such satellites was classified "Top Secret" and would not be declassified for more than twenty-five years. I wrote some of these articles, and in 1971 I authored the first book ever published on these "Top Secret" satellites *and their Soviet counterparts,* which was titled *Secret Sentries in Space.*

On March 23, 1983, President Reagan went on TV to announce his hope that the United States could develop an effective defense against a possible Soviet ICBM attack—which became known as "Star Wars." To try to achieve the President's objective, a panel of several dozen of the nation's top scientists was created to explore a variety of advanced techniques and concepts. In early October, the panel prepared its report for the White House, classified "Secret," which offered its recommendations. I personally read a copy of this report in the *Aviation Week* offices *several days before President Reagan's copy was delivered to the White House!*

If, as some claim, saucer-shaped craft can make abrupt right-angle turns, surely our latest military aircraft would be saucer-shaped. Yet they are not. In 1952, Avro Aircraft Ltd., in Toronto, initiated design studies of a saucer-shaped craft which would be powered by a jet-engine driven horizontal fan. With financial support from the U.S. Air Force and Army, the company produced two 18-foot diameter models in 1959 for flight test. But subsequent flight tests showed that the saucer-shaped craft wobbled and was aerodynamically unstable in high-speed flight. This was later confirmed by wind-tunnel tests and the program was terminated in late 1961. Despite significant advances in aerodynamic expertise in the last thirty years, the Pentagon has not developed any saucer-shaped aircraft.*

In 1960, with the advent of the Space Age and its exciting new technology, the magazine expanded its name to *Aviation Week & Space Technology*—*AW&ST* for short. Since then, *AW&ST* has published more articles on space travel and technology than any other publication in the world. In the forty-five years that I have been associated with *AW&ST*, the magazine has published many articles which caused discomfort in the Pentagon, the CIA, and the White House. *But AW&ST has never published a single article to even suggest the possibility that there is a UFO coverup or that the U.S. government has any evidence of ET visitations. If any of AW&ST's editors had received a rumor from a credible source of a UFO coverup or of even a single ET visitor, a task force would promptly have been created to investigate the claim. And if the rumor could be confirmed, "Aviation Leak" would have published the biggest story of all time.*

Despite my ten years with General Electric in its highly classified defense activities, and my forty-five years with *"Aviation Leak,"* the only credible evidence of a "UFO coverup" that I've been able to find is by *those who make such accusations against the government, and by producers of many TV shows. The evi-*

---

*An excellent summary of this unsuccessful saucer-shaped aircraft program, including photos and sketches from once-classified USAF files, can be found in the Spring 1992 issue of *Skeptical Inquirer*, published by CSICOP (Committee for the Scientific Investigation of Claims of the Paranormal). The article was authored by William B. Blake, an engineer in the Control Dynamics Branch of the USAF's Aeronautical Systems Division, Wright-Patterson AFB, Ohio.

dence of their coverup is plentiful. Their false charges needlessly undermine the confidence of our own citizens in our government and unwittingly aid those foreign dictators who seek to discredit the United States government.

Index